the
QUALITY
of
WORK

the
QUALITY
of
WORK
A PEOPLE-CENTRED AGENDA

Graham S. Lowe

OXFORD
UNIVERSITY PRESS

OXFORD
UNIVERSITY PRESS

70 Wynford Drive, Don Mills, Ontario M3C 1J9
www.oupcan.com

Oxford University Press is a department of the University of Oxford.
It furthers the University's objective of excellence in research, scholarship,
and education by publishing worldwide in

Oxford New York

Athens   Auckland   Bangkok   Bogotá   Buenos Aires   Calcutta
Cape Town   Chennai   Dar es Salaam   Delhi   Florence   Hong Kong   Istanbul
Karachi   Kuala Lumpur   Madrid   Melbourne   Mexico City   Mumbai
Nairobi   Paris   São Paulo   Singapore   Taipei   Tokyo   Toronto   Warsaw

with associated companies in Berlin   Ibadan

Oxford is a trade mark of Oxford University Press
in the UK and in certain other countries

Published in Canada
by Oxford University Press

Canadian Cataloguing in Publication Data

Lowe, Graham S.
The quality of work : a people-centred agenda

Includes index.
ISBN 0-19-541479-9

1. Quality of work life – Canada. I. Title.

HD6957.C3L68 2000   331.25   C00-930250-6

Cover Photo: Robert Landau/First Light
Cover & Text Design: Tearney McMurtry

1 2 3 4 - 03 02 01 00

This book is printed on permanent (acid-free) paper ∞
Printed in Canada

For Joanne and Jennifer

Contents

List of Figures

Preface

I'd been thinking about writing a book about the future of work for some years before a McCalla Research Professorship, awarded by the University of Alberta for the 1997–8 academic year, freed me from classroom teaching and made it possible to write three-quarters of this volume. For that I am deeply grateful. I could never have completed the project, however, without the support and encouragement of Judith Maxwell and other colleagues at Canadian Policy Research Networks Inc., where I have been Director of the Work Network since January 1999. Finding a publisher in Canada willing to take on a book that straddled the trade and academic markets was harder than I had expected. I thank Laura Macleod at Oxford University Press for giving my initial proposal a second look.

Once I became immersed in the project, I realized that the most pressing issue about the past, present, and future of work is, in a word, quality. Achieving a higher quality of work for all should be our overriding goal in charting the future of work. Second, I knew that the future of work is a subject of significant public concern in Canada. For this reason I decided to gear this book to a broad readership. Not that academic research isn't important— indeed, it is vital to understanding our present condition, and it is the under-pinning for what you are about to read. My decision was reinforced, however, by the experience gained in the course of giving more than a hundred public lectures and workshops on future-of-work issues since the mid-1980s. I know that people outside academe are eager to learn about how the work world is changing and what individuals, groups, and organizations can do to influence those changes.

I have accumulated many intellectual debts in researching and writing this book. I want to acknowledge the ongoing contributions to my thinking about work issues made by Harvey Krahn, with whom I have collaborated on numer-ous projects over the years. My work with Gordon Betcherman on a Canadian Policy Research Networks 1997 report, *The Future of Work in Canada*, helped me to crystallize some of the arguments presented here. Students in my winter 1997 graduate seminar on the sociology of work at the University of Alberta provided detailed critiques of this CPRN report, raising some further questions and issues that I have attempted to address in this book. Frank Graves, Karen Hughes, and Sandra Rastin, along with an anonymous reviewer, all provided useful comments on an earlier draft, which Sandra Rollings-Magnusson had already improved with her editing. I am also grateful to Kerri Calvert, in the Department of Sociology's Information Centre, for digging up all sorts of useful information. In addition, Sandra Rastin provided valuable research assistance for several chapters. Some of the data presented here, especially in Chapter 2, were provided by the Angus Reid Group's Calgary office and Ekos Research Associates Inc., Ottawa. Sally Livingston's copy-editing helped to make the book more readable. Phyllis Wilson at Oxford University Press expertly guided the manuscript through to publication.

Writing a book takes a toll on every author's personal life. Recognizing the need for balance between work and family is one thing; achieving it is another. This book is dedicated to Joanne, with the commitment to continue striving for that balance, and to Jennifer, whose generation has a huge stake in the achievement of higher-quality work for all.

An earlier version of Chapter 6 was presented at 'Restructuring Work and the Life Course: An International Symposium' (University of Toronto, 7 May 1998). I thank Frank Trovato for his helpful advice on demographics and Karen Hughes for her valuable comments on the conference paper. Some of the research presented in that chapter comes from the School-Work Transition Project, of which Harvey Krahn and I are Principal Co-investigators. Major funders of this project include the Social Sciences and Humanities Research Council of Canada and the Department of Advanced Education and Career Development and the Department of Education in the province of Alberta.

Chapter 9 is based on my article 'The future of work: implications for unions', *Relations industrielles/Industrial Relations* 53, 2 (1998): 235–57, and The Fourteenth Sefton Memorial Lecture, which I presented at Woodsworth College, University of Toronto, 27 March 1996.

Graham S. Lowe
Shelter Cove, Lake Okanagan
July 1999

Introduction

Work, jobs, careers, employment, unemployment—these have generated more worry among Canadians than any other public issues in the 1990s. Federal elections have been won and lost on the issue of 'jobs, jobs, jobs'. Public opinion polls have documented a nagging unease about economic security that reflects wholesale change in people's working lives. The future of work has become a booming cottage industry for writers, consultants, and media pundits. These futurists variously predict the end of work, with unemployment becoming a chronic economic disease; the decline of the lifelong career with a single employer; or the obsolescence of skills in the face of new information technology. The public's anxieties about work reached a crescendo in 1996 and 1997. The Toronto-based *Globe and Mail* ran two six-part series on how rapidly and fundamentally work has changed, and the difficulties that Canadians were experiencing in trying to adapt to these new realities.[1] Several newspapers reprinted Victor Keegan's article from the *Manchester Guardian*, in which he announced that 'organized work is an artifact.'[2]

Canada's economy rallied in 1997, in a bright prelude to a looming crisis in global financial and commodity markets. Growth was stronger, job creation picked up, the unemployment rate eased down, and consumer spending increased. By mid-1998, health care was replacing unemployment and jobs as the national issue on which Canadians most wanted national leadership. This prompted an executive of the Angus Reid Group, which conducted the poll, to proclaim the entire economic agenda on which the federal government had been elected to be 'dead, dead, dead'.[3]

Yet amidst the widespread anxiety about deterioration of the health-care system, work issues remained a source of deep concern for many. The two sets of issues converged in a wave of nurses' strikes in 1999. The strikes in Newfoundland, Saskatchewan, and Quebec, in particular, focused public attention on a bald contradiction: many health-care workers operate under very unhealthy conditions. In fact, high-quality working conditions—reasonable workloads, adequate resources to do a good job, absence of stress, professional respect, along with decent pay—go hand in hand with the provision of high-quality health care.

For more than a decade, Canadians have needed an informed, wide-ranging debate about the changing work world. My purpose in writing this book is to spark that debate—one that will critically assess the directions in which work seems to be headed, and determine how we can meet the aspirations that individual Canadians have for their work life. This book offers both a diagnosis of the problem of contemporary work and a prescription for making it better. Without public discussion of ways to improve the overall quality of work opportunities for all Canadians who want a job, the country risks faltering socially as well as economically. To ensure Canada's social viability and economic prosperity, it is essential that, individually and collectively, we come to terms with the public sense of crisis about work. Individually, people need to know that they can play an important role in shaping the future of work. Individuals, employers, communities, and governments can work together to fashion a coherent vision of work reforms that mirror the kind of society and economy we value.

I start with the belief that the future of work is the future of society. We owe it both to ourselves and to the young people who will soon move into the workforce to consider our options carefully. What kind of work do Canadians want? Is a shared vision of work in the future even possible? High unemployment and the spread of temporary and other insecure forms of work are indeed problems—but has our preoccupation with them diverted attention from other aspects of work that also need reforming?

Each generation has its own particular future-of-work fixations, always presented with a dire sense of urgency. In the 1950s it was the grey-suited spectre of mass corporate conformity, the 'organization man'. In the 1960s it was automation and the prospect of a 'leisure society'. In the 1970s it was worker dissatisfaction and the pursuit of a better work environment. What's different about the 1980s and 1990s is that work concerns have come to be shared by a broader cross-section of the population, and to involve a wider range of issues. Unemployment, tensions between work and family, the stresses of too much or too little work, growing job inequalities, retirement with dignity, jobs for youth: these are only some of the leading contemporary concerns.

These aren't just work issues. They are closely linked to public concerns about health care, education, social services, homelessness, standards of living, and the widening gap between the haves and have-nots. At a time when people's sense of security, predictability, and control in their working lives seems to have weakened, the pillars of the welfare state are also crumbling. Not only has the public health-care system been weakened by budget cuts and restructuring, but the safety net that used to provide a soft landing for those facing employment disruptions has worn threadbare. Cost-cutting in the name of reform has scaled back unemployment insurance (renamed 'employment insurance' in its last overhaul), public pensions, workers' compensation, and post-secondary education. As a result, more and more Canadians feel they're on their own when employment troubles arise.

Jobs remain the Achilles heel of the national economic agenda. If we believe that the future of work is the future of society, however, it stands to reason that to deal with work problems we must consider more than economic factors; after all, as the futurist Joseph F. Coates reminds us, 'economics is not one of the helping professions.'[4] We have to step outside the economic realm to look at the social dimensions of work. Individuals as members of workplaces, organizations like unions and professional associations, families, and communities can take steps to shape current work trends in positive ways.

The most visible human crisis in work is global unemployment. Calling the global employment situation 'grim', the International Labour Organization recently estimated that one billion people, or about 30 per cent of the world's workforce, are either unemployed or underemployed, leading to suffering on a scale not seen since the Great Depression of the 1930s.[5] Too often, the proposed solutions have revolved around economic decisions and policies. The response to Jeremy Rifkin's book *The End of Work*, in which he argues that technological change is creating mass joblessness, makes it clear that the work crisis is bigger and more complex than unemployment: his book became a runaway best-seller in the US at a time when unemployment rates were falling to their lowest levels since the Second World War. In Canada, corporate executives, consultants, and professionals of all kinds flocked to Rifkin's lectures, motivated in part by the realization that in the 1990s no occupational group was immune from unemployment or downward mobility. The concerns that drive so many segments of the public to buy books like Rifkin's reflect a range of changes in jobs, work environments, and labour markets that takes us well beyond the latest unemployment statistics.

How and by whom is work being reshaped? Which groups are winners and losers in this onslaught of change? A first step towards answering these basic questions is to offer a factual reality check, to counter both the gloomy pessimism and the wide-eyed optimism of the various writers who have constructed our common myths about the future of work. We may know that the transformations we have experienced in workplaces are often too fast and too disruptive, but we do not really understand them. And it is little consolation, when we are trying to figure out how to deal with the perceived crisis in work, to hear 'experts' admit that even they are baffled. In 1996 the federal Deputy Minister of Finance responded to a question about persistently high unemployment by admitting that 'Nobody knows exactly what's going on.'[6]

Under these circumstances it's hardly surprising that myths tend to supplant facts. For example, even though technological change has revolutionized the ways work gets done, it is one of many factors contributing to Canada's intractably high unemployment rates. Similarly, while part-time, temporary, and contract work is spreading, most Canadians still hold full-time jobs. Despite signs of increasing labour-market turbulence, the typical worker does not change jobs any more frequently now than in the 1970s. And although training and education still give people a leg up in today's competitive job market, they are not magic-bullet solutions to our economic problems.

Important changes are indeed happening on each of these fronts. Yet no single trend is sufficiently powerful to spark a full-blown crisis in work: that has taken the collision of a multitude of changes in labour markets and work-places over the past decade. Most of these trends reflect the changing organization of labour markets, jobs, and careers documented by Statistics Canada, the most careful tracker of work trends in the country, along with many other researchers. The unemployment rate is the most frequently used indicator of the strength of the job market. However, it restricts our field of vision when we are trying to grasp the full range of work problems. To say this is not to diminish the serious difficulties faced by the 1.3 million individuals whom Statistics Canada counts as officially unemployed (there are estimated to be several hundred thousand more 'unoffically' unemployed because they do not meet the criterion of having actively looked for work in the past two weeks). In far broader terms, though, the work crisis reflects inadequate opportunities for meaningful work that offers personal development, a social purpose, a decent living standard, and a sense of economic security. Equal priority must be given to the quality of all paid work. This requires a shift in thinking from the quantity of jobs to their quality, all the while pushing forward on the job-creation front to bring down the unemployment rate.

The 1990s has been a decade of transition for workers and workplaces, bridging the gap between the old employment system and safety net, devised in the post-1945 boom, and an uncharted future. Contrary to the claims of people like the Canadian economic trend-watcher Nuala Beck, it is not possible to design 'a clear roadmap to the future'.[7] However, the basic items on the agenda for renewing working life can be found in the challenges that today's work trends pose. More than ever, work and society are enmeshed. The personal challenge, for many individuals, of balancing work and family has increasingly come to public attention. Young people face difficulties first in paying for their post-secondary education and then in finding decent jobs. Baby boomers want more meaning in their work, and their older co-workers are seeking seamless transitions to retirement. Labour-market upheavals are dividing society into those with good jobs, those with bad jobs, and those excluded altogether from paid work. The capacity of the non-profit sector is straining at a time when volunteers are picking up the pieces of the safety net that government cut-backs have shredded. If current trends—temporary and part-time work, unemployment, underemployment, bottom-line management strategies, a yawning gap between haves and have-nots, technological change, plodding rates of organizational innovation, declining standards of living, the stresses of too much work or not enough, work–family tensions, inequitable treatment of women and minorities—are allowed to continue unchecked, they will have serious consequences for Canada's future. Social integration and economic prosperity will be more difficult to achieve, especially if Canada becomes a more competitive, unequal, and individualistic society in which job and career decisions carry greater personal risks.

According to public opinion polls, workplace surveys of employees and managers, and other social-science research, Canadians value a supportive community, fairness and equity, personal opportunities to grow and contribute through challenging and interesting work, a decent standard of living, and a balanced life. However, these are complex and contradictory goals. In an era of economic recessions and downsizing, many of the same individuals who want changes that will improve their working life are also fearful that any change will threaten their job security. Even though most Canadians want to preserve high-quality, accessible health, education, and social services, public opinion has by and large supported government efforts to reduce deficits and debt—often through cuts to those same programs.

The crux of the issue is not the end of work, nor the disappearance of the traditional full-time job. Rather, it is the kind of work we value and therefore want to create as a society. The creation of new work opportunities and the disappearance of existing jobs are part of the relentless evolution of capitalism—the process that, in the early decades of this century, the Austrian economist Joseph Schumpeter called 'creative destruction'.[8] In any recent year, the Canadian economy has lost and created hundreds of thousands of jobs. Government economic policies try, largely through passive and indirect means, to achieve a net gain in jobs. Yet this objective has proven elusive in a decade marked by jobless growth. To put the issue in a broader context: there are close to 16 million individuals in the labour force. If we don't expand the debate to include issues of job quality, as well as the quantity of work available and how it is distributed, we risk wasting the talents and abilities of the vast majority of Canadians who are working now.

Like all industrial nations, Canada must strive for full employment. Along the way, however, we must stop and ask: in what kinds of jobs are people employed? what is the nature of the work they are doing? and under what conditions are they doing it? In the US, where these crucial questions are beginning to move onto the public-policy agenda, 'full employment' means huge numbers of individuals toiling for low wages in barely tolerable work environments. Real earnings for working-class Americans have fallen since 1989 and the poverty rate has increased, with growing numbers of full-time workers earning poverty-level wages.[9] Long-standing social cleavages in American society have deepened to the point where the divide between rich and poor now seems unbridgeable. By contrast, European countries have traded off growth in low-wage jobs in favour of preserving existing good jobs and supporting their consequently large numbers of unemployed people through a more paternalistic welfare state. Typically, Canada stands somewhere in the middle: its unemployment rates are higher than those in the US but lower than in much of Europe, and its income security and labour-market programs are neither as comprehensive as Europe's nor as miserly as those of the US. We can continue to steer a middle course, tinkering with work problems around the edges, or we can muster the collective will to create a new approach to work.

All the current talk about globalization breeds fatalism and a sense of power-lessness. So I want to emphasize that even though the Canadian economy is becoming increasingly integrated into global markets, individuals in their communities and nations can make a positive difference. An example is the way popular, grass-roots opposition helped to scuttle the Multilateral Agreement on Investment (MAI)—a proposed set of global trading rules that critics perceived as shifting economic power from national governments to multinational corporations. Also worth considering is the surprising diversity in the ways national governments have responded to problems of employment and unemployment. These range from the 'leave it to the market' approach found in the US to France's experiment with legislating a reduced workweek to the long-established tradition of worker–employer consultations in Germany, Austria, and Scandinavia.

The language used to talk about work is coloured with moral overtones. We talk of good jobs and bad jobs as shorthand for the increasingly unequal distri-bution of wages and working conditions in a service-based economy. Underlying virtually all negotiations over the terms of employment, for both employees and employers, is a sense of rights: who deserves what? Management's language has been dominated by the concept of quality. Nowadays, 'quality' is everywhere: in corporate mission statements, in the famous 'quality circles' that Toyota transplanted to its Canadian factory, in the Total Quality Management craze that swept North American manage-ment in the 1980s, in the customer-satisfaction pledges included with virtually every consumer product, in universities' recent efforts to survey graduates as a way of assessing program quality. These are all top-down initiatives to improve quality, invariably with a focus on the customer or client. For workers, however, this focus can undermine work quality, as in the case of female retail or hospitality industry workers whose right to an environ-ment free of sexual harassment may be sacrificed in the pursuit of customer satisfaction.

It's time we thought about fusing the moral language of work with the concept of quality. The quality goal can serve more than the interests of management, or customers: we can expand the definition of quality to include the worker's right to a job that is more than just a means of survival. Indeed, what should distinguish affluent, highly developed economies like Canada's from others is the ability to ensure as a basic right the opportunity to do personally meaningful, socially useful work that promotes a sense of security and well-being. As I will show, this is a hallmark of the kind of society that large numbers of Canadians want. Employers too can find benefits in a high-quality work agenda, since these same conditions can contribute to performance, effectiveness, and profits. High-quality work as I will define it serves both humanistic and economic ends.

All too often, we react to the changes sweeping through our work lives with a sense of inevitability and personal powerlessness. Consequently, at the very time when we need to actively pursue alternatives, many individuals feel immobilized. Yet it is possible to redesign jobs and organizations, create a more people-centred working life, facilitate ongoing education and skills development, craft public policies that encourage workplace innovation, reduce labour-market inequalities, and increase meaningful work opportunities. At home and abroad, experience has shown that if workplace, labour-market, and public policies truly put people first, the society will reap the benefits of improved quality of work life and sustainable economic prosperity.

Of the many changes needed in workplaces, one of the most important—and one that occupies a prominent place in this book—is to make the best possible use of people's skills, knowledge, and abilities. Few organizations have achieved this goal—despite the best efforts of some human-resource managers, union representatives, and workers themselves. Yet the idea that human resources are the most valuable resource in a global economy that rewards knowledge and the creative use of information is far from radical. As employers and government policy-makers frequently say, national competitiveness depends on creating flexible workplaces, 'learning organizations', and effective education and training systems. Harvard University's business strategy expert Michael Porter, in his 1991 study for Canada's federal government and the corporate lobby group the Business Council on National Issues, put it simply: 'Upgrading human resources will be critical to Canadian firms' ability to become more competitive.'[10]

The operative word here is 'upgrading'. Such overtures ring hollow unless accompanied by sweeping reforms within workplaces that challenge conventional views of how work should be organized and rewarded. So far, because of workplace inertia, organizational barriers, and resistance from managers, such reforms have not happened. Individual workers can learn—but they need to be in environments that encourage and reward this activity. Similarly, providing more people with higher levels of education or training may create an even better educated workforce—but the effort will be futile if there is not a corresponding demand for those human resources. Employers, governments, corporate lobby groups, unions, and professional associations typically respond to a chaotic economic environment by first adopting new rhetoric. Changing how one talks about workplace challenges is a long way from taking action. 'Quality' has become a catchword, alongside 'empowerment', 'gainsharing', 'teams', 'learning organizations', 'employability', 'equity', 'diversity', 'balancing work and family'. Consultants sell management the vocabulary as a 'new paradigm' that symbolizes refocusing, re-engineering, realignment, or whatever the latest label may be.

It is time to look anew at people's needs in workplaces. We can achieve this by situating the goals of developing and using human resources within debates about the future of work. The renowned futurist Kenneth Boulding has observed that 'Knowledge about the future is perhaps the most important fruit of knowledge about the past.'[11] The management thinker Peter Drucker points in the same direction when he asks: 'what's already happened that will make the future?'[12] There is an abundance of information about work and labour-market changes over the past two decades. What it shows is that for too long workers have been treated as costs to be trimmed and controlled, while calls for meaningful work have been rejected as incompatible with concern for the bottom line. I would suggest that high-quality work is the common ground on which the interests of individual workers, unions, and employers converge. Arriving at that ground will require some adjustments to the balance of power in workplaces, so that workers can become equal partners in discussions about the future of work. But this direction is the only one that offers the possibility of social reform that will allow Canadians—employees and employers alike—to shape their working future together.

This book is intended to cast new light on some perennially difficult questions. It was a quarter-century ago that the American work consultant Fred Best introduced a book on the future of work with these words:

> It is important to realize that the future of work is more than a matter of work hours, occupational projections, and income levels. Ultimately it is a matter of how men and women of the future will seek to define and express their existence. . . . We find ourselves increasingly forced to ask fundamental questions. What are we? What do we really need? For what goals should we work? What is the meaning of work?[13]

Best's questions are tinged with 1970s humanism, evoking nostalgia in those who lived through that era. But they are not easily dismissed. These are questions that we must ask ourselves again today. In a decade when business and political élites have expressed deep concerns about Canada's economic prosperity and productivity, reflecting on the human dimensions of work is a good way of getting back to basics. If we are individually and collectively—in workplaces, communities, and nations—to shape the future of work, then the cornerstone of the renewal process must be the quality of that work.

To show that a focus on work quality holds out the greatest potential for shared benefits, meshing personal priorities with the larger social and economic good, my discussion is organized as follows. Chapter 1 situates the idea of high-quality work in earlier debates about the nature, purpose, and meaning of work. Chapter 2 outlines Canadians' most persistent concerns about work in the 1990s, using evidence from public opinion polls. This sets the stage for Chapter 3, which builds the case that Canadians generally want more from paid work than decent pay and economic security—that they also want the personal rewards that derive from the work itself. Chapter 4 looks at key labour-market trends and the 'new economy'. Chapter 5 then focuses on one crucial trend: the gap between the skills and education of the workforce and the actual requirements of jobs. Chapter 6 considers the kind of working life that today's youth—the next generation of workers—can expect. Chapters 7 and 8 together assess the role of employers in creating higher-quality work environments. Chapter 7 shows the contradictions and inconsistencies in management rhetoric to the effect that people are the key economic resource today, while Chapter 8 presents case studies of several innovative workplaces that put a strong emphasis on people. Chapter 9 addresses the role of unions in pursuing a quality-of-work agenda—an important issue in the light of current debates about unions' ability to adapt to a rapid changing work world. Finally, Chapter 10 pulls together the threads of these arguments into a model that I hope will serve as an invitation to further discussion and debate.

Chapter 1

The Future of Work

The future of work is one of the most frequently recycled issues in commentaries on capitalism. Over the past hundred years, a succession of social analysts have predicted that economic upheavals will either usher in a better society or unleash chaos. Karl Marx believed that the inhuman conditions in the 'satanic mills' of the nineteenth century would ignite a workers' revolt against capitalism. The French sociologist Émile Durkheim was alarmed by the rising suicide rates and other signs of social disintegration that accompanied rapid economic changes in the early twentieth century. At the same time, many North American commentators equated the rise of huge factories with nothing less than unbridled human progress. The Great Depression of the 1930s led many to believe that the machinery of capitalism had broken down beyond repair. Basking in the optimism of rapid post-war growth, scholars in the 1950s typically viewed mass-production industries as capable of providing ever-higher living standards and greater individual opportunities, while reducing social inequalities. The transition from an economic system built around the production of goods by manual labour to a service-based economy run by white-collar workers has generated heated debate since the 1970s. Was the emerging post-industrial economy spreading the benefits of better work and more leisure, or imposing new forms of work degradation and inequality?

And so the debate about work continues. The difference is that today there are many more commentators serving up a bewildering array of discordant messages. Often the changes that are reshaping workplaces do not fit the scenarios suggested by futurists. By critically assessing the divergent images of the future of work, we can understand better the trends that now define the trajectories of work into the twenty-first century. To their credit, the futurists have helped to identify important emerging issues for public discussion. However, putting faith in their predictions could distract us from a more fruitful search for solutions to today's work problems. That's because writers in the futurist genre typically extrapolate bold, sweeping predictions from a single trend. (As the *Economist* magazine wryly concluded about John Naisbitt's latest megatrends book, it appeared to have been written 'at one sitting by a man who had decided to stay up for a week, pounding at a keyboard, gulping down black coffee and working through a pile of press cuttings'.[1])

My approach is to replace speculation with factual assessment of the major forces already transforming workplaces. The absence of facts and rigorous analysis from many discussions about work means that individuals, employers, and governments may make future plans based on erroneous or incomplete information. I believe that the shape of tomorrow's workplace is visible today. In other words, the best starting point for discussions about the kind of work life we want in five or ten years is a detailed understanding of current trends.

Future Speculations

No one can deny that since the jarring 1981–2 recession, global economic changes have unleashed human dislocation and organizational turmoil. There have been enough winners—corporate executives, professionals running the financial markets—to buoy up sales of luxury imported cars and million-dollar recreational properties. For most people, however, work in the 1990s is defined by increasing personal risks through downsizing or employer restructuring, rising workloads, growing work–family tensions, and a declining standard of living. Workers have worried about their economic future for a decade as the 'jobs agenda' loomed over national politics. Managers, unsure about the best ways to achieve the elusive goal of competitiveness, see the need to innovate in the area of human resources, but too often revert to cost-cutting and restructuring. In the end, this approach sacrifices what organizations need most: people. In this swirl of uncertainty, each new personal career move and business decision seems more risky than the last. Little wonder that we are bombarded with contradictory speculations about the future of work.

Commentators on the future of work can be conveniently grouped into three camps: champions, doomsayers, and tinkerers. Champions are bullish about the future, seeing a silver lining of new opportunities in the dark economic clouds of the last two decades. Doomsayers, riveted on the gathering momentum of the information technology revolution, foresee widespread job loss and dehumanization. Tinkerers, usually government policy advisers and senior managers, advocate middle-of-the-road government policies and corporate strategies to even out the peaks and valleys of workplace change; their agenda is often couched in the language of competitiveness and productivity, flexibility and adaptability.

Typical of the champions is William Bridges. His best-selling book *JobShift* proclaims that 'the modern world is on the verge of a huge leap in creativity and productivity. But *the job* is not going to be part of tomorrow's economic reality. Although there will always be enormous amounts of work to do . . .

work will not be contained in the familiar envelopes we call jobs. In fact, many organizations are today well along the path toward being "dejobbed".[2] With wide-eyed optimism, Bridges depicts future opportunities in highly individual-istic terms. Tomorrow's winners will be those who have prepared themselves to ride the wave of change by developing strong entrepreneurial attitudes and pursuing market-oriented training.

Doomsayers dwell on the downside of the information technology revolu-tion. In their view, technology is first and foremost a management tool to boost productivity—regardless of the human costs. 'The information age has arrived,' asserts Jeremy Rifkin in *The End of Work*; 'new, more sophisticated software technologies are going to bring civilization ever closer to a new work-erless world.'[3]

The tinkerers, who operate within the existing framework of policy options, see themselves as pragmatic, advocating indirect ways to reduce unemploy-ment. Many economists take this approach; they believe that if the economy's vital signs (what they call the fundamentals) are healthy—if inflation, interest rates, government debt, and taxes are all low—and government takes a private-sector approach to its operations, then market forces will take care of the unemployment problem through growth. Occasionally, governments and their advisers seek specific policy interventions. For example, a 1994 federal Advisory Group on Working Time and the Distribution of Work recommended a voluntary redistribution of work hours to help lower unemployment.[4] The problem with this kind of tinkering is that it can create new tensions. In this case, such flexible work arrangements conflict with the classic employer's defi-nition of flexibility: namely, having a ready source of cheap labour. And, iron-ically, many full-time workers want more paid work hours, not fewer, to help shore up family budgets. A growing number of human resource managers and experts are advocating 'high-performance work systems', a comprehensive package of changes intended to make organizations more people-centred. Yet such initiatives can also have undesirable consequences for workers, as we shall see.

Taken together, these three perspectives on the future of work suggest that we are at a historic juncture in the evolution of work. However, both the cham-pions and the doomsayers tend to overstate their positions on the basis of paper-thin evidence, and the tinkerers are liable to miss the most negative indi-vidual and social consequences of the policies they advocate. I will show that while some of the changes pinpointed by futurists are evident in Canada, their magnitude and impact are not 'revolutionary'. Still, there is good reason to be concerned, because the trends identified in Chapters 4 and 5 have serious consequences for the quality of work—an issue that receives short shrift in futurist literature.

This lack of attention to work quality helps to explain why old ways of orga-nizing and managing work—what the management gurus call 'paradigms'[5]—

are faltering. It also suggests that the way is open for us to consider new ideas and approaches But newness is relative, judged in the context of current thinking. So another route into the future takes us back through earlier discussions about the human dimensions of work, raising issues that are more relevant today than ever.

Back to the Future: Recurring Concerns

Present speculations about the future of work tell us that individuals invariably react to any changes that threaten to disrupt the established patterns of their life, especially their work life. The ups and downs of the economy are quickly reflected in public perceptions that oscillate between optimism and pessimism. In the early twentieth century Canada had great expectations of its business leaders and politicians, as western settlement spurred economic growth. Industrial expansion during the First World War led to a wave of general strikes in 1919, as workers demanded their fair share of rising profits. With the spectre of Bolshevik-inspired revolution hanging in the air, governments clamped down on this labour unrest with brute force, but later they tried to find new terms for labour–management cooperation. Mass unemployment during the depression of the 1930s prompted fears that the social order was breaking down and led governments to begin constructing a social safety net. Unprecedented growth and rising prosperity during the 1950s and 1960s heightened expectations that a new post-industrial era had arrived, with living standards and industrial productivity soaring.

In the 1950s the rise of mass production, large corporations, and an apparently insatiable market for consumer goods prompted critics to decry the dehumanizing and alienating effects of these trends. The first wave of automation, in the 1960s, was met with hopes not only of reduced drudgery but of productivity gains that could be shared with workers and might even lead to the creation of a 'leisure society'. Yet by the 1970s, the dark side of automation was capturing public attention. The questions raised then—about job losses, machines running workers rather than the other way around, the work process losing some of its human dimensions—are still vital today.

So it is that each generation braces itself against economic upheavals as if they were brand-new challenges. We tend to think that whatever forces are currently disrupting our work lives are somehow far more serious than any previously encountered. This is not surprising, because accurate points of comparison are difficult to find in the 1960s or 1970s. Often lacking is information about workplace conditions and individuals' work experiences in earlier decades that is directly relevant to today's debates. The common post-industrial scenario (another term is 'post-Fordist', meaning that the mass production and consumption system inspired by Henry Ford is no longer viable) portrays the demise of a full-time employment economy that offered security and rising living standards. If we use as our economic benchmark the decades of relatively prosperous growth following 1945, the late 1970s marked a watershed. Since then, incomes have fallen (after adjustment for inflation), unemployment has hit levels surpassed only during the 1930s, and job security has been shaken by restructuring and downsizing in private and public sectors alike. But sceptical economists would point out that the 1950s and 1960s were the exception, not the rule. There likely never was a golden era of employment in Canada's past. Or if it did exist, it was golden only for very select groups: Anglo-Canadian male managers, professionals, and, less frequently, unionized manual workers in the leading manufacturing, resource, and transportation firms. For women and many immigrants to Canada, the post-war decades had little lustre. Today, especially among the baby-boomers, personal recollections and media images of the 1950s and 1960s suggest those were better times, and that things have deteriorated ever since. In the longer view, though, it is clear that work is ceaselessly being transformed.

Canadian magazines, newspapers, and academic journals, along with a smattering of government reports, between 1960 and the early 1980s show how the current questions about work emerged.[6] The commentaries in these publications were nowhere near as incessant or urgent as more recent analyses of work trends, especially since the 1981–2 recession. That period marked a turning point for most Western industrialized nations, separating three decades of relative prosperity from the current age of economic turmoil and anxiety. Yet the dominant refrains about work today were already emerging in the 1960s and 1970s. In the 1960s automation was the hot topic, gradually giving way to speculations about a coming 'leisure society'. Employment was not seen as a problem until the 1970s, when economic slumps, inflation, the oil crisis, and rising unemployment became causes for concern. In the early 1980s, economic recession, joblessness, and the digital technology revolution were increasingly prevalent worries.

Looking at representative articles from the popular media since the 1960s, it is difficult to find a consensus about where work was headed. Typical of the 1960s were articles such as 'Automation: servant or master?', 'How automation can kill society', 'Are people obsolete already?', 'Automation and the age of leisure', 'Leisure crisis: can we stand life without work?', '2000: age of leisure', and one that has a '90s ring to it, 'Education: the key to freedom in an automated society'. The 1970s brought even more speculation about the future of work: 'Here come the robots', 'Enjoy less work', 'Automation alienation', 'Insecurity and frustration in the era of leisure', 'Inventing the future', 'Compressed work week: pattern of the future?', 'Future of work: will Canadians always need to work?', 'New concept of work', 'Toward 2000', 'Don't be fooled by "new era choices": no work—no money, no leisure', 'Making work more human', 'Bringing back the future: it all looked so rosy 25 years ago'. The nostalgia of this last title is all too familiar at the end of the century.

Contradictory Trends

The majority of Canadians working today have spent most, if not all, their working lives inside institutional settings that are undergoing wrenching transformations. The economy, labour markets, workplaces, families, education and training programs, and the entire social safety net look very different now than they did at the end of the 1970s. Coming all at once, and often colliding, these changes underlie the present unease about the future of work. The Canadian economy has become highly susceptible to the forces of globalization, whether through formal arrangements such as the North American Free Trade Agreement, the proposed Multilateral Agreement on Investment, the Asian financial crisis, or fluctuating world markets for natural resources. At the same time, information technology has accelerated our integration into the global economy; equally important, it has had a huge impact on productivity, employment prospects, and how Canadians do their jobs.

Some Canadian employers have responded to increasing change, uncertainty, and globalization with new forms of management and work organization. Yet in both private and public sectors, the dominant response has been cost-cutting, resulting in massive staff reductions through downsizing, even in profitable firms. Working harder and longer each week has become the norm for the remaining employees in downsized organizations. To maintain their living standards in the face of declining real wages, in many families both parents must work, which introduces a host of new stresses and conflicts. Even though teamwork, training, and worker empowerment have become part of the language of management, in general employees have experienced few real improvements.

At a personal level, because the Canadian workforce is aging, retirement has taken centre-stage. And steadily rising educational levels mean that younger workers, in particular, expect decent, interesting, and well-paid jobs—the very things that the service-based economy has had difficulty generating in adequate numbers. Compared to earlier decades, the distribution of family and personal incomes is more polarized, with fewer in the middle, more at the bottom, and an increasingly affluent élite at the top. Contributing to this polarization is the spread of less secure part-time and low-paid forms of employment. Meanwhile, governments at all levels have attacked mounting debts and deficits, unleashing cutbacks in public spending that have yet to have their full impact on workers and communities. The social safety net that formed the cornerstone of post-war social policy can no longer be relied on to give solace and security to those in need. It's little wonder that individuals perceive a crisis in work. Virtually all Canadians are witnessing—or directly experiencing—work changes well beyond the bounds of what they have come to expect.

Understanding what's really going on in the work world is further complicated by the fact that many trends appear to move in contrary directions. This tangle of opposing changes confronts us with several over-arching issues: the number of jobs available; the capacity of the economy to create more good jobs; flexible ways of working; the use and impact of technology; healthy work environments that encourage a balanced life; personal economic security, and a decent living standard; the role of training and education; and workplace reforms to give workers more control over their work. One way to gain a clearer sense of what working life could be like in five or ten years is to think about the following trends and how the contradictions they suggest might be resolved:

- Some Canadians can't get enough work, while others have what they consider to be too much work. Many workers have no economic choice but to put in longer hours at a time in their lives when they want to work less, while 1.3 million are jobless and growing numbers of part-timers want full-time work. Total family work hours have risen to maintain living standards, and dual-earner couples have become the norm.

- Downsizing has been the management strategy of choice for the past decade, even in profitable firms, despite calls from business leaders for more people-oriented approaches to management. Revitalizing employees' morale, loyalty, and commitment is urgently needed in many large public- and private-sector organizations. Yet these issues still fall outside the box of most management thinking.

- At a time when health care is an overriding national concern, workplaces have been overlooked as sites for promoting good health. Growing numbers of workers feel the stresses of overwork and the competing demands of work and family. The costs of employer-provided drug and medical benefits and long-term disability insurance are only now prompting some large employers to examine how improving the work environment can reduce employees' health problems.

- Discussions about how to adapt workplaces to a changing economic climate have focused on big corporations and big government. Yet self-employment is rising rapidly, and small businesses have been the main sources of new jobs in the past decade. Despite these trends, issues of managing and developing human resources among self-employed people and small businesses have received little attention.

- Despite predictions that information technologies will destroy or degrade jobs, most Canadian workers think their jobs have improved because of computers and welcome the opportunity to develop and use new computer-related skills. And despite employers' complaints about a shortage of technological skills, far more workers are able to make productive use of computers than are required to do so in their jobs.

- Concepts such as the knowledge society, lifelong learning, and the learning organization have become part of conventional business wisdom. But Canadian employers still do little to provide employees with adequate training opportunities. Moreover, approximately one-quarter of the workforce has little opportunity to use their existing education or skills at work.

- While overriding personal concerns about unemployment demand economic policies committed to job creation, we also should not lose sight of the fact that the workforce has become increasingly female, well-educated, and older. These trends increase the pressure for more flexibility and personal challenge in work, as well as for the work environment to be supportive of workers' responsibilities for care of children and elders. A good number of workers want career changes, but their feelings of economic insecurity underscore the risks of such moves. Among employers, 'flexibility' means cutting labour costs through reliance on a 'just-in-time' workforce.

- As for the post-industrial, knowledge-based economy that many commentators claim has arrived, the broader picture shows that most of the jobs being created have low or moderate skill require-ments. While the demand for some professionals, technical experts, and managers is growing rapidly, in the larger context of the entire labour force this demand generates relatively few new jobs. The majority of all jobs will continue to require no more than a high-school education for the foreseeable future.

Each of these situations poses huge challenges for individuals, employers, unions, industry and professional associations, communities, and governments at all levels. What's more, they raise important questions about the visions of future working life held by Canadians, and the social and economic costs of getting there. The thread running through all eight situations is the quality of the work available in the economy. The issues they raise are closely linked. Resolving each of them will require us to think more holistically about how to create high-quality jobs for all individuals who want to work.

Automation and Leisure

The quest for quality work takes us back several decades to discussions about automation and the 'leisure society'. In the 1960s these debates posed impor-tant questions about the meaning and quality of work, questions that still haven't been addressed adequately. The idea that economic growth rates and living standards would climb steadily upward was attractive to most people. For the average person, automation held out the prospect of less work. Many welcomed automation as liberating, because it seemed reasonable to expect that one benefit would be more leisure time. Others anticipated mass unemployment and a less attractive enforced leisure that would lead individuals to reconsider the role of work in their life. Another school of thought looked forward to an escape from work, once individuals realized that it was not meeting their psychological and social needs; this school was inspired by Abraham Maslow's hierarchy of human needs, an influential psychological theory in the 1960s, which suggested that although the industrial system provided material necessities for individuals and their families, it didn't fulfil personal needs such as self-development.[7]

Lurking just below the surface of the discussions about a leisure society was a sense that all was not well with work. For some, leisure was preferable. This position reflected a Western philosophical tradition, dating back to Aristotle, according to which human potential was best developed by not working. The idea of escaping from paid work was doubly appealing to the masses. Media talk of 'blue-collar blues' and 'white-collar woes' in the 1970s voiced a growing dissatisfaction with humdrum jobs. High productivity, incomes, and economic growth were not enough to satisfy the personal desire for meaningful work.

Central to the concept of the 'leisure society', then, was the promise that in it both material and non-material needs would be met. But how? Proponents of the idea pointed to the gains in economic productivity (which, until now, business had simply reinvested to produce even more growth) and said that the time had come to spread the benefits of this wealth more broadly by reducing work time without reducing workers' incomes. Moreover, they argued, if this shift was not made voluntarily, it would be forced upon society by rising unemployment. As the British social commentator Jeremy Seabrook explains: 'The promise of leisure is industrial society's response to all the contesting visions that have been evolving since the 1960s. It belongs securely to the growth-and-expansion dynamic of capitalist society and it is an appealing prospect to people whose lives have for so long been shaped by labour.'[8]

In the eyes of its critics, leisure was no better than work, having become routinized and turned into a commodity by the very firms that deprived their workers of meaningful work experiences. This critique focused on the quality of leisure time, but it also raised probing questions about work. Leisure offered the illusion of freedom because the reality of work was unfreedom. By the early 1980s, social critics across the spectrum were beginning to think about how to respond to shortages of paid work. The business consultant and futurist Charles Handy, in one of the first concerted attempts to grapple with the future of work, warned that lifelong jobs would disappear and that there would be less work to go around because of technology.[9] The maverick French Marxist

André Gorz anticipated Rifkin's end-of-work thesis by at least a dozen years with his sweeping pronouncement that 'The micro-electronic revolution heralds the abolition of work.'[10] Gorz also anticipated our current debates about reduced work time and a universal basic income, suggesting that until that total abolition occurred, society should provide everyone with 20,000 hours of lifetime work (equivalent to ten years of full-time work) and a guaranteed income funded by taxing all automated production.

Gorz had little to say about the nature of the work that would remain after machines had cut a wide swath through the labour market, but the issue of a scarcity of work was now on the agenda. He believed that individuals needed liberating from alienating, boring work—the most common kind—just as much as they needed to share a shrinking number of work hours. The politics of work have not progressed much beyond where Gorz left off. This is especially true in Europe, where a broad coalition of worker and community groups have lobbied governments to reduce weekly hours and spread the remaining work around more equally. In April 1998, major European cities witnessed marches protesting against unemployment, job insecurity, and social exclusion. Hundreds of thousands of marchers demanded a decent income and an immediate reduction of the workweek across Europe to 35 hours, then gradually to 30 hours, in a bid to create more jobs.[11]

Canada also confronts the dual scarcity of quality work time and leisure or personal time, but the responses here are far less politicized than in Europe—perhaps, in part, because of an overriding concern to maintain living standards. For example, a recent survey of Ontario workers found that most did not see the reduction of work time as likely. They said they would welcome it as long as income levels could be maintained in future—but that prospect is highly unlikely.[12] Unskilled, lower-paid people working in tedious jobs were the most likely to express a strong desire to work fewer hours or not at all. By contrast, those with higher incomes wanted reduced work time in future; this finding suggests that the issues of work hours and quality of life is closely linked to the growing divide between haves and have-nots. Absent from the research on the idea of leisure, however, is any recognition that leisure is a gendered activity. Women with dependants to care for have less discretionary time than their male partners. Now that women constitute 45 per cent of the workforce, any discussion of leisure must take account of the need to integrate paid work with family responsibilities as the latter change over the course of a person's life.

There seems to be little doubt that creating more flexible approaches to work will benefit individual workers, employers, and society as a whole. The federal government's 1994 Advisory Group on Working Time and the Distribution of Work recommended greater flexibility in work hours, a move to a reduced workweek, and a more equitable distribution of existing work hours.[13] Others have advocated a universal income that would guarantee all citizens a minimum living standard. Even the Organization for Economic Cooperation and Development (OECD), representing the industrial nations that account for 75 per cent of the world's economy, sees this approach as contributing to the goals of increasing both economic flexibility and societal cohesion. If basic economic security is accepted as a right of citizenship—a proposition that free-market true believers would reject—then the next logical step is to consider a guaranteed basic income for all. Proponents of a guaranteed income argued that it would not only ensure an adequate living standard, but prevent the social disruption that would result if increasing numbers of people were unable to earn a living wage. As Sally Lerner explains: 'It can be argued that without a UBI [universal basic income] program embedded in a supportive civil society, the gradual disappearance of adequately-waged secure employment will inevitably be experienced as downward mobility and disgrace by those affected.'[14]

Even with such a program, however, the work needs of the vast majority would not be addressed. Certainly people would take psychological and physical comfort in knowing they would not be left hungry and homeless. Yet their needs for the meaning and personal growth that work can provide might still go unmet.

The Quality-of-Work-Life Movement

European discussions in the 1970s tended to centre either on leisure or on work time more broadly. North American concerns, by contrast, revolved around how to improve working conditions. Today the European focus is on job quality, whereas in North America the main goal is to generate lots of jobs, regardless of their quality. Even though US opinion polls going back to the 1960s show a willingness to trade income for more leisure time, the American ideal of a post-industrial society revolved around work activities. Indeed, Daniel Bell's influential 1973 book, *The Coming of Post-Industrial Society*, had surprisingly little to say about leisure.[15] At the same time, however, other American work analysts were criticizing the single-minded focus on economic growth that still dominates American thinking, and seeking ways in which an affluent society could also contribute to the non-material well-being of workers.

Questions about the American-style capitalist growth ethic came from some unlikely quarters. In the early 1970s Judson Gooding, an editor of *Fortune Magazine*, noted that the meaningless nature of many jobs presented a human problem with significant economic costs, including absenteeism, vandalism, resistance to change, strikes, and a weak work ethic. Detecting a palpable 'job hatred' across large swaths of the working population, especially younger workers, he urged managers to recognize that the incentive for work lay in a 'search for participation and fulfillment'.[16] He cited University of Michigan surveys showing that workers felt entitled to more than just a pay cheque, that they sought satisfaction in challenging and interesting work. Gooding called for 'a basic revision in managerial attitudes, bringing executives to the realization that a central purpose of every business enterprise must be not only to provide goods and services for the public and a return on investment for the owners, but also to provide good rewarding jobs for the employees'.[17]

Gooding's ideas were echoed in the quality-of-work-life (QWL) movement that enjoyed a brief heyday across North America in the 1970s. QWL sought to focus attention on the human dimensions of work. Its critique of working conditions could easily have been anticipated, given that capitalism had delivered several decades of economic prosperity. A guiding belief of the QWL movement was that 'the product of work is people.'[18] Thus workers were entitled to a healthy work environment that would encourage 'the practice of responsible citizenship'.[19] Central to the QWL movement was the belief that work should be healthy and safe, and should provide not only an economically secure future but equitable rewards, according to a worker's contribution to the service or product; opportunities for self-development and controlling how a job gets done; and workplace democracy—in other words, workers should participate in decision-making. In short, QWL proponents believed that work needed to be humanized.

These ideas struck a chord in Canada. A 1973 conference organized by the Canadian Council on Social Development, an Ottawa-based social policy think-tank that is still an influential voice on issues of poverty and income security, captured the tenor of these discussions. The conference's topic was 'new concepts of work', specifically how work was changing across the industrialized world, and how those changes deemed to be socially beneficial could be encouraged. With uncanny foresight, participants sought to expand the debate by asking what kind of society Canadians wanted. The conference proceedings make it clear that changes in values were seen as the driving force behind work changes during the 1970s; values were far more important than the economic forces that are paramount today. These value shifts raised questions about how work could be reformed. Creating more meaningful work was deemed a priority, although nobody attending the conference was able to define just what constituted meaningful work. The conference roundly dismissed media and employer claims that the work ethic was under threat from the anti-establishment attitudes of the baby-boomers who were flooding the job market. Changes were detected in the work ethic, although it was still robust: 'The big difference today is that people want their work to satisfy their own and society's needs more than it has done in the past.'[20] Twenty-five years later, this remains more an ideal than a reality.

Building a Work-Quality Agenda

Improving the quality of work has been raised as a public-policy issue in earlier debates about leisure, work scarcity, and proposals to humanize work. Today the need for support for a fresh approach to work, based on the concept of quality, is even more compelling. As the pollster Angus Reid has observed, 'Work—or at least half-decent, well-paying work—has slipped away from us.' [21] In his view, the quality of jobs is declining even faster than their quantity. Indeed, issues related to the quality of working conditions, job content, and job rewards are being linked to a larger set of concerns about the overall quality of life. In Alberta, the Quality of Life Commission, organized in 1997 by the Edmonton Social Planning Council on behalf of a coalition of community organizations, held 21 small discussion groups, each representing a diverse cross-section of the city.[22] Discussions identified growing concerns about social polarization and a lack of opportunities to obtain adequate jobs and education. Citizens participating in these discussion groups identified six related factors that enhanced the quality of life: meeting basic necessities; hope; self-determination; health and well-being; security; and community.

What's obvious about these characteristics of a decent quality of life is that all of them can be provided in large part by paid work. There are individuals who are unable to work because of age, poor health, or disability, as well as parents who choose to care for their young children instead of working, and they must be provided for though tax-funded income security programs. But for most people a job clearly does offer a way to obtain the necessities of life and a sense of security (however shaky that may have become). In other respects, however, many jobs are woefully deficient with respect to offering hope for the future, opportunities for people to control their work, health and well-being, or a sense of integration into the community. These are the dimensions of job quality, therefore, that require attention.

The organic links between work, community and an individual's overall well-being are often overlooked. But the Canadian poet Tom Wayman, for one, has contemplated them:

> Our employment has a major influence on who our friends are, and strongly affects our attitudes towards an enormous array of events, social movements, artifacts, environments, etc. And despite the silence in which our society wraps participation in the workforce, our jobs each day reconstruct society. Because of our efforts at work, the members of our community are fed, sheltered, clothed, educated, entertained, and much more.[23]

Wayman questions the value our society places on all work, and his comments highlight the need to rethink the criteria used for rewarding work. Even the most apparently mundane jobs—cleaning other people's houses, cooking food in an inner-city snack bar, or delivering newspapers—help society to recreate itself. What's more, workers in these jobs seek meaning from them. Yet such tasks have been undervalued, while executives' salaries continue to soar, even though what CEOs actually do hasn't changed much in decades.[24] In basic terms, then, 'decent' work means work that is socially valued and, therefore, adequately paid.

Another convincing argument for improving work quality emanates, oddly enough, from corporate boardrooms. Legions of consultants, executives, and policy experts have advocated better development of 'human resources'— people. Implicit in the notion of a knowledge society or an information economy is the belief that increasing productivity, competitiveness, and profits depend above all on making better use of workers' mental powers.[25] Many voices have joined this chorus. Take, for instance, the Alberta government. In numerous policy pronouncements, it states that the province's workforce is the most productive, literate, well-educated, highly skilled, and youthful in Canada. 'Skilled workers are essential to Alberta's economic health; all Albertans have a stake in building the labour force of tomorrow.'[26] The Conference Board of Canada, a corporate- and government-funded think-tank, has drawn much attention to 'employability skills': essentially, the kinds of skills that employers say they require. Firms need workers who can communicate, think, and continue to learn, who have positive attitudes and behaviours, who are responsible and adaptable, who can work with others. As MaryAnn McLaughlin of the Conference Board puts it, 'Well educated people who are committed to excellence and to lifelong learning are the key to the social and economic well-being of our country; they are critical to the survival and growth of Canadian business.'[27]

The former US Secretary of Labour Robert Reich has widely promoted human-resource development as a national industrial strategy. In *The Work of Nations*, he argues that in a global economy, a nation's best competitive advantage lies in the talents and skills of its people.[28] Most crucial for Reich, living standards and prosperity depend on how people's skills are used. In a Toronto speech, Reich told his audience that the real issue isn't jobs *per se*, but workers' capacity to add value: 'In an era of falling trade barriers and a shrinking global village, adding value will be central to the job market of the 1990s—in Canada and everywhere in the industrialized world. That means Canadians will not only have to be more skillful than they are now, but even more than their competitors in the years ahead.'[29]

Yet such arguments ring hollow, mainly because they fail to address the way human resources are actually used in workplaces. In a labour market where one-quarter of workers claim that they don't use their skills or education on the job, and in which the stresses of overwork or conflicting work and family demands detract from the productivity of many more, it is crucial to upgrade the content of jobs and improve working conditions. The fallacy of basing national economic strategies on human-resource development is that it assumes rising levels of education and training will attract more skilled, knowledge-intensive, and interesting jobs. But markets don't work that way; if they did, the Alberta economy would be a global competitor offering an abundance of rewarding knowledge-based jobs. While the province does boast a relatively low unemployment rate, its low minimum wage, low unionization rate, and weak social safety net all detract from overall job quality. The larger point is that higher levels of education and training in themselves mean nothing if, in response, employers simply raise their hiring requirements without raising the actual requirements of the job. And what about the 49 per cent of workers whose education has not taken them beyond high school? They may never be 'knowledge workers', yet surely they have more to contribute to their employers, and the national economy, than the narrow parameters of their current jobs permit. In short, improving the quality of work is important for all workers, not just the 'knowledge' élite.

This is a tall order, considering that most of the jobs created since the 1980s have been in the small firms (fewer than 20 employees) that have picked up the labour-market slack created by waves of corporate and government downsizing. This trend has helped to create a split labour market, in which the lower tier consists largely of jobs in small businesses. These jobs tend to be 'bad'— as opposed to the good ones offered by big employers in both the private and public sectors, because small firms tend to pay lower wages, offer fewer benefits such as pensions, have much lower rates of unionization (itself an indicator of better job rewards), and require less skill.

While evidence about the impact of firm size on wages, benefits, job content, and working conditions is convincing (as we will see in Chapter 4), there has been virtually no discussion of how small businesses can be encouraged to create higher-quality jobs. Researcher Grant Schellenberg neatly captures the paradox of job creation in the small-business sector in an article entitled 'Good work if you can get it?'[30] He raises a possibility that so far has not been picked up in Canadian policy debates, drawing on ideas from American academics who envision the rebirth of skilled, satisfying craft work (exemplified in the specialized manufacturing industries of northern Italy), as an alternative to employment in large corporations based on the outmoded logic of mass production.[31] This idea has its share of critics. Still, the possibility of creating quality work in smaller firms, especially in the expanding service sector, needs to be moved outside of academic circles into the public-policy spotlight.

The Moral Dimensions of Work

In recent years a moral discussion has arisen centred on issues such as workers' rights and the meaning of work for humans. These are old themes, admittedly, but they are even more important in today's global economic context. For years, the United Nations-sponsored International Labour Organization (ILO) has served as a global conscience, injecting a social perspective on work issues into international economic debates. At the core of the ILO's social agenda is the creation of more and better job opportunities. In 1944 the ILO adopted the

Philadelphia Declaration, a statement of its aims and principles that made improving the quality of work a priority, and committed all signatory nations (including Canada) to achieving this goal through public policies and programs.[32] Among its aims were the following:

- full employment and rising living standards;

- employment in occupations that enable workers to enjoy 'the satis-faction of giving the fullest measure of their skill and attainments and make their greatest contribution to the common well-being';

- a just distribution of wages, hours, and other benefits, including training opportunities;

- decent working conditions and a minimum living wage for all employed;

- recognition of the right of collective bargaining, and cooperation between management and labour; and

- safe and healthy work environments.

In effect, the Declaration sets out a basic workers' bill of rights. Like all rights, however, they must be more than written declarations or laws to be effective. Employers, governments, unions, and workers in a society must accept these aims as legitimate and enforceable goals. The ILO, and its member nations, articulated these goals in the aftermath of the twentieth century's two most traumatic events: the Great Depression of the 1930s and the Second World War. While post-war economic growth elevated living standards, extended rights, and improved working conditions for vast numbers of workers in industrialized nations, a new set of conditions have prevailed since the late 1970s.

Since then, the overall quality of work life for many segments of the working population has declined. When several Canadian provincial employee unions took their employers (i.e., provincial governments) to the ILO's World Labour Court in the early 1980s, complaining that the basic rights enshrined in the charter were violated by unilateral wage roll-backs and the curtailment of certain collective bargaining rights, court rulings in the unions' favour had no effect in Canada, where they were not enforced. No doubt this outcome was applauded by other employers who were getting tough with unions in the 1980s. More generally, though, it signalled an ominous erosion of basic rights, affecting even those workers with some collective power to resist such a trend. Every community across the country has its own stories of this slide. For example, in over 20 case studies of changing workplaces in Nova Scotia communities in early 1990s, a Dalhousie University research team found that many jobs had disappeared for good, and that the remaining ones demanded more effort for less pay and security.[33] Despite the lack of any evidence that workers' wage demands undercut economic growth, a wide range of employers had embarked on what the researchers called a 'race to the bottom', trying to compete by driving down the cost of labour.

In the four and a half decades since the ILO adopted the Philadelphia Declaration, it has continued to remind the world of its principles. Marking the fortieth anniversary of the declaration, an ILO official told readers of the *Monthly Labor Review* (a publication of the US Labor Department) that while it is economically and politically possible to create employment opportunities for everyone, 'what matters is not only the number of jobs created by the world economy, but also the quality of those jobs—what they offer in terms of productivity, skills, and social and physical working conditions.'[34] The official also cautioned that this social agenda for employment faces an uphill struggle, because the 'backlog of high unemployment and underemployment inherited from the past is a heavy burden to carry as a country proceeds to meet the challenges of the future'.[35]

In the most basic terms, the word 'moral' refers to the distinction between good and bad, between right and wrong. In Canada, the moral discourse about work is most frequently heard in the 'good jobs–bad jobs' shorthand used to describe the growing duality of the labour market in terms of the distribution of income and other job rewards. Although this shorthand implicitly expresses a moral judgement on the inequalities that exist in the labour market, we have not yet openly discussed what as a society we consider desirable and undesirable in a job, and therefore should be encouraging or discouraging through public policy. When the Economic Council of Canada used the term in its 1990 study of the service sector, it likely hoped to launch such a debate.[36] But 'good jobs–bad jobs' has merely become an easy catch phrase used to describe what's happening in the entire labour market. As a result, two questions remain to be answered: what are the qualities of good jobs that would be socially and economically most beneficial? and what actions could government, employers, unions, workers, and communities take to promote them?

Anyone hoping to answer these questions should revisit, as we did briefly above, the 1970s debates about automation and the 'leisure society'. More than any other discussions about work in the past quarter-century, these debates addressed the human purpose and meaning of work. These issues are resurfacing today in several countries. In Britain, for example, a commission chaired by the Bishop of Liverpool published 'Unemployment and the Future of Work—An Enquiry for the Churches' just before the national election in 1997.[37] An effort to extend public discussions beyond the issue of mass unemployment, the report challenges the assumption that high unemployment is here to stay. It also stresses the need to ask whether all jobs are worth doing, and how jobs with better working conditions can be created. In a related initiative, the Labour government of Tony Blair has established a policy unit to address the social exclusion that results when young people and less-qualified adults are shut out of the labour market altogether. This initiative was motivated by the belief that society has a moral obligation to provide all individuals with opportunities to participate fully in economic and social life, and that failure to do so would deny individuals a basic right.

In the United States, the moral dimensions of work are beginning to attract wider public attention, perhaps in response to the dehumanizing aspects of corporate downsizing. Their confidence shaken, many people in the world bastion of free enterprise have come to question the 'rightness' of corporate behaviour that places profits before people. This is hardly a surprise, given that close to three-quarters of respondents in a representative national sample of Americans surveyed in late 1995 by the *New York Times* reported that they or someone close to them had been laid off since 1980.[38] Large majorities of respondents to the same survey agreed that companies and employees are less loyal to each other than ten years ago, and that workplace relations are becoming more competitive and the mood angrier. Personal traumas, cynicism, and economic anxiety have also been deeply etched into the psyche of the Canadian workforce. The downsizing and restructuring of work organizations that have become so widespread in North America have been less common in Europe or Japan. Only recently, in response to the most serious economic crisis of the post-1945 period, has Japanese business turned to North American-style downsizing. The time is ripe, then, for critical reflection on how the human consequences of business decisions could be made a criterion for good corporate citizenship.[39]

A handful of employers have moved in this direction, placing greater importance on human values in economic decision-making. When Wellford Wilms, a California academic, conducted case studies of Hewlett Packard, Douglas Aircraft, the automotive maker NUMMI, and US Steel, he claimed that all four have found a new way of working.[40] According to Wilms, in the face of 'crushing change' those companies have forged a 'new compact' between workers and managers. This 'culture of cooperation' essentially redefines 'human resources'. Instead of seeking greater flexibility—an overriding management goal in all sectors nowadays—these firms have shunned the use of contingent workers; instead of contracting-out, they value their own employees—out of economic self-interest.

Far from rejecting the profit motive, this new contract draws its inspiration from a long line of conservative philosophers such as Hobbes, Locke, and Plato. Liberal-minded critics might well wonder if workers' best interests are served in these cases, whether humanistic values have actually become more important than purely market-based values, and to what extent power has been redistributed to workers. Still, Wilms's study does open up an avenue for debate to occur. A good starting point is his conception of a 'new social framework' built on mutual obligations, fairness, security, loyalty, and trust. As he writes:

A pervasive sense of mutual obligation must be at the center of such a new compact. Employees must be secure in the knowledge that they are important to their company's well-being, that they will be treated fairly (under terms of employment to which both employees and employers agree), and that they will share fairly in the fruits of their labor, also to be spelled out in such agreements. And to the degree feasible, they must be secure in their jobs. Only in this way will a vibrant, expanding economy provide a rising standard of living for everyone.[41]

We will see in Chapter 8 that some Canadian firms have also tried, with varying success, to construct their own versions of Wilms's new social framework. Although they represent only a small minority of employers—perhaps no more than ten per cent, based on estimates of the diffusion of people-centred human-resource management practices—such examples certainly offer grounds for optimism that a quality-oriented work morality is possible.[42] There have been murmurings in public-policy circles that this direction could be in the best interests of the nation, promoting both productivity and quality of life. For example, the authors of a 1995 review of the Canada Labour Code,[43] grappling with the changing context of employment, flag as a problem for both workers and employers the 'compaction of work', or doing more with less.[44] The report's proposed reforms to federal labour law underscore the need to strike a balance between social and economic values: 'Labour is more than just a commodity, to be auctioned off without regard to the underlying human condition. In addition to the income that it provides, employees see work as an expression of their humanity, as an outlet for their creativity.'[45] However, the report stops short of considering the specific changes that would be required to address the human aspect of work, other than giving workers more say through collective bargaining.

The American sociologist Alan Wolfe offers a thoughtful discussion of the need to realign social and economic values.[46] He reinterprets writers as diverse as the futurist Jeremy Rifkin, the social theorist Daniel Bell, the feminist Arlie Hochschild, and the social philosopher Herbert Marcuse as having framed a debate about the moral meaning of work. In a context of globalization, downsizing, welfare reforms, gender equity concerns, and a growing interest among Americans (mainly middle-class) in voluntarism, this debate revolves around whether work is degrading or ennobling. On one side are those who believe that work is crucial to the development of human potential, and needs only to be 'enriched' and 'balanced' with other commitments. On the other side are those, such as Rifkin and Gorz, who view work as 'oppressive' and 'stultifying' and advocate reducing work hours to improve the quality of life. Those critics are wrong, Wolfe argues, because work is not disappearing, and many new jobs need higher-order human capacities. People need work for all sorts of reasons, including a sense of personal identity, self-worth, and social ties with others.

Marxists believe workers are able to adapt to oppressive jobs because they don't know what is in their own best interests. Perhaps work truly is degrading for many people, and they simply don't realize it. Certainly it would be in workers' interest if, as Wolfe advocates, we could find ways of recreating jobs so they 'nourish our higher aspirations'. As he explains: 'The fact that there remain so many jobs that have little self-direction or that fail to contribute to people's moral development is not an argument to reduce our dependence on work, but to encourage precisely those kinds of work that contribute to "cognitive complexity", personal competence, and liberal democratic values.'[47] If we accept that work is not disappearing, then surely we must bring work into line with basic human needs and the values of fairness, justice, and equity. Only in this way will work acquire a moral purpose.

Conclusion

From a late-1990s perspective, one might think there is more concern now about the quantity of work rather than its quality. Poll after poll has documented public anxieties about unemployment and the need to create more jobs. For workers, the quantity of work—whether not enough or too much—has come to symbolize all that is wrong with the economy. Similarly, for employers who have pushed the do-more-with-less principle to the limit, quantity is the overriding concern. Yet the management-by-head-count strategy has had predictable, if unintended, consequences—as one management consultant put it, 'More damning than any overt negative reaction from employees to downsizing is quantitative compliance—people just doing exactly what they're asked, not investing themselves in the business.'[48] The preoccupation with quantity blinds both workers and managers to a host of underlying problems that can be addressed only by looking beyond job counts and work hours.

In fact, the quality of work is just as important to Canadians as its quantity. Even if we did miraculously achieve 'full employment' in the next few years by cutting the unemployment rate in half, Canada's problems with work and individuals' job worries would not vanish. The concept of work quality expresses what Canadians have wanted out of their jobs for decades, incorporating issues that have defined academic, policy, and public discussions about work for the past quarter-century. High-quality work—work that is respectable, meaningful, and life-enhancing—is worker-centred, but it also offers benefits for employers and national economic prosperity. The quality of work affects the quality of life in families and communities, as well as the economic vitality of the nation.

Chapter 2

The Crisis in Work

I often begin public lectures by asking audiences if they worry about the future of work. Hands go up and heads nod all around the room. Later, during discussion, people voice wide-ranging concerns: unemployment, downsizing, a fraying social safety net, more tenuous employment relationships, rising part-time and temporary work, reduced prospects for youth, job stress, work–family tensions, difficulties accessing education and training, retirement preparation, and more. Whatever the group—corporate and government executives, union and community activists, ordinary employees—all express a sense of powerlessness in the face of change. Their individual stories—whether based on people's own experiences or those of their co-workers, families, and neighbours—remind me of the American sociologist C. Wright Mills' famous dictum that the role of a sociologist is to turn private troubles into public issues. Most of the people I've met at those lectures haven't needed my help as a sociologist to do that. Indeed, the Canadian public has already started to make connections between personal work issues and the need to rethink both public policy regarding work and the fundamentals of work itself. This chapter will show that there is a forceful coherence to Canadians' work anxieties.

Probing the National Psyche

Exploring the depths of Canadians' collective psyche through public-opinion polls has become a national pastime. Yet their findings are often contradictory. Different polling organizations often produce very different interpretations of polling results. For example, Angus Reid finds that Canadians are becoming more individualistic, and that our society is moving towards an American-style survival-of-the-fittest social Darwinism.[1] But Alan Gregg counters this view, having detected a strong national commitment to liberal values that stand in sharp contrast to the conservatism of Americans.[2] And Michael Adams of Environics sees evidence of connectedness and empowerment among

Canadians at a time when other surveys suggest deepening fault lines in society and a pervasive sense of powerlessness to change our economic circumstances.[3]

The print media offer similarly incongruous perspectives. In January 1998 William Thorsell of *The Globe and Mail* intoned that 'there is a pessimism and wariness about Canadians that infects our domestic discourse at every turn, political, artistic and social'.[4] For many, says Thorsell, the approaching millennium stirs up a sense of foreboding, even though Canadians have many economic and political reasons to be optimistic. Yet *Maclean's* magazine, in its 1997 year-end poll, found Canada to be 'A confident nation . . . United by bedrock values—and a growing optimism.'[5] (Over the fourteen years of *Maclean's* annual polls, optimism has been a favourite theme, as we will see.)

Can we really be moving in such divergent directions at once? We need to be sceptical of what sells in the media (sex is another perennial theme in the *Maclean's* polls). More important, public-opinion experts have long recognized that making sense of people's attitudes is a messy business. To map the expansive terrain of public attitudes, polls ask questions on a wide range of topics, from political party preferences to views on the hot national issues of the day, personal economic security, priority areas for government action—and much more. Individuals often express logically opposite views on specific issues. Some people who want the system to get tough on crime may also oppose the location of prisons in their neighbourhoods; some men who claim to support gender equality may have less-than-egalitarian views on the sharing of housework and childcare. Of course, seemingly contradictory trends in public opinion on the same topic may simply reflect different ways of interpreting the data: the same glass can be half full or half empty, depending on who's judging. When the jumble of attitudes that individuals hold are combined to produce the 'big picture' of how the nation thinks, the potential for misinterpretation and outright confusion is even greater. And as any social scientist will tell you, the quality of public opinion data depends on how well the questions are constructed and the whether the sample is representative of the larger population being studied.

These are important qualifications to bear in mind. Nonetheless, the findings from most national surveys conducted by reputable polling organizations do, within limits, offer a fairly dependable barometer of Canadians' attitudes and priorities. Work issues have been a common subject of polls this decade, so there is an abundance of useful data. A review of the polls conducted by the Angus Reid Group, the Gallup organization, and Ekos Research Associates Inc., as well as the various firms that conduct the *Maclean's* polls, makes it clear that, as a nation, we have been fixated on jobs and the economy throughout the 1990s. This acute economic anxiety is both personal and public. It is personal in the sense that many individuals no longer feel secure in the labour market or confident about their future economic prospects, and have come to view education and training as their own best insurance in uncertain times. It is public in that jobs and unemployment have become urgent national priorities, raising the spectre of a society divided between haves and have-nots, and in that public trust in governments to deal with these issues has been undermined.

No government can single-handedly fix such seemingly intractable problems. This task will require all of the collective will and creative energy that we can muster. However, the Canadian public seems to be caught in a psychological quagmire in this respect. Not only is there widespread concern about the damage wrought by economic forces, but individuals are less willing than they used to be to trust either governments or the private sector to take leadership on these issues; instead they see these institutions as part of the problem. Not that this is unhealthy or even unexpected. The weakening of the social safety net that provided a basic level of protection against hard times, coupled with the demoralizing effects of downsizing, has shaken people's confidence in major institutions and in many cases given rise to cynicism. Public anxiety is heightened by the realization that there are no ready alternatives, no vision of a way forward that could unite us around a set of common goals. The first step in this direction, I believe, is a wide-ranging public discussion of the kind of working life Canadians want to achieve, individually and collectively, in the next five or ten years. This chapter, then, documents what we want to leave behind.

A Decade of Job Angst

Maclean's, Canada's self-described national magazine, began conducting its annual year-end polls in 1984. After reviewing the findings from these surveys and the accompanying commentary, it is easy to spot the main story line: job angst. These polls began when the economy was beginning to recover from the devastating 1981–2 recession. The first poll results in 1984 prompted *Maclean's* to proclaim on its cover that 'A confident nation speaks up.'[6] Inside, Peter C. Newman observed that the poll was a 'snapshot of a nation in a state of grace without pressure'.[7] No doubt their often painful memories of the recession made some people relatively satisfied with their economic circumstances and reasonably optimistic about the future. But a dark cloud hovered over this confident national mood. The official unemployment rate was over 11 per cent, and 18 per cent among youth. Fears about job loss overshadowed all other national issues in the public eye. There also was an openness to consider new approaches to organizing work, with 53 per cent of poll respondents expressing a willingness to give up some work hours and income to help an unemployed person find work.

The 1985 poll again showcased unemployment. It was becoming a recurrent worry, lurking just under the veneer of a general satisfaction with personal economic circumstances. At the end of the 1980s free trade and constitutional issues shot to the top of the political agenda, but the job angst persisted. The

1990s arrived with a crash, at least as measured by economic activity and employment opportunities. The public reaction to yet another recession was intensified by memories of the 1981–2 downturn. The seventh annual *Maclean's* poll, conducted in late 1990, reflected scaled-down economic expectations and a stark realization that individuals and families would have to cope on their own. Signalling this apparent self-reliance was the robust support expressed for government investment in education and training, even if this meant increasing the deficit. Support for this policy thrust far outweighed that for government deficit reduction, which would fast become the obsession of political and business élites in the 1990s.[8]

The 1992 survey, taken two years after the recession had cast its pall, documented 'profound concern about economic prospects over the next decade' and a 'crash of economic expectations'.[9] Two years later, with the country into a 'jobless recovery', the tenth annual poll offered occasion to reflect on the key trends of the past decade. Journalist Robert Marshall found one: 'It's *still* the economy, stupid.'[10] Respondents expressing economic optimism (a measure that tends to be high because it is so general) had dropped from 79 per cent in 1984 to 71 per cent by 1992. Unemployment topped the list of pressing national problems in eight of the ten years. Free trade and the environment took top spots in the late 1980s, when the economy was at the crest of its 1980s rollercoaster ride. The early '90s polls also showed that restiveness about declining incomes and rising social polarization had joined job and unemployment concerns. The economic fault lines were deepening, and by 1994 roughly one-third of poll respondents reported being in worse financial circumstances than ten years earlier, though another third felt better-off.[11] Then in 1995 the poll reflected widespread pessimism about the economy, the future of social programs, and personal financial security.

This troika of issues—the economy, social programs, and job security—forms the core of public opinion in the 1990s. These concerns have been measured in numerous ways, always coming up with the same bleak outlook. For example, the late 1995 poll found large segments of the population in a sombre mood looking ahead to the year 2000. Most foresaw minimal programs in the areas of unemployment, welfare, and health care, an emaciated public pension plan, a generally tougher job market for youth, reduced opportunities for anyone with only a high-school diploma, higher taxes, and a yawning gap between haves and have-nots. When the 1996 poll probed further into this millennial despair, asking respondents to imagine Canada in the year 2005, large numbers foresaw serious shortages of full-time jobs, longer work hours with fewer rewards, a deteriorated public pension system making retirement at age 65 unaffordable for many, charities running social services, and little or no government assistance for the unemployed.[12]

Allan Gregg, who has orchestrated the *Maclean's* polls, suggests that mounting anxiety about the economic future is creating a grudging acceptance of diminished opportunities[13] that he labels 'prolonged anxiety acquiescence'.[14] In other words, the grinding gears of the so-called new economy have simply worn people down. While large segments of the Canadian population may expect less economically, there also is a palpable backlash against a decade of layoffs and cost-cutting by big employers—public and private. We have become distrustful of large employers. There is a strong desire across the country for self-employment, or (second choice) work in a small firm.[15] The irony, as later chapters will outline, is that large employers on average provide better quality work than smaller ones, despite the fact that the potential to achieve the flexibility and autonomy many workers want is greater in small (i.e., non-bureaucratic) firms. What's more, Canadians are open to considering new public-policy options. Gregg singles out 'work' as the centrepiece of the post-deficit policy agenda, specifically 'finding permanent employment, the worth of work while employed, retirement income and income security in the event of unemployment'.[16] However, the public also has heightened expectations of corporate responsibility. Executive salaries soaring to stratospheric heights and employee lay-offs by profitable firms are being seriously questioned. The indications are that Canadians want corporations to be held publicly accountable for decisions that directly affect individual workers and communities.

Falling Expectations in a Divided Society

If you find this retrospective view of public opinion unsettling, brace yourself. Other research findings also document the trauma inflicted by the economic shock waves of the past fifteen years. Polls that repeat the same questions year after year can accurately track trends in public opinion. Since 1988, the Angus Reid Group has asked its survey respondents which issues they think are important for Canada, and therefore should receive the greatest attention from national leaders. When the top three (or fewer) issues on each respondent's mind were classified, they produced a list of some 23 issues.

Unemployment and the economy have been the public's leading concerns, except in 1990, when English Canada was preoccupied with national unity, and 1998, when health care became the overriding issue. Despite the urgency that political and business élites attached to reducing government deficits, this particular issue was far less important for the majority of Canadians. However, the public has reacted to the impact of government budget slicing and service reductions by placing greater emphasis on health care, education, and social services. Figure 2.1 shows that in all but one year since 1990, 20 per cent or more of those surveyed expressed concern about the economy in general, and since 1993 over 30 per cent have voiced similar concern about unemployment. Also relevant is that over the past decade, two other work-related concerns—education and poverty—have come to be seen as national priorities.

Other polls have also monitored Canadians' job insecurities. The Gallup organization has been tracking these concerns since 1982 (see Figure 2.2).

Figure 2.1 Work-related issues as national priorities Canada, 1988–1998

'Top-of-the-mind' responses to the following question: 'Thinking of the issues presently confronting Canada, which one do you feel should receive the greatest attention from Canada's leaders? What issues do you think are important for Canada right now?' In all, 23 issues were tracked, up to 3 per respondent. Only 4 issues are presented here.

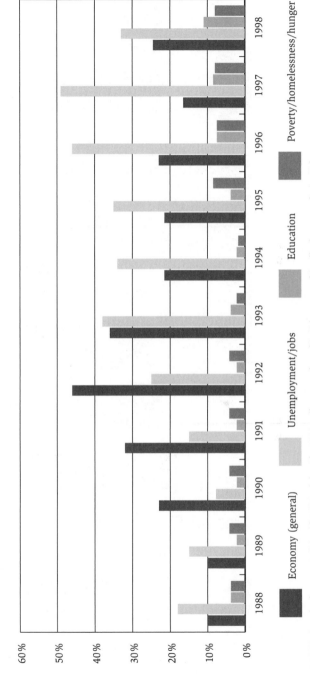

NOTES: Samples between 1,500 and 1,523 adults. The 1988 poll was conducted in February, and in all other years during July.

SOURCE: Based on *Angus Reid Report* (Nov./Dec. 1998).

Figure 2.2   Job insecurity, Canada, 1982–1998

'Do you think your present job is safe, or do you think there is a chance you may become unemployed?'

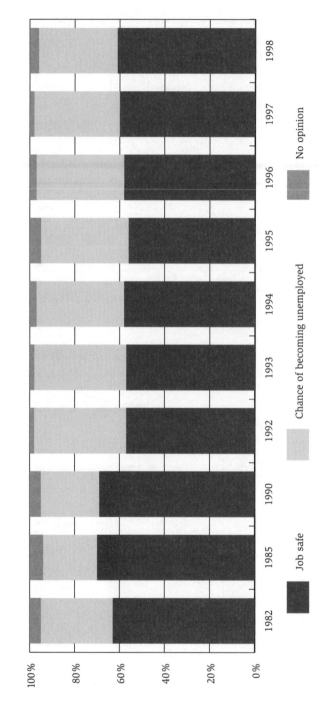

NOTES: Sample = 697 full-time and part-time workers. Polls for 1992–98 were conducted in August; earlier polls were conducted in March or April.
SOURCE: Based on *Gallup Poll* 57, 49 (26 Sept. 1997); 58, 70 (5 Oct. 1998).

Despite the high unemployment levels of the 1980s, between 24 per cent and 32 per cent of respondents in that decade reported concern about losing their jobs; between 64 per cent and 70 per cent felt that their jobs were safe. But the recession of the early 1990s altered these perceptions, possibly for the long term. Since 1992, when the recession was winding down, the gap between those concerned about becoming unemployed and those who felt secure in their jobs has closed considerably. In the 1990s, approximately four in every ten workers have feared that their jobs could vanish.

Linked to this sense of job insecurity is concern over declining living standards. These two issues go hand in hand. Real wages (after taking inflation into account) have been falling since the 1980s (a trend I will examine closely in Chapter 4) and concerns about social cleavages have been rising. As we can see in Figure 2.3, since 1989 between one in three and one in six Canadians have expected their economic situation to worsen in the coming year. But this is only part of the picture, for in most of these years slightly higher proportions of individuals have foreseen improved economic circumstances.

In other words, a decade or more of economic restructuring has widened existing class cleavages in Canadian society. We are becoming a more polarized nation. This issue is closely related to work, because whether people consider themselves rich, middle-class, or poor depends on their position in the labour market. Social and economic inequality reflects trends in employment income, which makes up by far the largest part of total income. In December 1995, the Angus Reid Group asked its survey respondents to locate themselves in an economic class.[17] One in six described themselves as poor, while only one in twenty considered themselves wealthy. The rest, or about three in four Canadians, clustered in the middle. When asked to assess their personal financial situation in the mid-1990s compared with a decade earlier, 40 per cent reported they were better off and almost as many (36 per cent) felt worse off. However, this general pattern masks huge differences across the social classes in which respondents locate themselves. More to the point, 64 per cent of the self-identified poor had become worse-off economically, as had 42 per cent of the lower middle class. In marked contrast, 67 per cent of the self-described wealthy reported being better-off financially, as did approximately half of the upper-middle (52 per cent) and middle (46 per cent) classes. However, between 15 and 28 per cent of the individuals in these better-off classes experienced deteriorating economic circumstances in the past decade.

In simple terms, the poor feel they are getting poorer while the rich feel they are getting richer. Furthermore, individuals who are lower down the social ladder are far more likely than those closer to the top to have felt the harsh impact of government cutbacks. The public is split on their overall assessment of whether government cutbacks have gone too far or whether they will create a better Canada in the end. There is considerable consensus, however, on three points: a clear majority feel that these cuts have hurt the poor more than the

Figure 2.3   One-year forecasts for personal financial prospects, Canada, 1987–1998

'What about you and your family? Do you feel that your own economic situation will improve, stay the same, or get worse over the next year?'

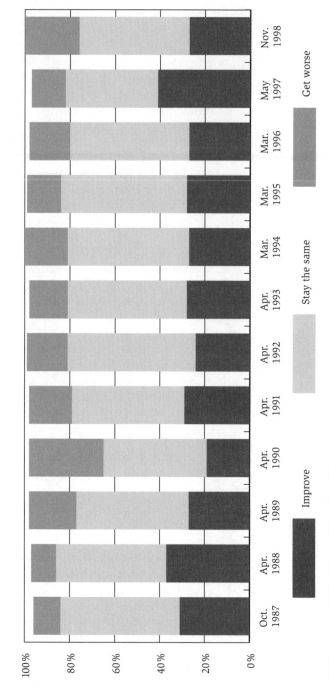

NOTE: Sample = 1,100 adults for 1987, 1,500–1,520 for other years.

SOURCE: Based on *Angus Reid Report* (Nov./Dec. 1998).

wealthy (six in ten) and believe that the poor have sacrificed too much (six in ten) and the wealthy too little (eight in ten) in the process.[18] While the winding down of the welfare state is not the main focus of this book, I do believe that these changes also affect our thinking about the future of work. In particular, they bring into sharp relief how closely the economic, political, and social spheres are connected.

Thus there is some convincing evidence that most Canadians see growing polarization in their society. What is striking about this perception of a nation dividing into haves and have-nots is that close to 80 per cent of respondents express concern about this trend, with little variation by demographic characteristics: generally speaking, region, age, education, labour-force status, and household income have little influence. If you live in one of the prairie provinces, are under the age of 30, have high-school education or less, or live in an affluent household, chances are that you are just slightly less concerned than other groups (see Figure 2.4). But even among Albertans, who appear to be the least concerned, some seven in ten worry about growing polarization.

When individuals feel they lack control over their lives, they experience stress. And they risk getting caught in a vicious circle of despair and helplessness, which feeds their sense of powerlessness. In a rapidly changing economic environment that leaves large numbers of individuals feeling victimized and helpless, the results can be traumatic. Sociologists have long documented that in times of economic turmoil, suicide rates increase, as does the likelihood that some individuals will turn to extremist political doctrines that offer simple solutions. Examples include the soaring suicide rates in parts of Eastern Europe after the collapse of communism, the support garnered by the ultra-protectionist Pat Buchanan in his bid for the US Republican Party presidential nomination in 1996, and the rise of the Reform Party in Canada as a reaction against a multitude of social and economic changes during the 1980s. Thus even as large-scale economic change transforms people's lives, one common reaction to that change—a perceived loss of personal control—can undermine the confidence that individuals need if they are to seek positive alternatives. This is a major barrier to the reconstruction of working life.

The End of Work?

Evidence collected by Ekos Research Associates indicates that experiences of economic and job worries have bred inertia across wide swaths of the Canadian public. When Ekos asked a representative sample of Canadian adults in its 1996 *Rethinking Government* survey whether they agreed or disagreed with the statement 'I feel I have lost all control over my economic future', 43 per cent agreed. Looking at Figure 2.5, we see that those most likely to feel this sense of economic powerlessness lived in the Atlantic region or in BC, had low educational attainment, were in the 45-to-64 age group, were unemployed, or had lower incomes. Even among the two groups likely to have the

Figure 2.4 Concern about social polarization, Canada, 1996

'I really worry that we are moving to a more divided society of haves and have-nots.'

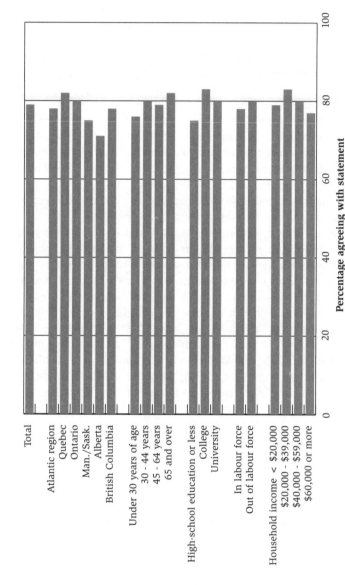

NOTES: Sample = 1,535 adults. Graph reports combined responses of 5, 6, and 7 on a 7-point scale where 1 = strongly disagree and 7 = strongly agree.

SOURCE: Based on Ekos Research Associates Inc., *Rethinking Government 1996*.

most opportunities and choices—those with a university education or a high household income—one in three agreed with the statement. Numerous polls conducted between early 1994 and early 1998 came up with similar findings.[19]

Of all the futuristic images of work portrayed in the media and in public discussions, the end-of-work thesis popularized by Jeremy Rifkin is undeniably the most prominent. Do Canadians share Rifkin's pessimistic view that new technologies are leading us ever closer to a workless world? Ekos Research Associates tested public support for the end-of-work thesis in one of its 1996 surveys. A 'very serious and permanent shortage of jobs' was considered very likely by 42 per cent of respondents in a nationally representative sample of adults. Another 23 per cent thought that this prospect was somewhat likely, while 32 per cent considered it unlikely. Those holding this bleak view of the future of work tended to live in the Atlantic region or BC, to be relatively young, and to report lower educational attainment and lower household incomes than others. But the demographic variations aren't great. Even among Albertans, who were the most sceptical about a Rifkinesque future, about one-third were pessimistic about the future of work. The same question asked in a March 1998 Ekos poll elicited similar responses.[20]

Thus the weight of public opinion tilts slightly towards Rifkin's view. This may help to explain why *The End of Work* became a best-seller. But there's more to these fears about the end of work than one could glean from his lectures. Ironically, what Rifkin presents as the driving force behind the reduction of job opportunities—new information technologies—is one aspect of the changing work world about which Canadians feel quite positive. In fact, as we will see in Chapter 4, the majority of Canadian workers welcome technological change. And to the extent that it has affected their jobs, its impact is seen as generally positive.

Why do so many Canadians fear an end of work? Here are further clues from the Ekos Research Associates' studies. Most respondents to Ekos surveys think the unemployment rate will remain high in the next ten years. Furthermore, respondents tend to view the problem of joblessness as more serious than the official unemployment rates reported by Statistics Canada would suggest. Indeed, 75 per cent of respondents to a late 1996 Ekos survey thought that the actual unemployment rate was higher than that reported. The same survey documented strong support (81 per cent) for having the federal government set targets for reducing the unemployment rate, just as it has for reducing the deficit—again, setting the direction for some pretty firm public policy. These findings signal that Canadians are starting to link private troubles and public issues when it comes to jobs.

Furthermore, Ekos asked its survey respondents whether they saw the gap between rich and poor becoming narrower or wider in the next ten years, more than four in ten believed it would become wider. And when asked to identify which 'differences' are most divisive for Canadian society—between rich and

Figure 2.5   Canadians' sense of economic powerlessness, 1996

'I feel I have lost all control over my economic future.'

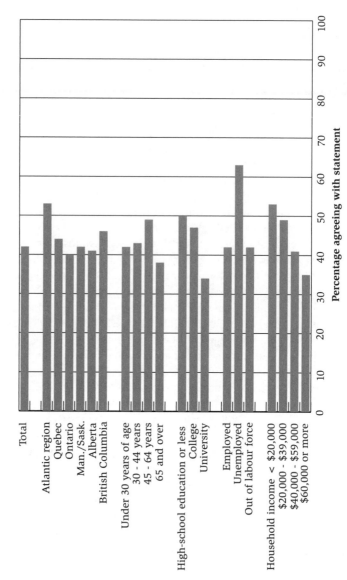

Percentage agreeing with statement

NOTES: Sample = 1,535 adults. Graph reports combined responses of 5, 6, and 7 on a 7-point scale where 1 = not at all likely and 7 = extremely likely.

SOURCE: Based on Ekos Research Associates Inc., *Rethinking Government 1996*.

poor, French and English, ethnic groups, generations, or men and women—economic inequality topped the list.[21] What's particularly interesting is that Ekos compared the general public's predictions of social inequality with those of a sample of 'decision makers' selected from the political and business élite. Over half of the élite expected a widening gap, although it is unclear how serious a problem they considered this to be.

There also is a personal angle to how we view the future of work. For most of us, work is at the core of our identity, and if our work environments are in flux, so too is our sense of identity. A resounding three-quarters of the Ekos survey respondents believed that 'people need the discipline and identity associated with traditional occupations and work in order to contribute to society.' In contrast, slightly less than one-quarter took the position that 'if people's full living needs were taken care of, the end of work could free individuals to focus on more important and interesting human activities.' The same survey found an entrenched desire for paid work, with 55 per cent indicating that they would continue working even if they had enough money to live comfortably for the rest of their lives, because 'my job is an important part of my life.'

Even though a sizeable minority of respondents would choose not to work in that situation,[22] this finding echoes the importance that, as we'll see in Chapter 3, Canadians attach to the work ethic. The Ekos *Rethinking Government* studies explored one alternative to paid work: participation in the 'third sector' made up of non-profit community and voluntary organizations. For most respondents, however, this option was a non-starter. While Canadians have traditionally valued volunteerism, and community organizations are seen as making vital and growing contributions to society, the third sector falls outside the range of what Canadians consider 'work'. In an age when declining living standards and the prospects of unemployment are all too real, turning what used to be volunteer activities into paid work is difficult for Canadians to comprehend—likely because it is unclear how such jobs would be funded. This part of Rifkin's scenario for the future casts a ray of light in an otherwise dark picture, but so far it has not resonated with Canadians.

In general terms, though, Canadians do seem ready to consider taking action on the job front. Ekos found that close to half of the individuals it surveyed in late 1996 expected to lose their jobs in the next few years, a finding that is consistent with the Gallup poll results reported above. Such a pervasive fear of job loss is prompting people to wonder if they should be preparing for what could be a future of shrinking work opportunities and expectations. Indeed, almost three-quarters of employed respondents to the Ekos survey agreed that 'we should be actively planning for how to manage the transition to a world without enough jobs for all those who want to work.' As for who should take primary responsibility for preparing society to face an era of work shortages: 47 per cent of those who agreed with the statement named the federal government; others named provincial governments (17 per cent), business (13 per cent), private citizens and households (14 per cent), and non-profit and voluntary organizations (4 per cent).

Ironically, at the very time when the public is growing ever more cynical about governments and suspicious of their motives, there is a consensus that when it comes to the future of work, the state has a leading role to play. In fact, it may be government's failure to address the 'work agenda' that in large part is fuelling public cynicism. For example, the remarkably popular federal Liberals led by Prime Minister Jean Chrétien have been highly vulnerable on one issue: failure to reduce unemployment.[23] Ekos Research Associates' ongoing surveys confirm that the public is very uneasy about the winding down of government's role in society. Although we may not want to return to old-style state intervention, there are areas where government action is essential. With respect to work quality, for instance, only government can legislate a renewed framework of employment standards guaranteeing an adequate minimum wage, hours of work limits, layoff notification, vacations, and so on. The same is true of public pensions and income support (appropriately combined with opportunities for retraining and career change) for unemployed workers.

On the economic front, then, it appears that a public increasingly jaded about government's ability to solve problems does want state action. Add to this volatile mix other factors, such as an aging and more culturally diverse society and the spectre of government deficits and debt, and it is understandable that Ekos would conclude that economic anxieties and public cynicism about government are mutually reinforcing. In the absence of a unified collective vision of how to respond constructively to the challenges presented by new work realities, individuals are adapting to economic transformations on their own by devising personal survival strategies.

The Training 'Solution'

The above discussion poses several paradoxes. Canadians in the 1990s are deeply troubled about the future of work, yet they still seem wedded to traditional models of work. Most people are dubious about government's ability to solve national problems and think that it is too beholden to corporate interests, yet they look to government to take the lead in job-related issues, especially in reducing unemployment. The perception that Canada is becoming a winner-take-all society, and that living standards are slipping, is widespread, yet in the public mind there appears to be only a vague connection between these trends and the changing work environment.

When it comes to personally responding to the new work realities, Canadians have a rather single-minded focus. One of the most common expressions of individualism in this country is the unwavering belief that education is the key that unlocks economic opportunities. Looking beyond their own immediate situation, Canadians in general see a hierarchical society in which the distance between top and bottom is growing. However, we still cling to the belief—regularly reinforced by government and business—that by acquiring more education or job-relevant training, we too can climb the class ladder and protect ourselves from the risks of an increasingly volatile labour market.

This personal reaction to societal problems is entirely rational. Employers' loyalty to their employees has been eroded, so many workers feel that they are on their own when it comes to ensuring career security. It is likely this understanding of the need for self-reliance that accounts for the signs of rising entrepreneurialism and resiliency that, as I will discuss in Chapter 3, some management commentators discern in employees' work values. Employees are taking responsibility for enhancing their labour-market prospects. When we look at the economic survivors and success stories, it is obvious that an individual's education and skills are increasingly decisive—though still no guarantee of getting and keeping a good job. For example, most of the full-time jobs created in the 1990s have gone to university graduates. In general terms, any kind of university degree continues to provide a bigger payoff in the labour market than any other kind of educational credential. At the same time, individuals with only a high-school education are facing greater difficulties finding and keeping a job. Aware that education still matters, Canadians also have come to question the ability of the education system, at all levels, to provide high-quality, relevant instruction. We could interpret this trend as reflecting a general tendency to think things were better a decade or two ago. However, a fairly pointed evaluation of the education system is found in a late-1995 Angus Reid poll. Presented with the statement 'the educational system in Canada is not paying enough attention to the skills and training that are needed in today's economy', close to four in five respondents agreed.[24]

We also could interpret this criticism of schools as reflecting the depth of Canadians' job worries. People who see the educational system as their only lifeline will naturally want it to function perfectly under all conditions. Evaluations of educational institutions parallel the health of the economy, getting harsher as the economy worsens. Yet in seizing on education and training as their economic survival strategy, many Canadians have prematurely foreclosed debate on other possible ways of renewing working life.

Perhaps the most extensive analysis recently undertaken of Canadians' views on education and training was Ekos Research Associates' *Reskilling Society* study.[25] An overwhelming proportion (94 per cent) of the workers surveyed in early 1994 believed that it is important to learn new skills throughout one's working life. And fully three-quarters expressed an interest in taking some kind of training over the next year or so. However, only about one-third had actually received any formal training in the past year, and the workers most in need of training rarely got it. The reason is that opportunities for employer-sponsored training are closely related to other desirable working conditions, all of which are concentrated in large organizations and skill-intensive industries—precisely the areas of the labour market that are closed to the least-educated. Still, the study's conclusion resonates with points made above: 'The idea of reskilling society has strong appeal in the economically anxious nineties. Training and skill investment are touted as a cornerstone foundation for labour market renewal.'[26]

Convincing evidence in this regard is the study's finding that the most common reasons for taking training are to reduce the risk of unemployment and to gain control over one's economic destiny. We need to realize, though, that people are turning to the training solution at a time when educational costs are rising and there are signs that employers, especially smaller ones, may actually be investing less in training than they used to.[27] Moreover, workers who do receive training, or financial support for further education, from their employers are usually the ones already in good jobs. Thus education and training are helping some sectors of the labour market, while others are completely cut off from these opportunities. The inevitable result is even greater economic polarization. Indeed, Ekos survey respondents cited cost as the main barrier to obtaining training.

The divisions between haves and have-nots are starkly evident in public attitudes about training. The Ekos study sorted survey respondents into five groups based on their attitudes to training. This produced a segmented model of the labour market that reflects the good jobs–bad jobs split. Trapped in the lower reaches of the labour market are the 'economically distressed' (the working poor with major skill gaps but little interest in training), and the 'traditional threatened' (mostly men in declining manufacturing and construction sectors who don't want training despite widespread unemployment). Together, these two groups comprise 29 per cent of workers. The 'bootstrappers or change-seekers' are also in bad jobs, but they want to acquire training in order to get ahead. This group, mostly female, accounts for 22 per cent of all workers. A fourth group, labelled the 'secure middle', makes up more than 25 per cent, and consists largely of middle-level workers with moderate desire for and average participation in training. Finally, the 'agile and aggressive' group comprises slightly under a quarter of all workers; these already highly skilled and well-paid professionals are the most committed to training and the most likely participants. In short, those who could benefit most from training tend not to recognize its value—a view that may reflect a lack of experience with formal training.

Viewing the labour market in this way draws our attention to a significant fallacy in the education and training solution. In theory, increasing one's 'human capital' (economists' terminology for training, education, skills, and work experience) by acquiring further job-relevant education or training should reduce the risks and increase the opportunities in today's labour market. If others are doing the same thing, however, the competition for better jobs will only increase. So far, most employers have not responded to the growing supply of better-educated workers by increasing the skill requirements of jobs.

A 'Working Canada'

Ekos Research Associates' 1997 *Rethinking Government* survey confirmed a strong preference for concerted federal government action on four issues, all of which involve investing in people: education, health care, job creation, and unemployment—in that order.[28] (Job training ranked further down the list, probably because of its common association with programs aimed at getting the unemployed back into the job market.) The fact that education outranked even health care shows just how strongly the 'education ethic' influences Canadians' responses to perceived crises in work.

When Ekos Research Associates probed these public views further, it discovered resounding support (85 per cent) for a 'national project' based on the theme of 'a working Canada'. This was the second choice for a national project, right behind 'a healthier Canada' (87 per cent). The survey did not define what 'a working Canada' would entail as a national project, but the idea is intriguing. We know that the current thinking would likely focus on education and training—a good direction, to be sure, but one that raises tough questions. How can we promote equal opportunities for training at a time when inequalities are increasing, both in the labour market and in society generally? Does 'working' mean a job for all takers? What kinds of jobs should be created? How can this goal be achieved in the context of stubbornly high unemployment? Above all, before we can consider directing our collective efforts towards the creation of a 'working Canada', we need to answer this question: what kind of work do Canadians want?

Chapter 3

What Canadians Want from Work

In August 1997, Jim Alexander and his construction crew, heavy equipment in tow, left unemployment behind in New Brunswick to search for work in Alberta's booming economy. When the *Edmonton Journal* interviewed them in December, the gamble had paid off: all fourteen men were hard at work. Asked why he and his crew trekked across the country, Jim was candid: 'If you can't work, you may as well be dead.'[1] This human-interest story was front-page news. After all, it exuded a determination and entrepreneurialism that seemed tailor-made for Alberta's popular mythology. For Premier Ralph Klein, the fact that Jim and crew headed straight for Alberta would be one more sign of the 'Alberta Advantage'. Realistically, though, most of the nearly one-and-a-half million unemployed at the time couldn't have followed Jim's lead, and likely would not have had his luck either.

When I read this story, I thought of the importance work has for Canadians and the ends to which many will go in search of a job. Jim's comment, juxtaposing work and death, reminds us that for many people, work *is* life, or certainly a huge part of it. This is my starting point for talking about what Canadians expect out of a job and the reasons why paid work is important for us as individuals. These work expectations and motivations offer a bold outline of the kind of working life that Canadians want—a vision of the future. But that vision has been obscured by the very problems that it has the potential to ease: the gnawing anxieties over economic security that have defined public opinion in the 1990s. In short, we have been looking in the wrong places for solutions.

Work Values

Some of the most insightful research findings on what Canadians want from their work are contained in limited-circulation reports, such as the Angus Reid Group's *Workplace 2000* survey commissioned by the Royal Bank, or employee surveys by human-resource management consultants such as Towers Perrin. This information constitutes a rich but largely untapped resource that can point us towards creative work options and workplace changes for the future.

In his 1996 book *Shakedown: How the New Economy Is Changing Our Lives*, pollster Angus Reid wrote that 'Rekindling a sense of hope and optimism is our most important challenge.'[2] How can we achieve renewed optimism after a decade of disquiet about economic change, and scaled-down expectations about living standards? How can the unemployed fishery worker on the East Coast or the underemployed coffee-bar server on the West Coast believe that a better future is possible? Buffeted by constant winds of change, many people are feeling helpless to control any aspect of their economic destiny, particularly their work life. But there is another layer of public opinion to consider, one that reveals considerable continuity in work values and expectations. Indeed, what individuals want out of a job and the importance they attach to paid work is remarkably stable, even though the context in which they work has altered dramatically. We saw in Chapter 2 that issues of job creation and personal economic security have become priorities, as they should. The problem is that these priorities have crowded out other concerns that also matter deeply to most Canadians: the quality of the work they perform and the environment in which they do it.

For now, consider just one example of how the job angst documented in Chapter 2 stands in relation to other, perhaps even more fundamental concerns. A recent poll by Ekos Research Associates asked a representative sample of Canadians what they look for when deciding whether they are interested in a particular job. Presented with three job characteristics—personal growth and development, salary and benefits, and job security—large majorities rated each highly. However, salary and benefits were seen as less important than personal and development, and job security was even less important.[3] This is not to say that having a secure, economically rewarding job is not important. Rather, what this research finding tells us is that Canadians put job quality very high on their wish list. Yet by focusing almost exclusively on job angst, most surveys in the 1990s have missed this issue altogether.

The Meaning of Work

That insight from the Ekos survey led me to think about our core work values. There is a long tradition in both Western and Eastern thought to the effect that work is an expression of our essential humanity. Who we are as individuals, and as a society, is defined in large part by what we do and how we do it. Urgently needed, then, is a plan to redesign working life in line with the twin goals of ensuring economic security *and* improving the quality of the work experience itself. Put simply, there must be enough jobs to go around, but that in itself is not enough: in addition to living wages, these jobs must provide opportunities to utilize and develop our human potential. So far, discussions about how to change work have focused too much on the former, to the neglect of the latter.

Theologians and philosophers have long asked questions about the meaning of work. For example, the theologian Matthew Fox argues that individuals should strive to make work more spiritual and less alienating.[4] Distinguishing between outer and inner work, Fox notes that the entire history of industrialization has revolved around the outer, or visible, aspects of work: the field, factory, or office where work gets done, and the pay cheque that people receive for their work. Fox claims that work has become dehumanized and soulless. So when he asks, 'What are the work needs of our time?' he is inviting reflection on how our spiritual needs can be fulfilled better through work, and how work must change to meet those needs.

The philosopher Edmund F. Byrne takes a different approach, examining how a capitalist society values work. What are the taken-for-granted values and ethics that underlie corporate decisions? For Byrne, work-related values spring from the community in which the work is performed. The contract that ties employees to an employer is also a social contract with the larger community. Thus, corporations are bound by community values about the dignity of work and quality of life. In Byrne's view, 'there is a critical need for a new social contract that will redefine corporate interests in relation to the primordial concern of any community to maintain the social welfare of its people, including workers and their families.'[5] Work values, then, are also community values that lay out normative guidelines for ethical corporate behaviour—yet those guidelines are rarely followed because corporations are more powerful than individuals and communities.

I agree with Fox and Byrne that work is alienating for many people—perhaps even most. However, it seems unlikely that things are any worse now in this regard than at any previous time in the past 150 years. A long line of thinkers going back well before Marx has criticized industrial capitalism because of its dehumanizing, alienating effects on workers. At the dawn of the industrial revolution, even Adam Smith, the intellectual father of modern capitalism, expressed concern about the effects on workers of a more detailed division of labour.[6] Fox's solution is to create a new spiritual order, out of which will flow the outline for a more meaningful kind of work life. Byrne's solution is to rebalance the social contract so that the values of workers and the communities in which they live are fully respected in corporate decision-making.[7] One draws our attention to individual's work needs, the other to the community basis of these needs. I believe that the individual and community are inseparable. Thus Fox's question, 'What are the work needs of our time?', and Byrne's question, 'Should corporations be required to build meaning back into jobs?', can be addressed simultaneously. As we will see, there is a basic continuity in

Canadians' work values that transcends time and space. When the beliefs about work held by individuals are widely shared, they can help to set the agenda for improving the structures and environments in which we work.

It is the conventional wisdom today that the world of work is undergoing rapid and incessant change; as Peter Drucker puts it, the only thing we can be sure about in post-industrial society is change itself.[8] True enough, work structures look different now than they did a quarter-century ago. Today, there are more part-time and temporary jobs, more self-employed people, more small businesses, fewer layers in big organizations, and corporate networks that span the globe. What people bring into the workplace is different, in large measure because the demographics of the workforce have changed. Workers in the 1990s have become increasingly well educated; more are women, visible minorities and immigrants; more are juggling job and family responsibilities. However, in the face of all of these workplace and workforce changes, one of the central characteristics of work remains constant: what individuals want from it.

Ask yourself this question: 'What is the most important thing I want from a job?' Chances are that you're thinking about work that is challenging and interesting, that gives lots of scope for personal development, lets you use your talents and education to make a positive contribution. Quite simply, you desire work that is personally fulfilling. The results from three Canada-wide surveys of workers in the mid-1970s, the late 1980s, and the late 1990s show that fulfilment in work was a national priority long before the current crisis began.

Surprisingly few nationally representative surveys have systematically examined work attitudes and satisfaction, even though these have been public issues for decades. There are lots of polls that ask a few questions about work issues or job concerns. For example, it seems that every few years there is a perceived threat to the work ethic. Usually some employer complains in the media that people, typically youth, just don't want to work as hard as they used to. So pollsters take a snapshot of public opinion on this single issue. But such snapshots are meaningless without a comprehensive monitoring of a range of work attitudes and individuals' work experiences over time. While the three surveys I will examine were not designed to be directly comparable, what's important is that they arrive at the same conclusions from different angles.

The Work Ethic

By the early 1970s, the long wave of expansion that had energized the 1950s and 1960s was beginning to ebb. Inflation was a problem, but there was no OPEC, no Japanese competition, no recession. Unemployment was running at just over 5 per cent—roughly half the rate of the 1990s. Even so, there was disquiet about work. In contrast to the 1960s, with its strong job creation and full employment (at that time, 96 per cent was considered 'full'—meaning a 4 per cent unemployment rate), joblessness was still seen as a growing problem. Huge numbers of baby-boomers were entering adulthood. Having come of age in the rebellious youth culture of the 1960s, many were ready to challenge the status quo. As unemployment nudged up despite strong economic performance, representatives of the business community began to wonder out loud whether some of the unemployed preferred not to work. Was the work ethic eroding, especially among the nation's youth? Were jobs no longer as satisfying as Canadians expected? The federal government's response to these questions was to launch a study of Canadians' work ethic and their satisfaction with employment.[9]

Gallup polls conducted between 1957 and 1975 consistently showed that two in five Canadians believed that most people they knew were not working as hard as they did ten years before. Yet in the 1974 Work Ethic survey, 70 per cent of the employed respondents said they felt a strong sense of commitment to their jobs. And everyone agreed with three statements: 'when things go well at work I am happiest'; 'I feel very good when I've completed a good day's work'; and 'at the end of the day, when I have worked hard, I have a sense of accomplishment'. Canadians in the early 1970s unanimously wanted to be productive at work. Thus the federal government study gave the work ethic a clean bill of health.

Unfortunately, solid research doesn't always put to rest popular myths. In *Maclean's* magazine's 1984 national year-end poll, close to two-thirds (63 per cent) of respondents agreed that the work ethic was eroding and, further, that the next generation would not work as hard as earlier ones.[10] A comparison of 1979 and 1988 national Gallup polls, which asked the same question about the work ethic, suggests that the intensity of work is creeping up, as are work hours in many cases. In the 1978 survey, 69 per cent thought that the people they knew were not working as hard as they did a decade before; ten years later, this view was held by only 50 per cent, with close to one-third saying that people were actually working harder.[11]

Almost a quarter-century after the first major national work-ethic study, the Angus Reid Group's *Workplace 2000* study revisited the issue. And by all indications, the work ethic in the late 1990s is just as strong as ever. Super lotteries didn't exist in the early 1970s, but if they had, researchers might well have asked what workers would do if they won a million dollars. When asked this question in 1997, only 17 per cent of workers said they would quit their job and never work again; 41 per cent would stay in the same job, 17 per cent would launch a different career, and 24 per cent would start their own business (these were the only response choices presented). That nearly one in four people chose the last response suggests that people want to exercise more control over their work.

Job Satisfaction

A national job satisfaction survey conducted in 1973 documented an inconsistency between what people want from work and what they actually experience in their jobs. As in virtually all other national studies of job satisfaction, in Canada and elsewhere, the responses to a question about overall job satisfaction reflected high levels of positive responses. One reason is that people's assessment of job satisfaction tends to be relative, often based on comparisons with the fairly small number of jobs held by people in their social circle—the minimum-wage fast-food server is not likely to be comparing her job with those of engineers or teachers. For some workers, having their present job is better than a limited range of alternatives, which may include being unemployed. Thus while close to nine in ten workers expressed satisfaction with their job in general, this number dropped when more focused questions were asked. Considerably fewer (6 in 10) said that they would definitely take their present job if they had the choice to make again. About the same number would recommend their job to a friend. Beneath the thin gloss of overall satisfaction, then, Canadians apparently did have some misgivings about specific aspects of their jobs.

When presented with a list of 34 job characteristics that contribute to satisfaction, interesting work was the top priority, ahead of salary, a chance to make friends, or even job security. The study's authors concluded: 'Above all, people do not want to work in a stifling environment. This is not particularly surprising given the amount of time we spend at our jobs.'[12] Pursuing this finding, the researchers discovered that people's interest in their work is linked to three other job features: being given opportunities to develop their abilities; doing the things they did best; and having lots of freedom to decide how to do their work.

Indeed, the desire to perform interesting work was almost universal. A mere 3.7 per cent of survey respondents considered interesting work unimportant. When given a choice between interesting (or challenging) work and higher pay, two-thirds of survey respondents opted for the former. This is all the more remarkable given the relatively high inflation in the early 1970s, which might lead one to predict the opposite response. And when the 34 job characteristics were listed in order of importance, only one item in the top ten—working with friendly people—did not have some connection with challenging and interesting work, or the resources needed to do the job. The study then asked workers how satisfied they were with each of the 34 job features that they had rated in terms of importance. The biggest discrepancies between what workers desired and what they got in their jobs were interesting and challenging work, promotion opportunities, and having adequate resources to do the job. Again, the quality of the work was valued most.

The 1980s

In 1987, the polling firm Environics conducted another national job satisfaction survey.[13] The overall level of satisfaction that Canadians reported in their job remained unchanged from the early 1970s. The economy had regained full stride after recovering from the 1981–2 recession. The raw acquisitiveness and excessive materialism that marked the end of the 1980s were at their height. Yet there were troubling signs that the labour market had become a far less hospitable place for many individuals.

Just as in the 1973 survey, half would opt for another occupation if they could choose over again, and half intended to change employers. Environics did not examine a detailed list of job characteristics. But it did find that, while more than seven in ten workers were satisfied with their pay and job security, this was not the case with promotion opportunities, or opportunities to participate in decision-making about their job. Workers under the age of 30 and professional women were especially dissatisfied, mainly with the lack of career advancement opportunities. Rona Maynard interpreted these findings in the *Report on Business Magazine*:

> The survey's message is clear. Today, employees expect not only the traditional rewards of job-holding, a steady paycheque and a secure future, but emotional rewards that are more difficult to quantify. . . . Whether they are janitors or general managers, most Canadians want appreciation for their skills, interest in their aspirations and information on the corporate goals that their efforts promote. They want to be treated like fully rounded human beings, not names on the payroll. Modest as their hopes may sound, too few employers are fulfilling them.[14]

No doubt Maynard's article was read by a good number of managers and executives. But the call for a more humane workplace was swept aside by a growing preoccupation in corporations and governments with bottom lines and deficits. In an era of downsizing and cost-cutting, organizational life was lean and mean, not nurturing or fulfilling. David Olive, editorializing in the *Report on Business Magazine* in 1991, voiced strong objections to corporate Canada's retreat from a 'putting employees first' ethos. 'Only yesterday, employees were held to be the most valued assets of a corporation,' Olive wrote. 'Then the recession began to do its work. Today the job market is awash with *curriculum vitae*, and people don't seem so valuable any more.'[15]

The 1990s

Does Olive's observation that workers are undervalued still ring true in the late 1990s? The lingering aftermath of the recession earlier in the decade, complicated by the revolution in information technologies and global economic trends, meant that government and business alike have remained straightjacketed in a downsizing mentality. And the evidence is mounting that downsizing de-emphasizes human resources, leaving employees feeling like disposable commodities. There are, however, glimmers on the horizon that a more people-centred approach to management has the potential to take root. Governments are becoming concerned about the renewal of their human resources in the midst of a massive exodus of older workers. Corporations are rediscovering the productivity payoffs of cultivating employee loyalty and commitment. But we haven't turned that corner yet.

How, then, are workers experiencing the workplace turbulence of 1990s? The *Workplace 2000* survey conducted by the Angus Reid Group in 1997, with the sponsorship of the Royal Bank,[16] is perhaps the most detailed national analysis of job satisfaction and work attitudes since the federal government's surveys in the early 1970s—nearly a quarter-century earlier. This is startling in an era driven by measures and evaluations all sorts of 'outcomes', and it certainly helps to explain why the quality of work has not received the public attention it deserves. (It is interesting that a major bank has made a connection between Canadians' satisfaction with their work life and the overall health of the economy. Then again, shell-shocked employees hiding in the corporate trenches are not free-spending consumers.)

The detailed psychological profile of Canadian workers that emerges from *Workplace 2000* echoes the 1973 and 1987 job satisfaction surveys. Although it is important to emphasize that the three studies are not directly comparable, because of differences in methodology and question wording, their findings converge around several key points. In 1997, workers expressed general satisfaction with their jobs (see Figure 3.1). On probing more thoroughly, however, it is easy to find signs of discontent. Or, to put it more constructively: the data illuminate areas where both employees and employers stand to gain from improvements. To this end, the *Workplace 2000* report urges managers to focus on creating a workforce of skilled, satisfied individuals who are made to feel appreciated and rewarded for their efforts. This is a major challenge, as the report explains, given that 'the dislocation caused by the recession, globalization, "right-skilling" and increased demands for productivity took its toll on workers in Canada. . . '.[17]

Most workers (86 per cent) who responded to the *Workplace 2000* survey expressed overall satisfaction with their job; this level was almost identical to those found in previous job satisfaction surveys. People tend to give positive responses to such general questions. Nevertheless, one in six workers was dissatisfied with his or her job. And if we look at other areas of the work environment, it is clear that other problems loom as well. For example, two-thirds of workers reported that their jobs were somewhat or very stressful. Heavy workloads that make it hard to keep up were the main problem, made worse by the long hours required in many cases. Lack of involvement and recognition was also a source of frustration for many employees. Many wanted to

Figure 3.1   Workers' ratings of jobs and workplaces, Canada, 1997

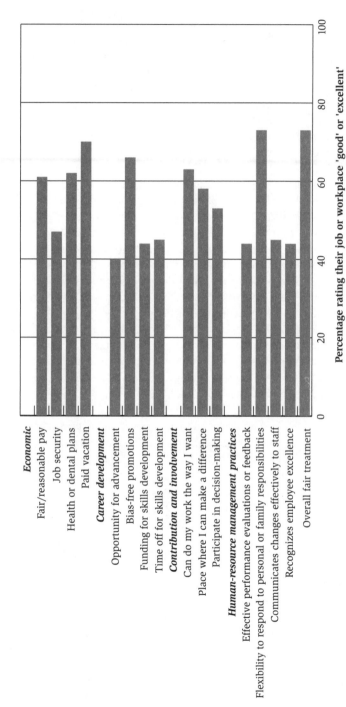

NOTE: Sample = 1,000 employed.

SOURCE: Based on Angus Reid Group, *Workplace 2000: Working Toward the Millennium. A Portrait of Working Canadians* (Fall 1997).

contribute more but felt discouraged from doing so by management policies and organizational structures. Some felt unrecognized and under-rewarded for the contributions they had made. Others felt that their talents were not being used. Indeed, 23 per cent of respondents reported that their job required skills significantly below their levels of expertise or experience (see Figure 3.2).[18] (This problem of 'underemployment' will be addressed in Chapters 5 and 6.)

Workplace 2000 tends to put a positive face on these findings. It emphasizes how workers are feeling more optimistic about the future, preparing themselves for workplace changes, and displaying 'entrepreneurialism'. True, some two-thirds of workers responding to the survey believed that 'they have what it takes to succeed in the 21st century workplace.' But what does this mean? A sizeable minority (28 per cent) felt that the workplace was changing so rapidly that they couldn't keep up. Barely half of the workers surveyed had a career plan. However, a slight majority felt very confident that they had the skills needed to find a comparable job if they were laid off. For these workers, personal preparedness for the next century means acquiring skills through further education and training. When asked to state the biggest challenge they faced in this regard, the most common response, cited by 43 per cent, was keeping up to date and learning. *Workplace 2000* shows that Canadians' personal responses to an unpredictable work future directly reflect the strong public-policy emphasis on education and training that I described in Chapter 2. In personal terms, if 'entrepreneurialism' means taking initiative for lifelong learning, then most workers seem prepared to be entrepreneurs.

The *Workplace 2000* findings suggest that it is not easy for workers to develop their skills. Training is a good example. About half of the respondents—considerably more than in other surveys of training[19]—reported having taken a course to upgrade their knowledge or skills for their current job in the previous 12 months. Yet in less than two-thirds of these cases did the employer pay for the course, and in just over one-third was the course held during working hours. Lack of time, money, and employer support were the most common barriers cited in this regard.

A good number of employers no doubt believe that employees themselves should pay for courses that enhance their general employability. Employees, however, would be quick to point out that the benefits of extra training also accrue to their current employer. This raises the question of how workers' skills, abilities, knowledge, and experience (or human resources) are actually being put to use within the workplace. We might expect employers generally to agree that all employees should have a work environment that enables them to contribute their best efforts. As things stand, though, this ideal seems a long way off. For example, only about one-tenth of workers have the authority to act alone on a new idea, or one that could save their employer time, money, or both. Only one-third had made suggestions for improving their job and/or the profitability of their firm at least once a month. Approximately four in ten

Figure 3.2   Selected evaluations by workers of their jobs and employers, Canada, 1997

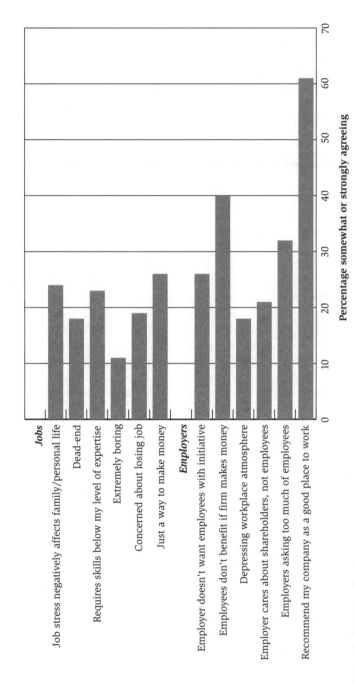

NOTE: Sample = 1,000 employed.

SOURCE: Based on Angus Reid Group, *Workplace 2000: Working Toward the Millennium. A Portrait of Working Canadians* (Fall 1997).

workers 'are encouraged and expected to think of new and innovative ways of doing things'—but six in ten, apparently, are not. What seems most likely to stifle such initiatives is a lack of rewards, time, and enabling structures that empower workers.

By looking at how workers rated their jobs and employers in the *Workplace 2000* survey, we can obtain a more detailed picture of the quality of their work life. Whereas 70 per cent agreed that their job was challenging and interesting, fewer (58 per cent) said they were encouraged at work to actively continue learning in their field of expertise. And sizeable groups (between 18 and 26 per cent) considered themselves to be in a dead-end job, underemployed, or not encouraged to use initiative (see Figure 3.2). Economic issues still figure prominently. One in four viewed their current job as just a way to make money, while just under half reported feeling that it was getting harder to make ends meet. When asked to rate their workplace on a scale of very poor to excellent, roughly half or fewer gave 'good' or 'excellent' ratings in the following areas: involvement in decisions affecting their work; job security; time off for training; effective performance feedback; recognition for doing a good job; and advancement opportunities (see Figure 3.1). Not surprisingly, only just over half felt that their company cared about them. Along the same lines, in the 1996 *Workplace 2000* study slightly over half (53 per cent) of respondents reported that their employer valued employees less then than a few years earlier. In contrast, only 19 per cent reported that their employers valued employees more and put a higher priority on protecting jobs.[20]

Putting all these trends together, we end up with an image of the workplace as awash with cross-currents. The most obvious contrast is the one between a high level of overall job satisfaction and various signs of discontent with specific job or workplace characteristics. But to expect otherwise would be to deny the complexity of social life, especially inside work organizations. This point comes across in many ways. Several years ago, I was invited to speak at a workshop for personnel professionals and career counsellors. Included in the workshop kit was a lapel button that read 'I Love My Job!' Everyone sported these buttons, and would most likely have agreed that in general terms their jobs were pretty good. Yet one unintended effect of the buttons was to open up coffee-time and lunch discussions about sources of job dissatisfaction. If consistently high overall job satisfaction levels were an accurate indicator of the full extent of work experiences, then, like the lapel button, this chapter would have a brief and happy story to tell; concerns about the future of work would be negligible. In reality, experiences are filtered through individuals' expectations, and work is multidimensional, meeting many needs from the economic to the psychological.

Several prominent themes emerge from the above studies of work attitudes and job satisfaction. Canadians have a deeply engrained commitment to work, and they generally like their work; yet when asked about specific features of their jobs, or to evaluate their employers, a good number tend to express discontent. These findings should be taken as constructive feedback, for they can be used to both employees' and employers' advantage. Most in need of attention is why organizations appear to have difficulty providing adequate opportunities for employee development, participation, and advancement. Pay and job security are also important, especially among those in low-paid and tenuous positions, but the majority of workers say that their main motivation is self-fulfilment. On this point Canadians are no different from people elsewhere. Many other surveys have shown that individuals place a high value on interesting work and the ability to contribute their ideas and talents to the organization in which they work. For example, studies that I conducted with my colleague Harvey Krahn among Edmonton high-school and university graduates in 1985 and 1996 show a strong preference for interesting, challenging, and self-fulfilling work, even ahead of pay and job security.[21] Most workers want to do their best on the job, and to develop their potential to do even better.

The New Employment Contract

One additional study confirms that the human dimensions of work are being neglected. Towers Perrin, a major North American human-resource management consulting firm, regularly surveys private-sector employees, and in 1995 it published a Workplace Index measuring how Canadian and American workers felt about their jobs.[22] Reading between the lines of that Index and reinterpreting the data, it is possible to extract a more critical perspective on what needs to change in workplaces.

Towers Perrin sets the stage for its Workplace Index by observing that in the 1990s, employers 'had to recreate themselves through reengineering and downsizing. Canadian companies have been laying off and redeploying thousands of employees. Demanding more from fewer people. And stretching to compete. . . .'[23] Instead of finding employees to be disillusioned, demoralized, or on the verge of burning out, Towers Perrin discovered 'a resilient workforce that is seeking a new employment relationship'.[24] This assertion naturally raises questions about just how resilient employees have become, and what kind of new relationship they are seeking with employers. After inspecting the survey results, I too would give employees credit for weathering the storms of corporate reorganization and downsizing. But I would suggest also that they want a rather different 'new deal' from the one proposed by Towers Perrin or other management consultants.

Most of the employees surveyed condemned downsizing and restructuring, which two-thirds had experienced in the two years leading up to the survey. Most did not think these strategies had improved their firm's business. While a solid majority (66 per cent) were optimistic about the firm's success in the coming year, they gave the credit not to management's efforts, but rather to their own. Many employees (46 per cent) were critical of their employers' attempts to cut waste and bureaucracy. Eight in ten saw their co-workers as hard-working and dedicated. And a similar proportion felt that personally they could have a positive impact on the firm's success through their daily work. On the basis of these findings, Towers Perrin advises employers to do more to 'engage employees'. The report then goes on to outline a new employment relationship, based on the six themes comprising the Workplace Index: career security; making a contribution; personal growth; alignment with business goals; management effectiveness; and customer focus.

Clearly these six themes reflect an employer's perspective; they say very little about how employees themselves feel about their jobs. Towers Perrin concludes that workers who rate their workplace high on all six dimensions are more committed than other employees and therefore more productive. This finding has direct implications for management. For a start, managers could rectify problems that detract from employees' satisfaction and performance; this means ensuring that employees are recognized and rewarded for their efforts, and given opportunities for personal and career development.[25] However, the new deal that employers are advised to offer their workers is couched in the language of 'employability' and 'personal responsibility'. This is what Towers Perrin hears employers telling workers: 'Don't expect a job for life. Do expect that your continuing employment will depend on providing continuing value and contribution to the organization. Recognize that you must take at least partial responsibility for guiding and maintaining your skills and applying those skills in the areas most critical to our profitable growth.'[26]

In the past, work was based on an implicit understanding along the lines of 'I'll be a loyal employee if you provide me with job security.' In its place, Towers Perrin proposes a new system based on individual initiative and merit. Workers who clearly contribute what managers now call 'value added', and who take the lead in honing their skills, should be supported and rewarded over the long term. This is the basic logic of the performance-based pay systems that are becoming more common. Towers and Perrin conclude that employees are accepting the fact that their continued contribution to the firm is the only reasonable basis for secure employment. This idea of a meritocracy in the workplace raises the spectre of individual winners and losers, with the potential to create the kind of social divisions that, as we saw in Chapter 2, really worry Canadians. If resources for employee development are allocated on merit, how will merit be defined? and by whom? These are serious issues, because if it follows the logic of the new employment contract, the economy could end up tapping the potential of only the top 15 or 20 per cent of workers.

The logic of performance-based pay assumes that employers can assess an individual's contribution fairly and equitably—never mind the even more difficult challenge of evaluating group or 'team' contributions. It also assumes that expectations in this regard are reasonable, and that all employees are given the opportunity to make a full contribution, including developing and refining the skills needed to do so. At stake, then, is what the employment relationship *should* be. I will return to this later; for now, let's concentrate on gaining a better understanding of what employees want.

The six indices that Towers Perrin used for employees' ratings of their workplaces and employers do offer some useful clues in this regard. The fact that most workers saw a link between their firm's financial success and their own job security raises the question of whether they felt they were encouraged to contribute fully. About three-quarters said they did. However, other aspects of the work environment may discourage them from making full contributions. For example, only 41 per cent of those surveyed believed that they had advancement opportunities in their firm; 53 per cent agreed that their interests were considered in corporate decision-making; and 59 per cent rated their immediate supervisor as effective in supporting their growth and development. Towers Perrin puts employers on notice that they need to address organizational weaknesses in these areas: 'Employees today equate fairness with a sense of participation, and failure to create a participative culture could, in the future, have a negative effect on employee commitment.'[27] But employees might well be sceptical. While a large majority of those surveyed perceived themselves and their co-workers as hard-working, only two out of three rated managers as doing an effective job. These findings underscore the two realities that co-exist in most workplaces: one for managers and another for everyone else.

Conclusion

This chapter has documented a gap between the kind of high-quality work that Canadians want and their actual employment experiences. In particular, Canadians want more opportunities for work that is challenging, interesting, that encourages personal development, and that engages them in decision-making. Why have work-quality issues not received more attention? The main reason is that Canadians have been preoccupied with the basic calculus of economic survival. Vanishing job security, high unemployment, loss of control over one's economic future, a fraying social safety net, declining living standards, a widening chasm between 'haves' and 'have-nots'—as we saw in Chapter 2, these concerns have been at the forefront of the public consciousness in the 1990s.

But job anxiety is far from universal. Some segments of the workforce— senior managers and the 'knowledge workers' in the information technology, financial services, and energy industries—see abundant opportunities on the horizon. The public mood is moulded partly by the information selectively filtered through the media, and partly through individuals' own experiences. But few people have the time or resources to run a 'reality check', testing their specific concerns about work in the future against the best available data. The next chapter provides this reality check, documenting what we know and what we need to know about the trends likely to have the greatest impact on the quality of work in the future.

Chapter 4

The 'New Economy'

Canadians want a better quality of work life. A steady stream of workplace surveys and public-opinion polls affirms that. So far, however, public policy on the work front has tended to focus on the scarcity of jobs as captured in a single statistic: the unemployment rate. Missing is any discussion of how the quality of work might be improved.

The 1990s began with the Economic Council of Canada sounding alarm bells over the emergence of a 'double-edged' labour market as Canada became a full-fledged service economy.[1] It was the Council that coined the 'good jobs–bad jobs' term that has framed much of the discussion about the changing nature of work. The Council's two main recommendations were a renewed emphasis on human-resource development and the provision of economic security for workers in the face of labour-market insecurities.

For the Economic Council, a good job was well-paying, secure, and skilled. However, this definition expresses only part of what most Canadians understand by a 'good job'. Also important is having a say, doing something that is interesting and mentally challenging, developing one's potential, and making useful contributions through one's work activity. Ideally, work should improve a person's overall quality of life. Yet too often, as we have seen, work is stressful, lacks meaning, and interferes with family and personal life.

This chapter offers a critical view of work in the 'new economy', showing that current labour-market trends are making quality goals more difficult than ever to achieve. The advent of information technology and economic globalization has contributed to huge shifts in the scale, location, and speed of economic activity. But these changes are evolutionary, not revolutionary. Many believe that the strength of the economy lies in its knowledge workers, and that continuous learning and adaptable skills are the key to prosperity. Workplace experiences, however, suggest that employment structures stifle the application of knowledge and active learning. In fact, there is a growing contradiction between image and reality. The economy is creating both skilled, well-paid jobs and unskilled, low-paid, dead-end ones. Sales and service occupations remain the largest occupational category. In 1996, these semi-skilled and unskilled jobs were held by more than one in four of all workers—3.7 million individuals in jobs that could hardly be called 'knowledge work'. The three most common male jobs were truck driver, retail salesperson, and janitor; for women, retail salesperson, secretary, and cashier.[2] Clearly, the work-quality issues that were central to debates about the future of work in the 1960s and 1970s—what the 'new economy' gurus consider the old industrial era—are more relevant than ever today.

There is a useful distinction to be drawn between a job and work. A job is an economic entity. Employers use job descriptions, economists refer to the number of jobs created or lost, workers compete for jobs in the labour market. Strictly speaking, a job is a 'piece of work' that one does for hire or profit.[3] The idea of work is more philosophical: our whole being is complexly related to work. While unemployment results in loss of income, then, a lack of purposeful work diminishes the human spirit, and can be equally devastating.[4] Certainly we need to create more jobs—but we also need to think about the kind of 'work' we want to create.

This chapter examines a cluster of trends that, by default, are now charting the future of work—and, unless we muster the political will to alter their direction, will continue to do so. Job insecurity, labour-market polarization, the problems associated with adapting work organization to new information technology, and work environments that have a negative impact on health and family life underscore the need to pay more attention to the human dimensions of workplace change. Together, ironically, they run against the grain of the people-as-competitive-advantage thinking that is so prevalent in public policy today.

Assessing Work Quality

Since the Economic Council's *Good Jobs, Bad Jobs* study, a number of other Canadian researchers have examined job quality. But their main focus has been on income. As Statistics Canada's 1998 labour market overview stated: 'From some perspectives, a "good" job balances a satisfactory level of pay with appropriate working conditions, task variety, co-worker interaction and other non-monetary characteristics. However, from the macroeconomic point of view . . . what makes a job "good" is simply how well it pays over a week. This aspect of job quality most impacts economic health.'[5] Obviously, a living wage is the only way to ensure that individuals, families, and communities are sustained. Yet work also contributes in more profound ways to human fulfilment.

A one-sided economic perspective must therefore be expanded to include the social and psychological aspects of work. For example, people with higher levels of education also tend to have higher current income and lifetime earnings than less-educated individuals. But education also tends to mean a better quality of work. Education is a good predictor of the levels of autonomy (making decisions) and authority (as a supervisor or manager) an individual enjoys in a job, even after taking into account the effects of gender, age, firm size, work experience, and industry on these two job-quality dimensions.[6]

Learning is another dimension of quality work. However, opportunities for additional job-related training—a hallmark of a knowledge-based economy—are unequal, and are closely related to a worker's income and level of education. Only some three in ten workers annually receive training related to their present or future employment.[7] University graduates are twice as likely to participate in such training as high-school graduates are. Only one in five workers earning less than $15,000 takes part in training, compared with half of those earning more than $75,000. Training also is more readily available in occupations requiring high levels of knowledge and skills: for instance, among managers, scientists and engineers, teachers, and health-care and other professionals.

The spread of various nonstandard forms of work has major implications for quality. Nonstandard work—part-time and temporary jobs, multiple jobs, and 'own-account' (solo) self-employment—contrasts with the traditional model of full-time, continuous employment with a single employer. Now accounting for about one in three of all jobs, nonstandard work on the whole has lower skill requirements, is more repetitive, and offers less decision-making autonomy than standard jobs. In some economic sectors, particularly in the lower-tier service industries (retail, personal and consumer services), a nonstandard job likely means not using your education, skills, and abilities.[8] At the same time, among the nonstandard workers are select groups—website designers who contract their expertise, self-employed professionals, business consultants—who benefit from the independence and freedom of not being tied to a single employer as an employee. These people are among the élite knowledge workers frequently held up by futurists as models for us all. In reality, though, this high end of the nonstandard work spectrum illustrates the polarization that increasingly divides the labour market.

While some senior managers and professionals can earn far more in the private sector, and enjoy better benefits too, for the average employee job quality is better in the public sector. Less bound by market forces, government has been more inclined than the private sector to make employment policy decisions on the basis of fairness, equity, and the community good. Thus whereas fewer than half of private-sector employees have pension plans, more than four in five of those in the public sector do. A similar split is evident with respect to benefits such as medical and dental plans and paid sick leave. The higher levels of unionization in the public sector contribute to the public–private 'job quality gap'.[9]

The size of an employer can also affect work quality. Statistics Canada researchers who examined the impact of firm size on wages, fringe benefits, and work schedules found a quality premium attached to employment in a large firm.[10] Even after accounting for differences in workers' characteristics and the industries concerned, large firms pay 15 to 20 per cent more than small ones. Pension-plan coverage is four times higher in large firms. And workers in large firms put in shorter workweeks, although more of them are likely to have shift work.

The above evidence challenges the conventional wisdom that smaller firms are preferable to big corporations and governments as employers. No doubt that wisdom is reinforced by the litany of hardships caused when large employers downsize. It may also reflect a desire to escape what the sociologist Max Weber called the 'iron cage' of bureaucracy that seems to come with size. In any event, the fact that in recent years net job creation has been highest in small firms suggests that it is all the more important to find ways of improving working conditions in the small-business sector.

How do workers define work quality? In the late 1980s, the American sociologists Christopher Jencks, Lauri Perman, and Lee Rainwater devised a study to find out what workers viewed as desirable in a job. While earnings were the single most important consideration for workers, they found 13 non-monetary job characteristics that, together, were twice as important as earnings. Among them were full-time weekly hours, on-the-job training, not getting dirty at work, longer vacations, a flexible schedule, little direct supervision, having a union contract, varied work, public-sector employment, few layers of management, high educational requirements, and job security. (Interestingly, with respect to labour-market inequality, the American researchers also discovered that the range of inequality in the distribution of these non-economic benefits was almost twice that found in pay.[11])

This view of job desirability echoes what various surveys show that Canadians want from their work. Some of the features associated with desirable jobs actually refer to the context in which such jobs are likely to be found. That is, working in a unionized workplace, for a public-sector employer, or in a non-bureaucratic organization tends to mean better pay, higher educational requirements, more influence on decision-making, and greater training opportunities.

Only one Canadian study has attempted to develop measurable indicators of job quality. Drawing on the above American research, Andrew Jackson, a Canadian Labour Congress economist, and Pradeep Kumar, an industrial relations professor at Queen's University, observe that pay is the most widely measured and reported quality indicator in Canada. By contrast, 'remarkably little is known about the characteristics of jobs in terms of meeting the needs and desires of workers to develop and exercise their skills and capacities, to work at a reasonable pace, to derive interest and satisfaction from their work, and to participate in a non stressful work environment.'[12] Trends in earnings, the distribution of pay, pension plan coverage, involuntary part-time employment, work schedules, permanent and temporary layoff rates, job stability, and union representation suggest a deterioration of job quality in the 1990s. However, more information is needed on issues like job satisfaction, benefits, access to training, stress, job autonomy, and participation in order to document how job quality is changing over time in Canada.

And even then we would not have a complete picture of work quality. To get at what Alan Wolfe calls the 'moral dimensions' of work, we need to cast a wider net. On this point the American sociologist Randy Hodson offers some insights. Reviewing many qualitative studies of how workers actually experience and respond to workplace organization, he concludes that maintaining dignity is an overriding desire. Hodson shows how individuals strive to 'defend or regain dignity in the face of work organizations that violate workers' interests, limit their prerogatives, or otherwise undermine their autonomy'. For Hodson, dignity means 'having personal space for one's individual identity'.[13] Worker dignity is greatest in work settings that provide participation, freedom, and opportunities for self-actualization.

Quality work is a multi-faceted and holistic concept that reflects the perspective of the person doing the work. The use and development of human potential, the work environment, personal fulfilment and meaning are just as important as the economic aspects of a job. No single study draws all these features together. But the research noted above indicates that quality may be declining. Some key labour-market and workplace trends, to which I will now turn, indeed suggest that, instead of enhancing overall job quality, the 'new economy' is erecting barriers to this goal.

Job Security

Unstable employment undermines individuals' economic security. This situation is made worse by a lack of adequate government programs to help workers make labour-market transitions, whether in finding jobs or changing careers, upgrading their skills, or entering retirement. Permanent layoffs have contributed to what economists call labour-market 'churning' since the late 1970s, so this is not a new trend. Nor is it restricted to large employers, as popular notions of downsizing suggest: in fact, a worker's chance of being put out of work is greater in a small firm than in a large one. Even so, during the 1992–3 recession the permanent layoff rate was 7.5 per cent of all employed, and the temporary layoff rate 9.3 per cent. To put numbers to these trends, in 1993, 1.165 million workers were permanently laid off and 1.8 million were temporarily laid off. These figures do not include workers who retire or simply quit their jobs. In a tight labour market, more workers put up with undesirable working conditions because voluntary quit rates decline.[14]

Between 1981 and 1994, the typical new job lasted about three and a half years. However, the stability suggested by this average hides unsettling undercurrents in job tenure. The polarization we have seen in other areas is also evident with respect to job security. On one hand, a growing proportion (64 per cent in 1994) of newly acquired jobs lasted less than a year. On the other hand, jobs lasting more than a year tend to extend beyond five years—a trend apparent across all groups and economic sectors. Thus job instability is greater for recent hires.[15]

Yet workers' sense of insecurity, outlined in Chapter 3, seems to be even greater than these layoff statistics might warrant. The explanation lies in the difficulty of finding a new job and the lack of income support while unemployed. For most of the decade the unemployment rate has hovered around 9 per cent of the labour force—about twice the level of what economists used to consider full employment.[16] Requirements for unemployment insurance eligibility were tightened in 1996 when the program was renamed Employment Insurance, supposedly to shift the emphasis from income support to training. Consequently, the number of beneficiaries declined from a high of 3.7 million in 1991 and 1992 to 2.9 million in 1996. By 1997 only 36 per cent of those officially unemployed collected benefits during any given month.[17] What's more, the number of people who have been jobless for more than six months has steadily risen.

Unemployment is symptomatic of a larger problem of under-utilized labour. The Centre for the Study of Living Standards, an Ottawa-based economic think-tank, documents that involuntary part-time workers increased six-fold between 1975 and 1995.[18] In the same period the unemployment rate went up from 7.2 to 9.5 per cent. If the hours lost by these involuntary part-timers (over 800,000 individuals in 1995) are factored into the unemployment rate, the latter goes up to 12.5 per cent in 1995. The part-time employment rate has remained stable in the 1990s, at around 19 per cent of all employed. What's new is the growth in part-time work that is involuntary, creating a growing pool of sub-employed. This trend has been fuelled by the increasing preference among employers for less expensive, more 'flexible' workers.

The poor quality of part-time jobs was brought into the public spotlight by two highly publicized strikes in 1997: the United Parcel Service strike in the US and the Safeway grocery store strike in Alberta. At issue in both cases were part-time workers' demands for longer hours, pro-rated benefits, and more personal flexibility. Some big employers, like the banks and various public-sector organizations, offer dental, medical, and disability coverage to their part-time staff. But most firms balk at the cost. Saskatchewan is the only province requiring employers to extend (on a pro-rated basis) all the benefits to part-time workers that are provided to full-time staff. (It's interesting to note that some Saskatchewan employers saw this regulation as beneficial in terms of staff loyalty and 'remaining competitive'.[19]) The fact that some workers choose part-time work for personal or family reasons—especially women, who account for more than three-quarters of all part-timers over the age of 25—

signals a desire for the flexibility it offers. So far, however, flexibility comes at a significant personal economic cost.[20]

The decline of permanent employment is another symptom of insecurity. In November 1995, 12 per cent of paid workers were in seasonal, temporary, casual, or temporary help agency jobs. Historically, most non-permanent work has been seasonal, but now temporary and casual workers account for 83 per cent of all such work. Permanent jobs provide higher average wages and better benefits than non-permanent ones. The permanent–non-permanent wage gap is $3 per hour. In 1995, two-thirds of permanent jobs had at least three of five benefits (employer-sponsored pension plan, health insurance, dental benefits, paid sick leave, paid annual vacation), compared with only 18 per cent of non-permanent jobs. Only 16 per cent of permanent jobs offered none of these benefits, compared with 60 per cent of seasonal, temporary, or casual jobs.[21]

If job security has become more fragile, though, claims that workers can expect seven jobs in their lifetime are exaggerated. While specific groups may have work histories that include many employers (for example, seasonal workers in some resource industries, construction workers, women who have moved in and out of the workforce to accommodate family responsibilities, and computer specialists whose skills are in great demand) the seven-job career is far from the norm. It may, however, become a reality for young people now entering the labour force.

In contrast, many older workers leave the labour force altogether when faced with workplace restructuring. This is why the average age of retirement has declined in the last decade. In a rapidly aging workforce, economic security in retirement has become a major concern. In 1997, only 44.5 per cent of 45- to 54-year-olds who filed tax returns, and only 30 per cent of all tax-filers, made registered retirement savings plan (RRSP) contributions.[22] Just over half of paid workers have employer-sponsored pension plans, and the people least likely to receive this benefit are those in the most precarious financial situations—part-timers, non-permanent and non-unionized workers, new recruits receiving low wages, and those working in small firms.[23] This is a strong argument for maintaining, or even strengthening, public pensions.

Self-Employment

A leading labour market trend of the 1990s is the expansion of self-employment. In 1998, self-employed persons accounted for 18 per cent of all employment in Canada, and between 1989 and 1997, self-employment accounted for about 80 per cent of all job growth. Canada leads the industrial nations in this shift to self-employment; in the US, by contrast, self-employment over the same period rose only 10 per cent.[24] Like the rise in job creation among small businesses, the boom in self-employment is related to the trend among large organizations to reduce their workforces or restrict hiring. Generally speaking, the jobs both of the self-employed and of those working in small firms are of lower quality than the ones that large employers are eliminating, although a small number of individuals in these situations do have high-quality work.

A few of the new self-employed run small firms that employ other workers. ('Small businesses' are defined as having gross revenues under $5 million. In 1995, there were over 1 million small businesses in Canada, concentrated in retail trade, construction, business services, and personal services.) About two-thirds of self-employed people, however, work alone. These freelancers and contract workers form a growing pool of flexible labour available to large organizations as they downsize and outsource. According to 1997 Statistics Canada data, only about 12 per cent of self-employed people were pushed into creating their own jobs because they lacked other work options. By contrast, 42 per cent said they chose self-employment because they wanted more independence. Fewer than 10 per cent said the main reason they went into self-employment was to make more money.

Although on average the self-employed earn about the same as those working for other people, in the 1990s their earnings have fallen relative to those of employees, and they are far more polarized. In 1995, 56 per cent of own-account self-employed made less than $20,000, compared with 31 per cent of self-employed employers. Only 2 per cent of the own-account workers earned more than $80,000 that year, compared with 9 per cent of employers. This pattern reflects the fact that self-employment is highest among the most and the least educated. Similarly, the female–male wage gap is greater among the self-employed than among employees. In 1996, full-time female employees earned 73 per cent of what full-time male employees did. The gender gap was even greater among the self-employed: female (small business) employers earned only 69 cents for every dollar their male counterparts did, and the rate for solo (own-account) self-employed women was even lower (67 cents). This is not surprising, given that the recent growth in self-employment is especially strong at the top (engineers, accountants) and bottom (domestic cleaners, sales people) of the service sector, and that the concentration of women is higher in the latter category.[25]

Working hours among the self-employed raise further quality concerns. Increasingly, moonlighting means being self-employed on the side. Specifically, 38 per cent of multiple-job holders are self-employed in their second job—an accelerating trend. Furthermore, long hours are common among business owners. As Statistics Canada comments: 'Although it is not known how many business owners consider themselves overworked, many work long hours.'[26] Work hours also have become increasingly polarized, with more part-timers at one end of the hours continuum and more workers putting in very long work weeks at the other. Self-employment partly explains the overall rise in long work hours: in 1995, one in three self-employed individuals worked 50 or more hours a week.[27]

In addition, self- or small-business employment tends to mean reduced opportunities for worker training. The self-employed are on their own when it comes to finding and paying for training or career-related education, while the average revenue of an incorporated small business is only about $400,000 annually (considerably less for unincorporated businesses),[28] most of which goes to wages. Thus additional investment in workers is not a viable option for most small firms, even though it would likely help to 'grow' the business. Without significant government support, the goal of creating a knowledge-intensive or learning organization is clearly beyond the reach of most small firms.

With the assistance of new information technology, self-employment is helping to make the idea of the traditional all-under-one-roof workplace obsolete. Excluding individuals working on farms, in 1996 there were 819,000 Canadians working at home, comprising 6 per cent of the employed labour force. Well over half (58 per cent) of this group is self-employed. In fact, 30 per cent of all self-employed individuals work at home. Furthermore, working at home is more likely to be a part-time than a full-time activity, especially among women.[29] Although the trend towards decentralization is in its infancy, it is not too soon to raise concerns about the working conditions of home-based workers. For example, these workers fall outside of the usual employee-protection legislation, such as employment standards and occupational safety and health legislation, even if they are working on contract for another business.

Winners, Losers, and Those In-Between

Media images are constant reminders of extremes in wealth and poverty. Stories about homeless people and single mothers relying on social assistance are juxtaposed with reports of CEOs cashing in lucrative stock options. While Canada has not moved down this path as far or as fast as other countries, especially the US, opinion polls show that the public is very concerned that we are drifting towards a two-tiered society. Many individuals and families have endured a daily struggle over the past 20 years against sliding living standards. Despite some modest productivity gains, the Canadian economy has failed to deliver higher wages.

Economic anxiety deepens among those facing an uncertain economic future or a reduced living standard. Average after-tax earnings dropped 2.4 per cent for dual-earner families and 9.6 per cent for single-income families between 1989 and 1995, according to Statistics Canada data—and that decline would have been worse had the labour force not been expanding and increasingly well-educated. In the 1985 to 1995 period, individuals treaded economic water, having lost any wage gains from the latter half of the 1980s during the recession of the early 1990s. For families the story was similar, although two-earner families experienced only a 1 per cent drop in their living standards, compared with 10 per cent for single-earner families. In fact, most families now need two incomes to survive: in 1995, 60.5 per cent of two-partner families had both partners working.[30]

Poverty has grown wider and deeper as the labour market has become more competitive and income support programs have been reduced. In the first half of the 1990s, the low-income population grew 29 per cent, while the total population increased only 6 per cent.[31] Low-income families increased in the same period, from 13 per cent to 16 per cent of all families: 12 per cent of husband–wife and 48 per cent of female-led lone-parent families were below the official low-income line. Without the earnings of wives, 21.4 per cent of two-earner families would fall below the official low-income line, compared to the actual figure of 10.5 per cent.[32] In 1995, one in four children under age six lived in low-income families, up from one in five in 1990. And most welfare recipients are receiving lower benefits now than in the mid-1980s.[33]

What's happening to the poor reflects a larger pattern of income inequality.[34] In 1975, the average earnings of workers in the top 10 per cent of wage earners were 3.21 times those earners in the bottom 10 per cent; by 1990, the ratio had increased to 3.97:1. At a time when in Canada average wages were not rising, the cumulative effects of inflation meant that the poor became relatively worse off. It was in the countries with the best job-creation records in the 1980s that less-educated workers experienced the greatest drop in wages.[35] Instead of attaching a premium to the earnings of the better-educated, rising educational credentials tended to drive down the cost of less-educated labour. Such trends do not bode well for job quality among less-educated workers.

In particular, younger workers and lower-skilled and less-educated males under the age of 35 are doing far worse now than 20 years ago. Earnings gains have tended to go to older workers, often those with higher levels of education. As well, women's earnings have slowly increased, but this rise in part reflects the relative drop in male earnings in the 1990s. Since the 1981–2 recession, workers, especially males, in the 15-to-24 age group have been more affected than any other age group by declining wages, as we will see in Chapter 6. Interpreting these trends is complicated by the fact that some of the ups and downs in earnings trends for specific groups may cancel each other out in national averages. It's also important to recognize that, since participation in the labour force dropped in the 1990s, some people who might be earning lower incomes aren't included in these earnings calculations.[36]

A more polarized distribution of work hours—shorter hours for part-timers and longer hours for some full-time workers—lies behind these earnings trends. The young, less skilled, and less educated have faced increasing difficulties finding enough work at a living wage. Not only did full-time employment become scarcer, but at the same time average hourly earnings dropped. For the better-educated, however, full-time job opportunities increased. For growing numbers, 'full-time' has come to mean a longer workweek.

Approximately 17 per cent usually work more than 40 hours in a typical week. And in 1997, 2 million Canadians worked overtime, of whom more than half were not paid for their extra effort.[37]

The backdrop to these shifts in earnings inequality is the process of job loss and job creation. Most recent job growth has been in industries and occupations that pay above-average wages. When hiring for such jobs, employers often require applicants to have post-secondary credentials. Job loss has been felt the most in low-paid and low-skilled jobs.[38] Even though job creation was strongest in occupations and industries that pay above average, new workers start at the lower end of the pay scale. Furthermore, these good jobs are offset by large job gains in low-paying areas of the labour market. Consequently, growing segments of the population are excluded from the good jobs that are being created by virtue of their education, skills, gender, geographic location, or age. For this group, the quality of work may be beside the point; they simply want an opportunity to earn a living wage.

Information Technology: Fact and Fiction

Information and communication technology is a driving force in the transformation of work. The digital revolution, especially computer technology, has made huge changes in how and where we work. The spread of this technology raises the stakes for workplace reform, without which its potential to improve both productivity and the quality of work can't be unleashed. Access to computers themselves and the training needed to use them is creating new forms of inequality and reinforcing old ones. These developments have implications for the quality of work. Critics envision an information age marked by mass unemployment and—for the lucky few who do have jobs—dehumanized work.[39] Technology boosters counter that computers are creating a knowledge-based economy with widespread benefits. In fact, these debates have been going on since the 1960s, with new refrains and a faster tempo.

The Canadian evidence suggests that on balance, information technology has created more jobs than it has destroyed. When the Conference Board of Canada compared firms that made extensive use of information technology with other low-tech firms, it found that the former created more jobs than the latter.[40] At the same time, technological change can shake up workplaces, pushing workers in some industries onto the street, and reducing the skills or working conditions in others. Inadequate investment in technology and the accompanying skills may hinder the competitiveness of certain firms, making them vulnerable to low-cost producers in developing countries. Between 1986 and 1991, for example, 100,000 manufacturing jobs were lost in industries that used little information technology (for inventory control systems, product design, or in the manufacturing process itself); these were mainly fabricating and assembling jobs—the kind of work that can be done more cheaply in Mexico or China.

Studies of the impact of computers on work show both winners and losers. The labour force as a whole has undergone overall upskilling with some polarization. Within particular workplaces, however, there are signs of deskilling. And among individual workers we find 'considerable skill disruption'.[41] In other words, technological change means different things for the labour force, workplaces, and individuals. While policy responses should address all three levels, it is especially important to focus on workplace organization and management practices, since these can either stifle or encourage adaptations that are positive for workers.

The Conference Board, among others, urges careful consideration of what individuals and businesses can do to make information technology an enabling resource. But enabling for whom? So far, the emphasis has been on improving profits and efficiency for the employer. Paradoxically, though, the more sophisticated the hardware and software are, the more important become the skills and abilities of the worker who makes the technology function. Thus technology can be enabling for workers as well, in the sense that it may increase the need for skill, discretion, creativity, and learning on the job. The end result is greater productivity.

The Conference Board doesn't pursue the link between technology and organizational change, despite evidence of the importance of organizational context to technological innovation.[42] However, it does criticize industrial nations, including Canada, for underestimating the importance of overcoming two major barriers to successful information technology implementation: the quality, skill, and flexibility of the labour force; and the failure of many firms to integrate changes in organizational structures and processes with the introduction and effective use of technology. Failure to address these issues, the Board warns, 'will critically hamper the ability of Canada to compete in an increasingly knowledge-based global economy'.[43]

This point draws our attention to the quality of the work environment in which technology is used. Current working conditions and organizational structures can make it difficult for individuals to access and use technology. Here are three examples. First, let's consider why so many large-scale computer systems don't function properly despite their state-of-the-art technical features. Some organizations have learned an expensive yet valuable lesson: to pay more attention to the people side of technological change.[44] When corporations or government organizations introduce all-encompassing information systems with the goal of seamlessly linking financial, personnel, and customer data, it is often realized too late in the process that such systems require a total revamping of job descriptions, departmental organization, channels of communication—in short, the ways people work with information.

Second, consider teleworking. Mobile or decentralized work is made possible by advanced computer and telecommunications technology. According to the 1996 Census, very few employees are teleworkers, and the numbers remain small even when self-employed people who are home-based and technology-dependent are included. Some firms are beginning to encourage teleworking. Yet even at Northern Telecom Ltd, a high-tech leader, only 3,700 of 80,000 employees around the world actually work from home. There are many hurdles, ranging from traditional management assumptions (for instance, that if you can't see your employees you can't trust them to work hard) to the logistics of adapting work procedures, relationships, and schedules to accommodate 'virtual' work. We need to know more about what happens when an employer adopts teleworking or sets up satellite offices to improve the quality of life for employees by reducing commuting time in congested urban areas, as a few firms have done in Vancouver and Toronto.

Third, consider the gap between workers' computer abilities and actual on-the-job computer requirements. Put simply, computer skills are advancing more rapidly than opportunities to use computers. Between 1989 and 1994, the rate of computer literacy (the ability to perform work-related computer applications) among all workers increased from 59 to 68 per cent. These abilities exceed their use in workplaces. In 1994, just under half of all workers used computers in their jobs—a marked increase from 35 per cent five years earlier. There is scope for more knowledge-intensive work using computers in all sectors of the economy, but this would require employers to increase the skill content of jobs—a strategy that I will discuss in Chapter 5.

Despite dire warnings that we're moving headlong into a digital Brave New World, Canadians see technological change as having mainly positive effects on their jobs. This is a sign of receptivity to what could be productivity-boosting change. Between 1989 and 1994, 34 per cent of employed people reported that their work had been greatly affected by the introduction of computers or automated technology. Many of those affected stated that their jobs had become more skilled and interesting. Only one in five felt their job security had been reduced by technology in itself. Attitudes like these could be mobilized to help ease organizations over the pitfalls of technological change. To take advantage of them, however, employers would have to give employees affected by technological change a role in charting its course. According to a 1996 Angus Reid poll, two-thirds of the adults surveyed thought that technology would make life a bit easier in the future.[45] One possible explanation for this openness to technology is that workers like the prospect of acquiring the new skills and knowledge that technological change calls for, through either formal training or informal learning.[46]

In fact, many Canadians are taking the initiative and acquiring new skills at their own expense and on their own time. The *Workplace 2000* survey in 1997 found that computer training was among the most common types. Learning on one's own with the help of friends, co-workers, and family members is often an unacknowledged source of computer expertise in the workforce. Employers and public policy alike should support these activities. However, other workers are left out altogether.

In short, Canadians have high expectations that technology will improve work. What do workers see that managers, business owners, and policy makers don't see? Perhaps they sense the potential for what US workplace technology expert Shoshana Zuboff calls 'informated work'[47]—work in which individuals can make decisions, take risks, and acquire the skills they need to make use of the information computers can generate. The key here is not the technology itself, which can be readily purchased and installed, but an approach to innovation that ensures workers are trained to use the new technology. Adapting organizational processes, management styles, and workers' skills are equally important ingredients for a high-tech route to success. Without innovations in these areas, even the latest computer is nothing more than an expensive plastic and metal box.

The federal government's Information Highway Advisory Council (IHAC) claims to have charted a course towards an information society,[48] based on job creation through technological innovation, universal and affordable access, and lifelong learning. The reference to access points to the fact that household income is a key determinant of access to computers, modems, cellular phones, and other tools of the information age. The computer penetration rate in the top household income quartile was four times the rate in the bottom quartile, and the gap for Internet usage is even greater. When income and education are combined, the divide widens.[49] Clearly inequality of access should be a pressing social concern.

As for lifelong learning, the IHAC states: 'Learning and training comprise an integral part of the knowledge economy. Canada will provide an environment for lifelong learning in which all Canadians will have access to the widest possible variety of learning opportunities and tools in order to succeed in such an economy.'[50] In practice, though, the shift from old low-tech or no-tech industries to the new high-tech, information-based sectors requires major adjustments in any work organization. If organizational innovation is slow or absent, technological innovation will falter.

Work and Well-being

The quality of our work affects the quality of our personal, family, and community life. If the work environment does not support mental and physical health, if it interferes with family and personal life, or if it detracts from community involvement, then as a society we suffer.

According to the International Labour Organization, 'stress has become one of the most serious health issues of the twentieth century.'[51] Canada has experienced rising workers' compensation claims for job-induced psychological stress. Stress is a difficult problem to address. Its causes are embedded in work environments, especially organizational structures and the content of jobs—

precisely the things that managers are reluctant to change. But employers should be concerned, because stress can inhibit productivity through job dissatisfaction, low morale, increased absenteeism, and antagonistic industrial relations.

Employers are beginning to address the human costs of stressful and otherwise unhealthy work environments. Rising health benefits—in particular, prescription drug and long-term disability claims—have prompted actions in a number of public- and private-sector organizations. The Canadian Business and Economic Roundtable on Mental Health acknowledges that people's brains, not technology, are the foundation of the economy. The objective is to create resilient workers who can cope with multiple and often intense demands. In the light of research showing that workers are twice as likely to report stress or mental-health problems than physical illness, the Roundtable sees stress as a huge waste of human resources, and it is trying to educate business that mental health affects economic performance. Bill Wilkinson, co-founder of the Roundtable, calls mental health 'the ultimate productivity weapon'.[52]

The Toronto-based Institute for Work and Health also documents the economic costs of employee illness and injury: absenteeism, turnover, reduced performance, increased workers' compensation premiums and health-care claims. The Institute's research shows work-related musculo-skeletal injuries and disabilities (e.g., sprains, strains, inflammation of muscles, tendons and ligaments, as in repetitive strain injury or lower back injury) account for over 60 per cent of all workers' compensation claims. These costly problems are products of the physical, social and psychological aspects of a work environment. Direct workers' compensation costs in Ontario were $2.6 billion in 1996 and total costs, including indirect costs such as lost productivity, are four times this figure.[53]

Ironically, part of the problem is new information technology, which workers welcome because it offers the prospect of more skilled and interesting work. With new computer equipment and software comes an avalanche of information to be reviewed and processed. As a result, repetitive strain injury and muscle tension, upper back pain, and headaches have become standard occupational hazards for information workers. There's no question that these health problems reflect awkward work positions, lack of ergonomic equipment, repetitive work, and fast-paced work. Perhaps even more fundamental, though, is job control—the opportunity to make decisions. On one hand, lack of job control has been identified as a risk factor in heart disease. On the other, it is one aspect of a workplace's psychosocial environment—along with flexible work schedules, absence of role conflict, job security, good relations with co-workers, empowering styles of management, and a supportive organizational culture—that can enhance an employee's well-being. Consequently, occupational health experts are advocating organizational changes including communications and problem-solving training, job enlargement and redesign, and participatory decision-making. People's environments directly influence their health, so changing the conditions of work and content of jobs can go a long way towards making work health-enhancing.[54]

Recently, workplace health-promotion programs have become popular. These are generally aimed at encouraging workers to develop healthier lifestyles and work habits. This approach is very individualistic, viewing workers' attitudes and behaviour as both the source of the problem and the solution. Some novel approaches have been taken. For example, when one rapidly expanding BC computer game design firm—part of an industry that is prone to excesses in work pressures, hours, stress, and burnout—was planning a new facility, it designed it to include movie theatres, recording studios, a subsidized cafeteria, a gym offering aerobics and Tae Kwan Do classes, and a basketball court. As the president explained, 'When you've got people going 20, 21 hours a day, working their butts off, they'll work better and be happier if they've got the stuff they need to get the job done.' [55] Even so, evidence shows that, over time, long work hours and an intense work pace can have negative effects on workers' health and productivity. According to the Harvard economist Juliet Schor, such 'long hour jobs' are the result of the system of rewards and incentives in capitalist economies.[56] The price for prosperity has been reduced leisure time, sleep deprivation, and reduced quality of life.

Time, Balance, and the Quality of Life

Workers want a choice in when, where, and how much they work, but they're reluctant to risk their living standards to gain it. Even in the mid-1980s, Canadian workers seemed more willing to trade off pay for leisure or family time.[57] In any case, employers have staunchly opposed a shorter workweek, expecting higher overhead costs if more workers are added to the payroll; as Jock Finlayson, of the Business Council of British Columbia, explains, 'it is normally less expensive to increase hours of work for existing employees than to hire new ones.'[58] There are alternatives, however. For example, Tom Walker of the Shorter Work Time Network proposes rewarding seniority with more time off rather than more pay.[59]

A major flash-point for work time pressures is the conflict between work obligations and family responsibilities. In 1988, the Conference Board of Canada documented that employers attributed about a quarter of their absenteeism, stress, and productivity problems to employee work–family conflicts.[60] When it conducted a ten-year follow-up, it discovered that balancing work and life outside work had become an even greater problem for employees. Stress and health-related problems had increased, mainly because of employers' single-minded focus on cutting costs and boosting productivity and quality—strategies that especially affect the quality of life for an aging workforce, a large segment of which still has young children along with growing elder-care obligations.[61] One argument for providing workers with flexible schedules and supporting family responsibilities is that recruitment and retention, especially of women, will improve. US and Canadian research shows that the adoption of programs designed to help workers balance work and family are frequently part of a more comprehensive human-resource management strategy. The particular set of reforms known as the 'high performance' work organization will be outlined in Chapter 8.[62]

If indeed employment flexibility and family-supportive policies have economic and social benefits, as research suggests, then it seems short-sighted that when the federal government reformed the unemployment insurance system in 1996 it restricted women's access to UI (now called employment insurance) during maternity leave.[63] Generally, Canadian governments have provided few solutions to work–family balance problems—with the exception of Quebec. In fact, that province leads the country in the area of family policy, providing a range of programs to support working families, including $5 a day child-care, free full-time kindergarten, 18 weeks of maternity leave, and another 12 weeks of combined paternity and parental leave. While the political goal is to boost a declining francophone birthrate, for workers these programs help to lessen the conflicts between work and family. But these programs are largely external to the workplace, and do not move inside work organizations to get employees, employers, and unions talking about how workers could exercise more control over their work schedules and jobs in general. (Nor has any government in Canada addressed the fact that child-care is one of the lowest paid occupations in the country. Like nursing, it is a traditionally female job in which poor work conditions make it difficult for the care-givers to care for themselves and their families.)

The costs of not addressing this problem could be substantial. Among people aged 25 to 44—in their prime working and child-rearing years—approximately one-third of married mothers and fathers considered themselves 'workaholics', according to Statistics Canada's 1992 General Social Survey. Feeling trapped in an unrelenting work schedule was even more common among married workers of both sexes in the 45–64 age group. More than half of all workers over the age of 25 said they ended their workday feeling they had not accomplished what they set out to do. Half of the married parents in the 25–44 age group felt they did not spend enough time with family and friends. Even more telling, 52 per cent of married mothers and 39 per cent of married fathers agreed that they were constantly under pressure, trying to accomplish more than they could handle.[64]

Since the beginning of this century we have come a long way in reducing work hours, from around 60 hours weekly to 37 in the 1980s. And in the 1990s, despite increases in part-time work and unemployment, the average workweek has not changed much. The reason is that work hours have become far more polarized, with more people working either shorter or longer hours. In 1995,

24 per cent of workers put in less than 35 hours weekly, while 22 per cent worked more than 40 hours. In 1995, about one in ten employees over the age of 25 usually put in 50 or more hours weekly. Overtime is also on the rise: in 1997, 10.7 per cent of all Canadian employees (some 1.9 million individuals) worked unpaid overtime.[65] It may not come as a surprise to learn that over one-third of workers responding to Statistics Canada's General Social Survey reported that too many demands or too many hours had caused them excess worry and stress.[66]

More is expected of workers in less time. Downsized organizations often attempt to 'do more with less'. Sweeping staff cuts have shrunk government bureaucracies, and across the country government employees are scrambling to deliver 'core' services with diminishing resources. As Roberta L. Jamieson, the Ombudsman for the Province of Ontario, noted in her 1998 annual report: 'Coping has become a major preoccupation. Burnout in the public service is a fact of life. It is common for public servants to feel that neither the public nor government decision-makers appreciate their work. The continuing departure of colleagues, combined with long hours in an atmosphere of low morale and a sense of insecurity about their own future, are not conditions that promote productivity.'[67] In fact, increased workloads could backfire on employers, as mounting stress affects the health and well-being of workers, raising operating costs.

At a time of generalized economic insecurity and a slight decline in average after-tax incomes, it's hardly surprising that, when presented with the stark option of working more hours for more pay, or fewer hours for less pay, most Canadians opt for the former.[68] The present economic environment has not been conducive to a public debate about redistributing work time.

Still, it's puzzling why these problems haven't prompted employers and governments to encourage greater flexibility in work schedules and in the distribution of work hours. 'Flexibility' is an economic catchword in the 1990s, but in practice it has contributed little to improving the quality of work. Typically, flexibility has meant increases in temporary work, long work hours, part-time work, weekend work, shift work, self-employment, and multiple-job holding. Other forms of flexibility—job sharing, home-based or telework, flex-time, compressed workweeks—trail behind. While flextime is growing (from 16.6 per cent to 23.6 per cent of paid workers between 1991 and 1995), it is mostly available to core workers who put in longer-than-average hours.[69] These are usually managers and professionals, who have more control over their work schedules in any case, and are seen by employers as more responsible and trustworthy than lower-status clerical, service, or manual workers.

Work absenteeism is another problem. Some half a million full-time paid workers (not to mention large numbers of other workers not counted in the statistics) were absent in any given week during 1997: the average full-time worker lost 6.2 days for illness and disability and another 1.2 days for personal or family responsibilities (these figures exclude maternity leave). Women take more time off than men, and women with preschool children take three times as much personal or family time as other women. It appears that giving workers more say over their work schedules—flextime—is associated with reductions in absenteeism;[70] this should be an incentive for employers to extend the practice.

Finally, excessive workplace demands are affecting our ability to volunteer at a time when many social and community services are being downloaded to the voluntary sector. According to a 1997 Statistics Canada study of volunteering and civic participation, 31 per cent of Canadians 15 years of age and older volunteered their time. Although this rate represented a slight increase from the 27 per cent documented in a similar survey ten years earlier, the average annual hours volunteered had declined.[71] One aim of workplace reform—and a criterion of quality work—might be to facilitate community participation for those who want to volunteer but have been constrained by the demands of their jobs.

Conclusion

Certainly knowledge-based industries are creating good jobs. But such jobs are not abundant. They are available only to a select group of highly qualified knowledge workers, and the new information and communication technologies are double-faced, with the potential either to improve or to detract from the quality of work. More important, the labour market is becoming increasingly polarized between high- and low-paid jobs, while the rise of a contingent workforce of part-time, contract, temporary, and solo self-employed individuals suggests a further deterioration in the overall quality of work—a trend that is exacerbated by the growing divide between large employers and the small businesses and solo self-employment where most new job creation is taking place. Meanwhile, work-related stresses are increasing, with negative consequences for workers' health and family life.

Together, these trends suggest that we are at a turning point in the evolution of work. If we fail to address the impact of current changes in working conditions and contexts, not only will individual workers and their families and communities be worse off, but so too will employers and the economy. It is in nobody's interest, therefore, to ignore work-quality issues.

Chapter 5

Education, Skills, and the Knowledge Economy

Daniel S. Levine's on-line magazine *Disgruntled* chronicles what he calls the darker side of workplaces. The San Francisco-based workplace critic has given a voice to many rank-and-file employees who feel victimized by their employers' decisions or trapped in dead-end jobs. Levine's real-life stories often have an edge of desperation and anger that pushes them far beyond the satire of Scott Adams's comic-strip Dilbert in his campaign against the idiocy of life in a corporate cubicle. One of Levine's tales comes from a letter he received from a former engineer. 'One day,' writes this engineer,

> I was riding down the elevator with an older engineer whom I'll call Joe. Joe was retiring after 30 years with the company. This was his last day. I asked Joe what the highlight of his career was. He stared at me for a solid minute over the box of personal belongings he carried. He looked away. His face got cloudy. As he walked out the door for the very last time, he shook his head and mumbled, 'what a waste, what a waste'.[1]

The letter-writer quit the next day. Joe's poignant story is an allegory for the wasted human potential in the modern workplace. How many Joes are there in Canadian offices, stores, or factories? How many well-educated people are frustrated in their efforts to put their brainpower to use and contribute to the economy because of narrow job descriptions, dysfunctional bureaucracies, or poor management decisions? And how many capable people with modest formal education don't even get a chance to show their potential?

One of the central themes of this book is that achieving quality in work means giving workers opportunities to use and develop their skills, knowledge, and abilities. This chapter explores the expansive terrain of education, informal learning, skills, and job requirements. Its main point is that the rising numbers of public-policy experts and employers urging human-resource development are slightly off the mark. That's because so far they have missed the central issue: workplace organization, particularly the content and design of jobs. This is the axis around which the 'people and prosperity' strategy revolves.

'People and Jobs'

In 1976 the Economic Council of Canada published a landmark study, called *People and Jobs*, that was one of the first to focus on the importance of people's skills for the Canadian economy. Its arguments still resonate today. Indeed, some of the key challenges posed by the Council more than two decades ago have yet to be met. When we compare the 1970s with the 1990s, there is no denying that human-resource issues have become far more prominent in business and policy discussions. *People and Jobs* provides a benchmark for judging progress on this front. The Economic Council advocated a holistic approach to the labour market, in which it included the work environment—a consideration missing from many subsequent discussions of employment issues. It pointed to the growing demand among workers for challenging and interesting jobs, while noting the difficulty employers faced in creating such jobs. The Council speculated that 'if employers are unable to increase the challenge or the skill requirements in the jobs they offer, they may simply have to pay more to have the dull work done'.[2] Detecting a growing emphasis among workers on the non-monetary rewards of work, the report concluded with an uncannily accurate prediction: 'Looking to the future, the evidence suggests that the pressures on Canadian employers to make jobs interesting and rewarding are likely to become more acute than ever.'[3]

For workers, one of the ironic twists of the 1990s is that people-management strategies have moved in two opposing directions. Downsizing and workplace restructuring inflicted hardships on some employees. Yet at the same time others benefited from a growing recognition of the importance of human-resource development, especially within large corporations. The President of Xerox Canada, for instance, told a Conference Board audience in 1991 that education and training were the most important determinants of business success or failure in the 1990s, urging corporations to provide workers with more opportunities to use their skills, along with more responsibility and authority, and to become more involved in the educational system.[4] These ideas have been widely promoted in public policy. Nearing the end of the decade, the federal government has centred on two goals for labour policy in the new millennium. The first is to promote workplace productivity, especially through workplace innovation, improved human-resource management, and investment in people. The second is to improve the quality of working life, mainly by making it easier for workers to balance work and family, ensuring a greater sense of economic security, and supporting a learning culture.[5]

The Economic Council's point has been restated many times, it seems. Yet its goal remains almost as distant today as in the mid-1970s. The big difference now is that the workforce in general is much better educated, which raises the ante for workplace reform. Better-educated workers want more skilled and interesting jobs. Instead of seizing this challenge, business leaders, educators, and governments have reacted either by criticizing the educational system for failing to prepare students for the new rigours of work, or by encouraging individuals to get even more education or training. David Livingstone, of the University of Toronto's Ontario Institute for Studies in Education (OISE), proposes that it is time to reverse the optics on this debate: 'We need to scrutinize our notions of work, as well as the actual job structures and performance requirements of contemporary workplaces, as closely as educational system structures and performance standards have already been reviewed in many countries. Paid work reform should now be considered at least as seriously as educational reform has been.'[6]

It is fanciful to think that increasing the average level of education in the workforce will enable Canada to succeed in the global productivity race. For many people, a university degree, college diploma, or apprenticeship certificate is not a realistic goal—whether for personal or financial reasons, or because the cash-strapped post-secondary system is simply incapable of absorbing large numbers of new students. Rather, we should concentrate our attention on the 60 per cent of today's workers who have not gone to college or university, and ask how their jobs can be made more skill-intensive. This is especially urgent for those young people who, for various reasons, are not college- or university-bound. Remember that this group still comprises the majority of high-school graduates today. Their ability to learn and develop new skills is the raw material for economic productivity in many occupations.

Because these issues have largely been ignored in Canadian public-policy debates, it is instructive to look to the US. The report of the Commission on the Skills of the American Workforce gets to the core of the issue in its title: *America's Choice: High Skills or Low Wages!*[7] The report alerts policy-makers to the weak link between job requirements and workers' skills, especially for the majority of young people in the US who do not go on to college or university. Its prediction that economic growth will be concentrated in jobs not requiring a college education, and that these low- or semi-skilled jobs will remain 'the backbone of the economy', applies equally well to Canada.[8] Contrary to the common complaint from US boardrooms, educational think-tanks, and government officials that workers are not equipped to meet employers' current needs or, worse, ill-prepared for the high-tech service economy of the twenty-first century, the Commission determined that what 'skill' meant for eight out of ten employers was simply a good work ethic, reliability, and a pleasant personality and appearance. The same pattern is common among Canadian businesses.[9]

High-tech Skill Shortages?

Claims that Canada is facing skill shortages, then, need to be critically examined. By all accounts the high-technology sector, which creates the software and hardware of the digital revolution, has been facing an acute shortage of skilled labour. As Ron Zambonini, President of Cognos Inc., an Ottawa-based computer software manufacturer, explained his use aggressive and offbeat recruitment strategies: 'My No. 1 issue is people.'[10] Cognos brings in prospective recruits from universities for free pizza and beer nights, and it's become commonplace for firms in this sector to offer college and university graduates generous signing bonuses. The reason: at the end of 1998, the Canadian software industry claimed to have 20,000 unfilled jobs. It is important to note that high-tech firms can be found in a wide range of industries, not just computers. What sets these firms apart from low-tech firms is their rapid growth, which in turn is fuelled by constant innovation, their use of advanced information technologies, and their investments in workers' skills.[11] High-tech firms employ a small fraction of the Canadian labour market, however—even though their labour problems get extrapolated far more widely.

A 1997 survey by the Angus Reid Group for the Canadian Advanced Technology Association found that close to nine out of ten Canadian high-tech companies faced a skill shortage, which often resulted in difficulties filling positions.[12] The most pressing shortages at the time of the survey were in programming, management, and database design and analysis. One-third of the companies responding to the survey considered this situation very serious, as it prevented them from meeting rising demand for their goods and services. The main response to this skill shortage had been to recruit offshore, even though few firms felt that foreign workers were better than Canadian workers.

The same survey suggested that other options were not being pursued to anywhere near the same extent. Only 40 per cent of advanced technology companies had programs in place to upgrade the skills of current employees to move into areas of critical shortages. That firms dependent on specific skills don't do more to develop them in-house is all the more puzzling given the high levels of general education in the Canadian labour market, which should give most workers with post-secondary education a solid foundation for expanding their skills repertoire.

Labour-market analysts would likely reply that you can't put square pegs in round holes: someone trained in chemistry, for example, can't easily parachute into the digital world of software development. Yet many of the skills developed in college or university programs, from communicating to analytic thinking, are widely applicable. Certainly graduates in one field require some initial specialized training if they are to make the leap to a different one, and obviously there are limits to this sort of skill transfer. But isn't it the basic argument of lifelong-learning advocates that knowledge and skills are cumulative and laterally adaptable?

So let's consider this scenario. What if the high-tech sector put less emphasis on lobbying government for immigration-rule exemptions, or on creating strategic partnerships with universities to pump out more computer-science graduates? What if, instead, these firms tapped into the existing talent pool and trained its own staff, or graduates in other disciplines, to move into some of their vacant positions? If indeed learning and continuous innovation are hallmarks of the high-tech sector, then its businesses should create the conditions for these to take place among its workforce and new recruits. For example, firms could build on transferable skill sets in related disciplines. Students in biological science use advanced computer systems to analyze complex laboratory data; social-science students learn about relational databases through statistical software packages. Both backgrounds could be seen as stepping stones into some high-tech jobs.

Strategies like these would not eliminate all skill shortages. But they could result in the recruitment or redeployment of educated workers with appropriate aptitudes and interests, as long as the firm in question provided training in the specific skills it needed. Some software Internet developers do this: I recently saw two sociology graduate students, self-taught on Web-based technology, take full-time jobs in this sector and receive 'industry standard' training. But such arrangements are rare. High-tech employers may point to expensive training investments they have made in particular employees, only to see these workers lured away by rival firms. But the same thing can happen with imported job-ready computer professionals. What Canada needs to do is make high-tech education and training more widely accessible. This could be achieved though industry-wide programs funded by an employer-run training fund and involving post-secondary institutions as the training providers.

A final issue relevant to skill shortages is the so-called brain drain. The loss of well-educated workers to the US is another reason to take a close look at the potential to improve the quality of jobs, particularly in terms of skill use and development.[13] Among the possible reasons for this drain are the mismatch between the education system in Canada and labour-market opportunities, increased ease of movement because of NAFTA regulations, and higher pre- and post-tax earnings in the US. Most of the media coverage devoted to the brain drain has centred on the image of the US as a high-wage and low-tax haven. However, a much larger factor is likely the shortage of jobs of desirable quality for highly educated professionals. The shortage of challenging positions in Canada reflects structural differences in the two economies. For example, in most industrial sectors there is a higher concentration of research and development activities in the US, generating good jobs for more managers, engineers, and scientists. Firms operating within Canada (many of them branches of US-based corporations, which may be part of the problem) tend to underinvest in product and service innovations.

This should be a major public-policy issue, particularly as Canada is relaxing immigration rules in order to attract foreign engineers for computer and communications firms. It has also become an issue in the health-care sector, where after years of cutbacks and deteriorating working conditions, nurses, doctors, and other professionals are seeking better prospects elsewhere, creating staff shortages in some regions of the country. Many examples of this trend have come to light during recent nurses' strikes. Quebec nurses, for example, documented long lists of colleagues who had 'gone south'; in one Montreal hospital ward alone, in the year before the 1999 strike three nurses had left to go to Florida, and three to Texas.[14] Working conditions are invariably cited as the driving force behind such moves.

Are Canadians Overeducated?

Compared with the people of most other major industrial nations, Canadians are highly educated. In economic terms, this means we are rich in human resources; in laypersons' terms, it means we possess an abundance of talents, knowledge, skills, and creative potential. According to the 1996 Census, 9 million Canadians were post-secondary graduates. The latter accounted for 40 per cent of the population 15 years of age and older—a huge jump from 29 per cent in 1981. Some 35 per cent of the adult population, mainly older individuals, had not finished high school, but this group had still shrunk in relative terms, down from 48 per cent in 1981. The Census counted 3.5 million university grads, comprising 16 per cent of adults. If we look only at individuals who were employees (excluding the self-employed) in the fall of 1998, 18.5 per cent held a university degree and 34 per cent some other kind of post-secondary credential, while 21 per cent held a high-school diploma, and 17 per cent had some high school. Generally speaking, then, when we use the term 'employee', chances are better than 50 per cent that we are referring to an individual with a technical institute, college, or university education.[15] This fact should be borne in mind by employers when they think about human resources.

The workforce of the early twenty-first century will be even more highly educated, given that 51 per cent of women and 42 per cent of men now in the 20–29 age group have a post-secondary degree or diploma,[16] and average education levels will likely rise further still among current junior-high and high-school students. Surely this is reason enough to find ways of making work more challenging, interesting, and capable of stretching the minds of young workers.

For close to two decades, one strong motivation for younger Canadians to stay in school longer has been the difficult job market they have faced (discussed more fully in the next chapter). If we look more closely at post-secondary enrolment figures, however, there are signs that the vision of a learning society may be threatened. University undergraduate enrolment peaked in 1992–3, and by 1997–8 had dropped 8.6 per cent. Younger full-time students continued to flock to campuses, despite rising tuition costs that saddled them with growing debt loads. The group most likely to defer or scrap their university plans (generally for part-time study) were older individuals already in the labour force or hoping to return to work. While full-time undergraduate enrolments have been steady, part-time undergraduate enrolment for the 25–44 age group plummeted by approximately 30 per cent in the five years up to 1997–8.[17] These part-time university students are typically members of the workforce pursuing the 'lifelong learning' that Canadians say they see as the route to a better future. Yet the reality suggests growing barriers to such efforts.

Degrees, diplomas, certificates, and other measures of formal education are the most obvious indicators of a nation's human potential. That's why employers use these credentials to screen job applicants, even if the jobs do not really require that particular kind or level of education. However, if we limit our focus to those with post-secondary education we leave out close to half of these individuals in Canada's labour force who have a high-school diploma or less. If public policy is to make improving the quality of work a realistic goal, it must be inclusive, finding ways to ensure that the talents of all workers can be more fully used. Otherwise we risk accentuating the growing distinction between good and bad jobs.

The 1994 Adult Education and Training Survey, conducted by Statistics Canada, found that in 1993, 27 per cent of the working population participated in job-related training, that is, training taken for a person's current or future job, in a credit or non-credit course, on or off the job. We have already seen that workplace structures and policies tend to favour those already in good jobs. Training patterns are consistent with this tendency: workers who receive employer-sponsored training have higher incomes and formal education than those who do not. University graduates are twice as likely as high-school graduates to participate in job-related training. And while only two in ten workers earning less than $15,000 took part in such training, five in ten of those earning more than $75,000 did so. Furthermore, the people taking training tend to be concentrated in occupations with the highest knowledge and skill requirements: management and administration, science, engineering, social-science occupations, teaching, medicine, and health-related professions.[18]

Business leaders and policy-makers agree that developing people's skills and knowledge is essential for the new economy. But figuring out how to achieve this goal is difficult.[19] For one thing, despite rising educational attainment, productivity and income growth have been stagnant. For another, there is a basic contradiction between the short-term focus of business planning and profit horizons and the much longer-term goals implicit in arguments for promoting lifelong learning within the workforce and creating 'learning organizations'. Adopting a much broader conception of human resources that captures the full range of workers' actual and potential skills is one way that we might resolve these difficulties.

An Expanded View of Workers' Skills

With respect to skills, a recent national survey by a research project entitled New Approaches to Lifelong Learning (NALL), under the direction of OISE's David Livingstone, sheds important new light on the informal learning activities of Canadians—learning that takes place outside organized educational courses, adding to a person's knowledge, skill, or understanding. As Livingstone explains: 'our organized systems of schooling and continuing education and training are like big ships floating in a sea of informal learning. If these education and training ships do not pay increasing attention to the massive amount of outside informal learning, many of them are likely to sink into Titanic irrelevancy.'[20] I would add that it is equally important for employers and public policy-makers to pay attention to these findings.

Specifically, the NALL survey found that workers and unemployed people alike invested an average of six hours weekly in informal learning related to their current or expected employment. In most cases, such learning included keeping up with the new information in their specific area, acquiring new computer skills, adding to their repertoire of specific job tasks, and developing problem-solving and communication skills. The time devoted to informal learning varied by geographic region and social group. Still, it is important for employers to realize that it is not just their highly paid professionals or managers who are learning job skills on their own after work hours; lower-paid workers with less formal education also actively engage in this form of learning.

There is a pent-up demand for formal education, even among high-school dropouts. In addition to time and costs, however, the least educated face a third stumbling-block in that their informal learning is not recognized by educational institutions. Similarly, employers don't acknowledge self-taught skills, mainly because they are difficult to assess. Thus they miss out on the potential economic contributions of a large group of workers. Far from being over-educated, Canadians may well lack the challenges in their work life that would make fuller use both of individual potential and of public investments in education.

The NALL research expands our understanding of education and skills beyond what is acquired in classrooms. Employers who assume that people with nothing more than a high-school education are unskilled overlook the fact that such individuals may have combined their basic education with personal interests and motivation to learn, creating advanced skill sets. Take, for instance, the refined expertise that some high-school students have in repairing computer systems. It would not be unusual for your local computer shop's backroom expert to be a 17-year-old computer nerd. Computer skills are not the only ones that people often acquire informally, whether on their own or from co-workers, friends, or family members.

This sort of informal learning is well documented in research that I conducted with my University of Alberta colleague Harvey Krahn among groups of 1985 Edmonton high-school and university graduates.[21] When we did a follow-up study in 1992, more than six in ten of the employed high-school graduates, and over half of the employed university grads, had received informal job-related training in the previous 12 months. Rates of formal training were much lower. Improved computer abilities were among the main benefits of this informal training. Another important source of informal skill development is volunteer community work. There is clear evidence that high-school students, to take just one group, are developing useful work-relevant skills and knowledge through their voluntary activities.[22] This domain of skill development needs to be fully explored, and public-policy discussions of future human resource development directions must take it into account.

More generally, we are in urgent need of a more complete definition of what 'human resources' are, along with measurable criteria for assessing how well the economy is using people's full range of skills. Much of David Livingstone's critique of the use the economy makes of existing human resources rests on what he labels the performance gap: the gap between the knowledge a worker brings to her or his job and the knowledge actually needed to do it. Livingstone estimates that when formal and informal learning are combined, about half the workers in North America are underemployed in this sense.[23] In other words, we are underutilizing the productive capacities of people who could make significant contributions to national economic prosperity.

'Employability Skills'

The most frequently cited definition of the skills needed for the new (read information-based, technology-intensive) economy is the list of academic, personal management, and teamwork skills that, according to the Conference Board of Canada's *Employability Skills Profile*,[24] employers now require. Employability, as this 1993 document defines it, depends on seven essential skills: communication, thinking, ability to learn, positive work attitudes and behaviour, responsibility, adaptability, and ability to work with others. This list is not the product of systematic research into changing job requirements and employers' recruitment criteria—a study that still needs to be done. Rather, it was developed mainly on the basis of discussions with employers. Despite this limitation, the profile had taken on larger-than-life proportions with many policy-makers and managers, and has often been uncritically cited as evidence of what the workforce for the new economy should look like.

The Conference Board, for its part, recognized that the profile was merely a 'work in progress', and convened further consultations with government, business, and academics to flesh it out. A more recent Conference Board statement on employability skills makes it clear that defining and measuring these skills is indeed fraught with difficulties.[25] For one thing, many skills are tailored to specific work contexts. For another, the broad categories of 'communications', 'reasoning', and 'computer skills' encompass a potentially unlimited range of actual abilities. To be meaningful, such measures would have to be very finely calibrated—which raises the question of how to devise assessments that are not only accurate but useful for both workers and employers.

It is important to recognize that the term 'skills' can refer either to attributes of a person (on the supply side of the labour market) or to job requirements (on the demand side of that market). The problem, simply, is that the labour market is an imperfect mechanism for finding the best balance between the supply of talent and actual job requirements. We need to go further in our thinking. Confining discussions about current and future skill requirements to the matching of workers' skills with job requirements in the context of labour markets is far too vague. Such discussions need to move right inside the workplace—where the conditions for the utilization of workers' skills are laid down by management in terms of recruitment processes, job descriptions, and career development and training opportunities.

Let's shift our attention now to how workers view the use of their skills and education, an important perspective that is often missing from discussions of employability skills. Asking individuals how they evaluate the skill content of their jobs, or the extent to which they are overqualified for their work, offers a reasonably accurate picture both of human-resource utilization and of the actual skills demanded in particular jobs.[26] I have chosen two standard measures of human-resource utilization from Statistics Canada's 1994 General Social Survey, examining only those individuals who are currently employed and whose main activity is not going to school (focusing on non-students provides a more rigorous test of skill use and overqualification in the labour market, since student jobs are temporary and tend to be low-skilled). Figure 5.1 shows that over one in five employed non-students in 1994 reported that their job did not require a high level of skill. A profile of workers in low-skill jobs can be created from these data. The people most likely to be in low-skill positions are women, younger workers, those with less than high-school education, and those reporting no relationship between their job and their education. In terms of occupations, the largest proportion of people reporting low-skill work were in clerical, sales, and service jobs, and when the latter category was broken down, it was the lower tier of the service sector, which includes industries such as personal and consumer services and retail trade, that fell at the low end of the skills spectrum.

In short, close to two in five of the workers in a large chunk of the labour market, essentially the lower reaches of the service sector, report low skill requirements in their job. Of all the workers in low-skill jobs, 29 per cent hope to escape this trap by getting more education or training in the next five years (see Figure 5.1). This personal boot-strap approach has a lottery logic to it: get more education to improve your chances of landing a higher-skilled job.

Figure 5.1   Workers who report that their job is low-skilled, Canada, 1994

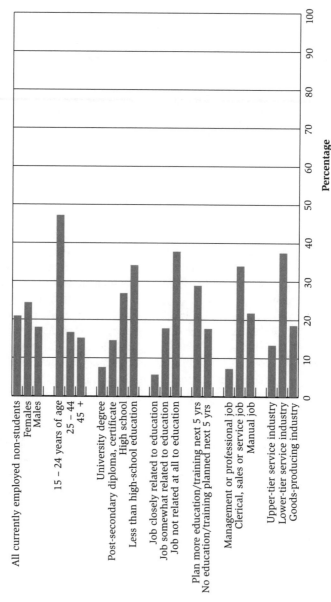

NOTES: Sample = 4,385 employed non-students. Based on responses to the question 'Do you agree or disagree...[that] your job requires a high level of skill?' (Strongly agree/somewhat agree/somewhat disagree/strongly disagree). Responses of 'strongly' and 'somewhat disagree' are combined here. All differences are statistically significant at the p < .05 level, chi-square test.

SOURCE: Based on *1994 General Social Survey*, microdata file, Statistics Canada.

More than one in five workers who aren't full-time students feel overqualified for their jobs (see Figure 5.2). As in the case of job skills, younger workers and those in clerical, sales, and lower-tier service jobs were the most likely to report that their experience, education, and training exceeded their job's requirements. Remedies to the problem must address how jobs are designed and the organizational environment in which they are performed, placing greater emphasis on the development and use of workers' skills. The fact that more than one in four workers with a university degree felt overqualified for their jobs is a singularly powerful indication that Canadian workplaces have not kept pace with the rising educational levels of the workforce.

How might we begin to rethink job design so that workers' abilities are put to better use? Figure 5.2 shows that 40 per cent of the workers who felt overqualified also reported low levels of job skill requirements. While there is more to discover about the broad range of factors contributing to overqualification, it is possible to examine in more depth how job skill content is part of the problem. I rely here on a survey of more than 6,000 university graduates from Alberta's four universities that Harvey Krahn and I conducted for the Alberta government's 'Key Performance Indicators' initiative in the post-secondary system. We tracked down 1994 graduates in early 1997, more than two-and-a-half years after they had completed their programs.

We asked these recent university graduates about the use of six specific skill sets in their current jobs. Figure 5.3 compares those graduates who reported being overqualified (the question was the same one asked by Statistics Canada's General Social Survey) with those who did not feel overqualified. On all six skill sets—speaking, writing, problem-solving, creative thinking, computers, and information management—the graduates who reported feeling generally overqualified also reported less extensive use of these specific skills. The use of three higher-order skills vital to an information economy—writing, problem-solving, and creative thinking—seem to most clearly differentiate underemployed graduates from those whose tasks make use of their education.

This study takes us much further, because it also asked graduates about their satisfaction with particular aspects of their job. Figure 5.4 makes it clear that university graduates who felt overqualified for their jobs also reported little satisfaction in terms of career advancement opportunities, decision-making authority, chances to develop their potential, or having interesting and challenging tasks to perform. Overall, less than 40 per cent of the overqualified were satisfied with their jobs, whereas more than 80 per cent of those who were not overqualified were satisfied. In short, as in the case of low job skill requirements, overqualification is symptomatic of a more pervasive problem of poor job quality. Such limitations on workers' productivity should be a major cause for concern among employers and policy-makers.

Figure 5.2   Workers who feel overqualified for their job, Canada, 1994

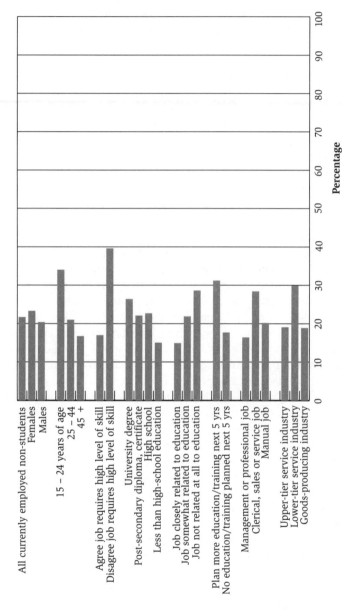

NOTES: Sample = 4,379 employed non-students. Based on responses to the question: 'Considering your experience, education and training, do you feel that you are overqualified for your job' (yes/no)? All differences except gender are statistically significant at the p < .05 level, chi-square test.

SOURCE: Based on *1994 General Social Survey*, microdata file, Statistics Canada.

Figure 5.3   University graduates' use of skills, knowledge, and abilities by perceived overqualification in current job, Alberta, 1997

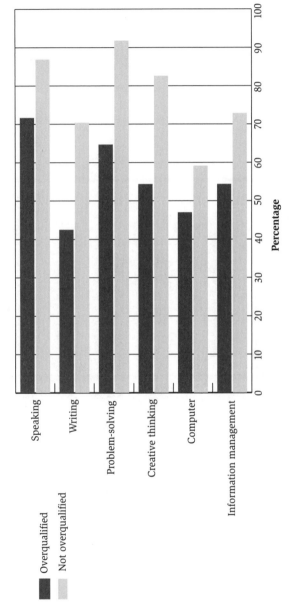

NOTES: Sample = 4,204 employed 1994 Alberta university graduates no longer in the educational system, surveyed in 1997. Based on responses to the question: 'Now we would like to assess to what extent you actually use the following skills, knowledge and abilities in your current (main) job. Using a scale of 1 to 5, where 1 is "not at all" and 5 is "to a great extent", to what extent do you use each of the following?' This graph reports responses of 5 ('to a great extent'). All differences statistically significant (p < .001, chi-square test).

SOURCE: Based on 1997 Alberta Graduate Survey, microdata file (Harvey Krahn and Graham S. Lowe, *1997 Alberta Graduate Survey: Labour Market and Educational Experiences of 1994 University Graduates*. Edmonton: Alberta Advanced Education & Career Development, 1998).

Figure 5.4   University graduates overall job satisfaction and satisfaction with job content by perceived overqualification, Alberta, 1997

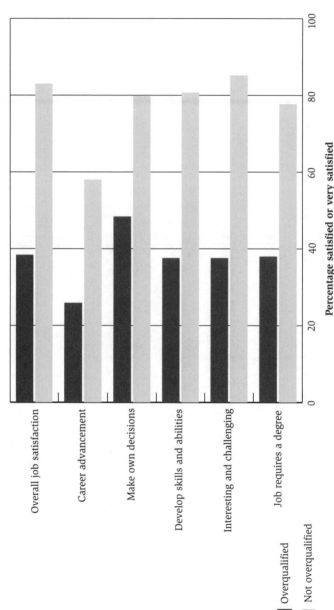

NOTES: Sample: see Figure 5.3. All measures (except job requires a degree, which was answered 'yes' or 'no') are based on a scale of 1 to 5, where 1 = 'very dissatisfied' and 5 = 'very satisfied'. This graph reports responses of 'very satisfied' and 'satisfied' combined. All differences between the overqualified and not overqualified categories are statistically significant (p < .001, chi-square test).

SOURCE: See Figure 5.3.

Literacy

Although debates continue over how to define and measure employability skills, there is a consensus that literacy is the foundation on which other important abilities rest. Increasingly, national governments, with encouragement from the Organization for Economic Cooperation and Development (OECD), are linking literacy, workforce skills, and lifelong learning. Echoing the policy thinking in Canada and other major industrial nations, the OECD has adopted from orthodox economics a 'human capital' view of literacy: at a time when the knowledge and skill requirements of jobs are increasing, and workers must engage in lifelong learning if they are to adapt to a rapidly changing labour market, high levels of literacy are essential. As the OECD puts it, literacy 'is the *sine qua non* of workplace learning'.[27]

The policy implications of this position are clear: every adult must be provided with adequate reading, writing, and mathematical skills. An OECD literacy report underlines two reasons. First, 'Poorly trained adults who cannot adapt to new conditions and labour market demands face increased risks of social alienation and economic exclusion.' Second, 'People are the key resource and their level of literacy is a powerful determinant of a country's innovation and adaptive capacity.'[28]

In 1996, following discussions with business and labour, the education ministers of the OECD countries agreed to promote lifelong learning as a response to globalization, information technology, the increasing importance of knowledge and skills, and the ongoing shift of economic activity to service industries. This broad policy thrust was intended to help individuals and families, workplaces, and communities actively participate in the process of economic change and renewal. At the same time, the OECD was also aware of the social implications: 'there is a risk of new polarization emerging between those who participate fully in the acquisition and use of knowledge and skills, and those who are left on the margins.'[29] Therefore it emphasized the importance of improving foundational skills such as literacy and helping people to make the transitions between learning and work. In addition, recognizing that workplace change is a key ingredient in lifelong learning, the ministers drew particular attention to 'the connections between new technologies, innovations and work organisation, and their implications for human resource development'.[30]

The problem with this conventional view of the link between human-resource development, lifelong learning, and workplace literacy is that it focuses exclusively on the levels of literacy in the workforce. Nobody would deny the importance of ensuring that all citizens have the opportunity to attain the basic literacy they need for full participation in economic and social life. But an equally pressing issue from an economic perspective is whether the literacy skills already in abundant supply among the majority of workers are being put to good use. If they are not, the link between literacy, lifelong learning, and economic prosperity breaks down. One could say, then, that the use of these bedrock literacy skills in the workplace is another indicator of job quality.

Literacy in the Workplace

The question of the fit between workers' literacy levels and the literacy requirements of their jobs was addressed in a study by my colleague Harvey Krahn and myself. Analyzing the Canadian results from the 1994 International Adult Literacy Survey (IALS),[31] we found a new twist on the link between literacy and success in the labour market and overall social well-being. Instead of focusing on individuals with low literacy, we redefined the term 'literacy gap' to refer to highly literate and numerate individuals working in jobs that don't use these skills. Our study found some tentative evidence that if these skills aren't used, over time they may atrophy. Social scientists have produced a long list of studies documenting the dehumanizing effects of routine and unskilled work, all emphasizing that improving the quality of this work is a human imperative. Now we can add to this list evidence that a good job also promotes the use and development of literacy.

The IALS used extensive practical tests to determine an individual's proficiency in three kinds of literacy: prose (understanding and using information from texts such as editorials, news stories, poems, fiction); document (locating and using information on job applications, payroll forms, transportation schedules, maps, graphics, and tables), and quantitative (that is, numeracy: applying arithmetic operations to numbers in print material, such as balancing a chequebook, figuring out a tip, completing an order form, or determining the amount of interest on a loan). The results were organized in four categories: 12 per cent of employed people scored at the lowest level (1) for all three kinds of literacy; approximately 25 per cent were at level 2; between 35 and 37 per cent were at level 3; and 26 to 29 per cent were at levels 4 and 5 combined. Literacy experts view level 3 as the one required to deal successfully with the everyday demands of living and working.

How literate and numerate are the jobs available to Canadians? Based on workers' reports, just over half read or use letters and memos in their job daily, but 20 per cent rarely or never do so. Just over one-third read or use information from reports, articles, magazines, or journals daily, whereas 29 per cent rarely or never do. Equal proportions use manuals, reference books, and catalogues daily and rarely or never. In terms of writing, 35 per cent of workers write letters or memos daily, while 32 per cent rarely or never do this. Some 30 per cent write or fill out forms, bills, invoices, or budgets daily, compared with 40 per cent who rarely or never do this. One in four write reports or articles on a daily basis, while 44 per cent rarely or never do. While just over one-third reported using math to calculate prices, costs, budgets, or to measure or estimate the size or weight of objects, a slightly larger group reported rarely or never performing these activities. The use of literacy skills is higher among workers who have supervisory responsibilities, are self-employed with employees (as opposed to own-account self-employed), in a full-time job, in a permanent job, or in a large firm. In short, the chance to use one's literacy skills is another feature distinguishing good jobs from bad jobs.

But these observations tell only part of the workplace literacy story. We also need to know how well individual workers' literacy skills mesh with their job requirements. This is a crucial test not only of how successful employers have been at using the most basic abilities that workers bring to their jobs, but of the labour market's success at matching literacy supply and demand. Comparing workers' skills on the three literacy dimensions with their job requirements in the same areas, we found that more than 20 per cent of workers are in jobs that underutilize their literacy skills: that is, the literacy requirements of the job are two or more levels below the worker's own literacy level. Figure 5.5 shows how well workers' literacy skills fit with their job requirements by combining the above measures of each into high, medium, and low clusters. The figure focuses on document and quantitative literacy, which can be seen as the building blocks of employability skills. In a high-skill, knowledge-based economy that effectively uses and develops its human resources, we would expect most workers to be in the medium-medium and high-high categories.

By this yardstick, Canada has a long way to go. Approximately one in four of workers surveyed in the Canadian IALS had high document and quantitative literacy skills and were in jobs with high literacy requirements in these two areas. One in three had moderate document literacy and were in jobs that placed comparable literacy demands on them. The same can be said for one in four regarding quantitative literacy. Yet these fit clusters don't account for even half of all workers or jobs.

The low-high cluster captures the standard view of the literacy gap, which has informed government policies for decades. Here workers have literacy deficiencies, to the extent that these skills are at a low level while their jobs require considerably more. But this low-high cluster accounts only for one in twenty workers in terms of document literacy, and slightly more than one in ten with regard to quantitative literacy. More important is the low-low cluster. This area of the labour market has low-skilled workers performing unskilled jobs—a situation in which between 15 and 17 per cent of workers find themselves. Typically these are older people, males, or workers with less than high-school education. There is a need to upgrade low literacy skills, as government literacy policies have rightly pointed out. But if this literacy enhancement strategy is pursued, it is equally essential, where possible, to upgrade the skill content of the jobs occupied by these workers. Otherwise these workers will soon find that their jobs do not permit the use of their newly acquired literacy skills.

Most important, however, Figure 5.5 shows that just over one in five workers is in the high-low cluster, possessing literacy skills considerably in excess of

Figure 5.5   Workers' literacy skills and workplace literacy requirements, Canada, 1994

Percentage of workers with the following 'fit' between their literacy skills and their workplace literacy requirements:

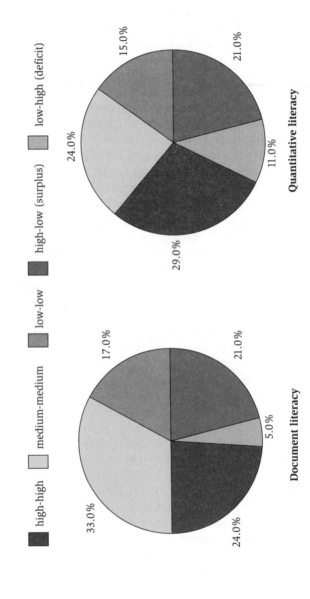

NOTES: Sample size = 2,604.

SOURCE: Based on 1994 International Adult Literacy Survey (Harvey Krahn and Graham S. Lowe, *Literacy Utilization in Canadian Workplaces* [Ottawa: Statistics Canada and Human Resources Development Canada, 1998]: 35).

what their jobs require. This condition of literacy surplus reflects more broadly the quality of certain jobs, and thus becomes a source of inequality in the labour market. For example, women are more likely than men to be in jobs that do not use their literacy skills, particularly if they are highly educated. A staggering 55 per cent of women with 17 or more years of education (most likely a university degree) are in the literacy surplus cluster with respect to prose and quantitative literacy (compared with 15 and 32 per cent, respectively, of similarly educated men). Surprisingly, we find untapped literacy abilities in some rather high-status jobs, ones that otherwise may have good rewards, such as decent pay. Technicians and semi-professionals (e.g., skilled technical workers, teaching assistants, health-care assistants) have the highest chance of being in the literacy surplus category. While one in five professionals has a surplus of document literacy, there also is a literacy surplus among workers in skilled and unskilled blue-collar occupations. This finding stands in sharp contrast to claims made about skill shortages in manual trades.

Literacy, Lifelong Learning, and Work Reform

Fostering higher literacy skills has become an important policy objective across the industrialized economies, and it is even more urgent in the developing countries. Reviewing the arguments supporting a more literate and numerate society, one is struck by the implications for improving the quality of work. An international perspective helps, and this is the real value of the IALS. For example, Sweden has considerably higher literacy levels than the US, Canada, or Germany. And Swedish workers report the highest use levels for all types of workplace literacy, reflecting more extensive use of literacy in hobbies, recreation, community activities, and other areas of daily life, but in particular at work. Looking at document literacy skills among Canadian workers, 16.4 per cent of sales/service workers, 24.7 per cent of skilled crafts workers, and 27.7 per cent of machine operators/assemblers report the lowest literacy skill level (level 1). This compares with 5.5 per cent, 6.7 per cent, and 11.7 per cent respectively in Germany, and 5.9 per cent, 8.4 per cent, and 7.3 per cent in Sweden.[32]

The literacy requirements of these jobs should—at least according to literacy experts—be a powerful motivator for those Canadian workers to upgrade their skills. But there's another perspective. Research on literacy in less-industrialized nations suggests that 'literacy skill is demand driven'[33] in the sense that if the need for these skills is low, there is little incentive for workers to acquire them. Pursuing further education or training is not a good investment because there will be no labour-market rewards. This logic likely operates among some Canadian workers who feel trapped in low-skilled jobs. Unlike the large numbers of other workers, mentioned above, who see skill upgrading as an escape route from dull jobs, the least literate workers in the least skilled jobs may simply be resigned to their limited circumstances, feeling powerless to change things.

People with higher literacy skills tend to earn higher incomes and have a lower chance of unemployment. In other words, an economy that has successfully tapped into the skills of the workforce will be more prosperous and productive than one that leaves workers' literacy skills underutilized. Canada still falls well short of this goal. For instance, manual craft workers in Canada are far more likely to score at level 1 (the lowest) on the document literacy scale compared with their German counterparts (25 per cent versus 7 per cent), a difference that reflects the German apprenticeship system's emphasis on developing and using skills.[34]

Furthermore, a person's literacy skills are useful only if they are regularly practised. A lingering concern among literacy experts is that literacy skills, much like other skills, such as conversing in a foreign language or playing the piano, may be lost over time if they are not exercised. Although there has yet to be a definitive test of this argument, Canadian literacy expert Stan Jones suggests that 'If literacy practices do maintain and enhance skill, then work organization itself can contribute to literacy skill.'[35] There is great value in the basic literacy training programs run by Frontier College or the workplace literacy upgrading provided by employers such as Syncrude Canada Ltd at its remote oil-sands plant in Fort McMurray, Alberta. However, many more people, including those with low literacy, would benefit if jobs were designed to use and develop skills and if work environments supported literacy activity.

This argument is a hard sell politically. A focus on literacy deficiencies has been deeply engrained in official government thinking. This view of the literacy 'gap' places the onus on individuals and educational institutions to remedy the situation. By the same token, employers are not likely to accept the responsibility for providing working conditions that make optimal use of literacy skills. Yet the economic stakes are high indeed. As we have seen, the OECD, in promoting the theme of 'literacy skills for the knowledge society', has argued that national productivity will suffer and individuals with poor literacy will be increasingly marginalized, both socially and economically. The OECD draws our attention to the fact that in the 12 countries now part of the IALS, one in four adults do not reach the minimum level of literacy considered indispensable for meeting the demands of everyday life and work.[36] As the OECD states: 'Jobs in knowledge societies require high levels of literacy skills for which demands are expected to increase. The fact that many members of the population possess only low skills poses problems for both countries and individuals, and affects families, communities and employers.'[37] If we restrict the idea of a knowledge-based economy to professional, managerial, or other high-status white-collar jobs, we will miss out on an opportunity to make meaningful changes in all areas of work. As the OECD itself points out, there are substantial numbers of blue-collar workers in the industrial nations with good literacy skills. This large pool of talent is either overeducated or lacking adequate challenge in their job, or both. Training and education alone will not solve this problem. What is needed even more, I would argue, is an approach to literacy that ensures all workers ample opportunity to apply and expand these skills in the course of their work.

It is widely recognized that literacy is a prerequisite for a citizen's active participation in all areas of social, economic, and cultural life. At the same time, we must recognize that, especially in the economic sphere, the process of participation itself should help to strengthen literacy skills. One of the main economic arguments for improving the overall literacy of a population is that a 2 per cent improvement in national literacy increases tax revenue roughly 1.8 per cent.[38] Perhaps it is worth considering the use of incentives—for example, tax credits—to encourage employers to create literacy-enhancing work environments.

Conclusion

Investing in 'intellectual capital' is the latest human-resource management mantra. Although this view of human potential may seem crassly economic, equating people's talents with business assets, one point seems beyond dispute: the stakes for developing and using the innate and acquired talents of workers will only become higher. If we accept that the so-called new economy is based on knowledge-intensive economic activity, then we need to think about how people can be given opportunities to apply their talents in their jobs on a daily basis, and how workplaces can encourage the development of untapped talents.

Public-policy discourse about education and skills that merely bashes educational institutions (usually universities), or their graduates, for not adapting to the realities of the global economy is not constructive. But when Ontario Premier Mike Harris told a summit on the future of universities that, in his view, humanities and social science graduates 'have very little hope of contributing to society in any meaningful way', there was one kernel of truth in his statement. Of course, he was dead wrong in terms of the overall economic returns to society of a liberal arts education: most arts graduates can look forward to high future earnings and a very low probability of ending up driving taxis or waiting on tables.[39] It is true, however, that many university graduates want to make a more meaningful contribution to the larger social and economic good than their jobs allow. Employers have a responsibility to these individuals (and to their shareholders and taxpayers who have footed much of the education bill) to make this possible.

If we look beyond the general demand for skills and educational credentials, we find unsettling signs that this intellectual capital is not effectively used, and that large groups of workers have inadvertently been defined out of the discussion. On the one hand, job requirements often exceed what daily work activities require from a worker. On the other, though, many jobs are not designed to encourage the development of the 'intellectual capital' now perceived by business as so important.

The solution to this problem can be found in workplace reform that gives priority to the overall quality of work. Returning to the Economic Council of Canada's 1976 *People and Jobs* report, one of its conclusions takes on even greater urgency today: 'the pressures on Canadian employers to make jobs interesting and rewarding are likely to become more acute than ever . . . it seems fair to observe that Canadian enterprises have done little experimenting with providing more enriching jobs or work methods. . . .'[40] The end-of-the-century update of this argument, as put forward by the Canadian Policy Research Networks,[41] is emphatic about the importance of reforming work organization and job design. It is possible for organizations to achieve a 'high-skill equilibrium' by designing work environments that are flexible, and that encourage worker innovation and initiative. This path to higher productivity requires business strategies founded on high-skilled jobs and ongoing learning—on conditions closely associated with high-quality work.

Chapter 6

Youth and Work

Young people occupy a curious place in public discourse about the future of work. They are at once invisible, misrepresented, and prominent. Many leading future-of-work writers don't address the concerns of younger workers at all; William Bridges is typical of the career-advice givers who market their ideas to the older baby-boom generation that is grappling with mid-career burnout and job angst.[1] Others present inaccurate stereotypes, as Jeremy Rifkin does in *The End of Work* when he speculates that technological job loss has fuelled 'a violent new criminal subculture' among the young.[2] Even under the more rigorous scrutiny of policy researchers and academics, future work trends are not considered from the perspective of young people struggling to begin their working life.[3] In sharp contrast, proponents of a high-tech future, like Don Tapscott, see the youth of today as riding the crest of the digital-revolution wave.[4]

Yet most members of the Canadian public harbour real worries about the future job prospects for young people. As public-opinion polls in the 1990s clearly showed, concerns about work frequently revolved around youth. Unemployment is the leading public-policy issue for Canadians, and among the unemployed the group that generates the most worry is youth. In the public mind, the difficult economic conditions today threaten to be even more difficult for the next generation.

This chapter places youth front and centre in debates about the future of work. I will explore what the transformations in labour markets and work-places mean for young people who have recently graduated from high school or a post-secondary institution, or will do so in the next few years. We need to take a careful look not only at how individuals in their teens and early twenties experience school–work transitions, but at how changes in the work world have affected the quality of the jobs available to graduates. So far, public policy has attempted to address some of the most visible problems that the changing relationship between the education system and labour markets have created in young people's transition to adulthood. The main policy initiatives have focused on creating more entry-level employment opportunities or promoting self-employment (to address high youth unemployment), raising the high-school completion rate (so that dropouts will not become a social problem), and increasing the work relevance of school programs (on the assumption that this is inadequate). Far too little attention has been devoted to the quality of work that the next generation of workers will experience.

Canada and other Western industrial nations have witnessed two decades of massive labour-market disruptions—rising nonstandard work, chronically high unemployment, declining incomes, job polarization, the information technology revolution—that have profoundly affected the employment opportunities for young people. All the while, policy experts, educators, and political and business élites have called for more effective human-resource development as the key to global competitiveness. The most crucial intersections between human capital and labour markets occur at the various exit points from the education system. But this is precisely where the argument that economic prosperity can be achieved through more effective human-resource development breaks down. The litmus test for a knowledge-based, high-skill economy is how well employers recruit and utilize recent graduates, providing opportunities for ongoing skill and knowledge development.

Is this happening? Not as much as it should. There are too many weak links in the education-work nexus. If we accept that, as Robert Reich asserted in *The Work of Nations*, a nation's most valuable assets are the talents and skills of its workers,[5] we must critically appraise how effectively these skills and talents are put to work, especially among those who are just beginning their working lives. More than anything, a country's economic future hinges on the young people who will become the next generation of workers.

After many years of studying school–work transitions in Canada, I keep being drawn back to several fundamental points. Regardless of how well schools, technical institutes, colleges, or universities fulfil their mandate to provide high-quality education, the organization of work and prevailing people management practices within firms prevent the optimal application of this education within the economy. The fact that each new generation of youth enters the workforce equipped with more education than its predecessors increases the risk of underemployment. Unemployment may be the most visible symptom of an economic system that does not make efficient use of human resources, and youth unemployment has been a pressing public issue in Canada for over two decades. In the 1990s, however, rising educational levels and economic globalization have drawn attention to the more pervasive problem of underemployment.

It also has become starkly evident that what appear to be the most urgent problems faced by young people—unemployment, underemployment, inferior job quality, barriers to further education—are the early warning signals of work-related problems for adults. As David Foot and Jeanne Li argue, youth unemployment today becomes young adult unemployment tomorrow. This is a demographic fact now made more inevitable by labour–market trends that exclude the least educated from mainstream economic and social life.[6] It is all the more important, then, to pay attention to research documenting the way labour-market difficulties in the early stages of a person's work life can have a lingering negative impact—what economists call a 'scarring' effect.[7]

Youth labour markets have long exhibited higher levels of instability and volatility—the economists' term is 'churning'—than adult labour markets. Since the early 1980s, transitions from school to work have become more protracted, diverse, difficult, and non-linear. Does the average high-school or college grad eventually settle into a stable work pattern or a career, simply taking longer to do so than their parents did, and arriving there in a more roundabout way? Or are there new forms of labour-market insecurity and uncertainty that extend well beyond the mid-twenties—the point in the life course when most policy-makers and social scientists assume that 'youth' ends?

These are certainly vexing questions, all the more so because the future shape of work may well be reflected in the work experiences of contemporary youth. Today, youth employment problems do not end with 'youth' itself, because they are mainly rooted in the ways work is organized and managed.

A Recurring Crisis

Before jumping to the conclusion that youth are the millennarian vanguard, for better or worse, let's put things in historical perspective. Every economic era has spawned a sense of urgency about how the next generation will fare. The decade of the 'dirty thirties' is a case in point. The Great Depression created an army of jobless youth, leading the government of the day to curtail their civil liberties with armed force and confinement in remote work camps. The counter-culture rebellion of the 1960s set off different alarm bells, but stopped short of raising the fears of economic collapse that had loomed in the 1930s. As the baby-boomers came of age, there was pervasive concern among élites and the general public about youth's role in the work world. The counter-culture values of the baby-boomers would, according to popular opinion, undermine their willingness to perform conventional work. In the 1970s many believed that young workers weren't as committed to the work ethic as earlier genera- tions had been. Yet as we saw in Chapter 2, when a 1974 federal government study tested this proposition it pronounced the work ethic healthy. That study quoted a Canadian Chamber of Commerce official who suggested that the problem lay in outmoded job structures: 'It is not that youth is unwilling to work. . . . It is simply that they have rejected the tightly circumscribed envi- ronment that the older worker has come to accept. . . . Instead, the younger people seek more creative roles for themselves and they want to influence the goals of the enterprise.'[8] This criticism of employers is especially telling, coming as it did from their own camp.

Almost identical observations were made about American youth in the 1970s. The *Work in America* project tackled claims about a declining work ethic head-on. It found that dissatisfaction among young workers was a justifiable reaction to insufficient use of their skills. Much of this problem resulted from employers' practice of credentialism—jacking up entry-level requirements to what the market will bear, so that the same job that last year required a high-school education now demands a two-year college diploma.[9]

The labour unrest at General Motors' new Lordstown, Ohio, factory in 1971 was unprecedented by American standards. It became emblematic of a generation in rebellion against demeaning, physically exhausting, and mindless mass-production work systems. American work analysts of that era offered an astute diagnosis of the problems faced by young baby-boomers. Expectations of personally rewarding work, they argued, had been stifled by bureaucratic work organization and a relentless managerial pursuit of efficiency. As Harold Sheppard and Neil Herrick predicted in their influential 1972 book *Where Have All the Robots Gone?*, 'If young people are willing to adapt and to accept the values of the hierarchical work situation . . . we can be assured that little attention will be given to restructuring work.'[10]

Sheppard and Herrick were correct. Today, the problems young workers encounter when seeking work that is both humanly and economically rewarding stem in part from the acquiescence of their parents' generation. This is a new twist on generational equity: the boomers' children inheriting their parents' failed revolution in the workplace. In the 1990s we have heard much talk of innovation in work organizations and management thinking. Yet while this management rhetoric sounds more people-friendly, it has not led us to higher ground. The reasons are rooted in the economic turbulence of the past two decades, especially the anti-people strategies that executives in both the public and private sectors have cobbled together in crisis-response mode. It is these managerial and public policy decisions, more than anything else, that lie behind the restructuring of youth labour markets.

The Youth Labour Market

Now let's consider the broad sweep of the youth labour market since the late 1970s. On a global scale, the Organization for Economic Cooperation and Development reported in 1996 that it views young people as among the primary victims in an era of high unemployment and deep economic restructuring. A young person's chance of being employed or unemployed largely depends on a nation's, or region's, aggregate rate of unemployment; demographics and the shifting industrial mix of employment have little effect in this regard.[11] But even though the problem is bigger than youth unemployment alone, the fact remains that specific groups of youth face significant barriers to finding jobs once they stop being students. The least-educated—not only high-school dropouts, but increasingly also high-school graduates, teenaged males, and Aboriginal youth—are at greatest risk of outright economic exclusion.[12] These young people need more active policy interventions to prevent them from joining the permanent economic underclass as adults.

Double-digit unemployment among youth (defined as those aged 15 to 24) has been a feature of labour markets in Canada, the US, Britain, and Australia since the mid-1970s.[13] Starting in the recession of the early 1980s, adult unemployment rates have spiked up, creating a larger problem that directly affects youth. In the 1990s, a trio of forces—government deficit-cutting, public- and private-sector downsizing coupled with a host of other wage-reduction strategies, and high overall unemployment—constricted the job market in Canada. In response, Canadian youth, like their counterparts in other industrial nations, withdrew from the labour market in droves, either returning to school or staying on longer. In the worst-case scenario, they drifted in a twilight zone between school and work. This is a deeply worrying sign of socio-economic exclusion that has gone largely unnoticed in Canada, even though the proportion of youth with no job experience jumped from 9.8 per cent in December 1989 to 24.6 per cent in December 1997. As Statistics Canada observes, this trend accentuates the barriers that a growing segment of the youth population faces 'trying to break the "no experience, no job—no job no experience" cycle'.[14] In other countries, such as Britain, where over one-third of 18-year-olds were neither employed nor in school in 1994, this exclusion of youth has attracted more attention.[15]

Young people are working less and getting more education. In the 1990s, the previous decade's rise in employment to population ratios for 15- to 24-year-olds has been reversed.[16] The youth share of the total Canadian population has declined, from 19.1 per cent in 1981 to 13.4 per cent in 1996.[17] Yet their share of total employment has fallen even more, from 25 per cent to 15 per cent between 1980 and 1995.[18] At the same time, post-secondary enrolments have swelled. As a result, educational attainment has risen steadily. In 1980, 13 per cent of 15- to 29-year-olds had a post-secondary degree or diploma; by 1995 this figure had almost doubled to 25.1 per cent (or from 19.9 per cent to 38 per cent of all 15- to 29-year-olds).[19]

In today's hyper-competitive labour market, young people who do not possess post-secondary credentials often face insurmountable obstacles to making a decent living. This is the downside to the knowledge economy. Average real wages have eroded over the last two decades. The distribution of work rewards is now more polarized, creating a yawning divide between good jobs and bad jobs. These trends are most starkly evident among youth. Youth wages have been falling relative to adult wages in all OECD nations except Sweden.[20] Education widens the disparities on a range of labour-market outcomes, with university-educated young people getting most of the good jobs created by the Canadian economy in the 1990s. While a university degree is no longer a job guarantee, it is still the best insurance against unemployment, part-time employment, low wages, and other labour-market insecurities. The new problem is that rising tuition fees, growing debt burdens upon graduation, and a shortage of part-time student jobs have started to push a post-secondary education out of reach for sizeable numbers of qualified young people. The inequities in access may only widen the growing gulf between university-educated youth and those with a high-school diploma or less.

Full-time employment for an indefinite term is often seen as the definition of a 'good' job. The spread of nonstandard or contingent employment, as employers seek flexible, low-cost staffing, is directly equated with 'bad' job conditions.[21] However, the quality distinction between standard and nonstandard work situations is far from clear. For example, part of the reason the US has low unemployment is that the bottom layer of the labour force toils in poverty-wage jobs, many of which are full-time. When certain employees, particularly women, are asked their views on flexibility, they often express a desire for part-time work with pro-rated benefits in order to balance work with family responsibilities or further education. And in the student labour market, it has always been the case that contingent jobs are virtually the only paid work available. Low wages aside, such work fits the rhythms of the school term, and most students assume that they won't be stuck selling burgers forever.

Part-time work (defined as less than 30 hours weekly) grew at the expense of full-time jobs in the 1980s, although in the 'jobless recovery' of the 1990s the part-time share of total employment stabilized at roughly 19 per cent. Despite declining employment rates overall since 1989, youth have become more heavily concentrated in part-time jobs.[22] By the mid-1990s, over half of female part-time workers were under 25, as were 40 per cent of their male counterparts. Most of the growth in part-time work, then, has been among youth who are no longer in school, resulting in a jump in involuntary part-time youth employment from 16.4 per cent to 26.5 per cent between 1990 and 1995.[23] The flexibility of a part-time student job quickly becomes an underemployment problem after graduation. Yet the risk of unemployment or involuntary part-time work is reduced considerably as young people acquire more education, with university graduates well below average on both counts.

Demographic Factors

These profound changes in youth labour markets are occurring at a time when the youth cohort comprises a considerably smaller share of the Canadian population than it did in the past. The American demographer Richard Easterlin has suggested that the smaller youth cohorts of the 1980s and 1990s should fare better in the job market than the larger generations ahead of them.[24] But in fact what we are witnessing is the reverse: worsening employment conditions for the smaller school-leaving cohorts since the early 1980s.

As a consequence, the issue of generational equity—public resources directed to meet the needs of older generations at the expense of younger ones—is destined to become a major public-policy challenge. This challenge will extend well beyond the recent issue of fairness in reforms to the Canada/Quebec Pension Plan, which require younger workers to pay considerably higher premiums than did those currently receiving pensions. An early warning signal of the potential for cross-generational friction is that most young people today seem to realize they will not have the same living standard as their parents' generation; they are the first cohort since the Second World War to face this reversal of fortunes.[25] A recent article in *Canadian Business* magazine conjures up images of 'a battle between the generations' over the fact that workers in their late thirties or older entered their jobs with lower credentials than are now required of new recruits. Ambitious twenty-somethings see this kind of credential-based gatekeeping as an effort by older workers to block their careers.[26] (It's interesting that this issue was even raised in a mainstream business publication.)

But then things are getting tighter all around for aspiring young workers. The Canadian labour force expanded by 7.2 per cent between 1990 and 1997, yet the youth labour force contracted by 11 per cent.[27] In the 1990s, full-time employment has nudged up only 3.3 per cent, while part-time employment jumped 18.5 per cent, signalling further erosion in 'standard' work. But among 15- to 24-year-olds full-time employment fell by a staggering 27.1 per cent; this drop was in no way offset by the 6.1 per cent gain in part-time employment. Even with a relatively smaller youth cohort, such a decline in youth employment opportunities is unprecedented. The only other cohort to experience a similar decline is the 55–64 age group. Workers in this older group are exiting the labour force for the same reasons that make it difficult for youth to enter: a reduction in levels of management and downsizing of large organizations. While the average age of retirement has dropped, then, the average age of transition to work from full-time education has risen. The labour market has been compacted by the delayed entry of youth and the earlier exit of older workers. It's as if the front and back ends of the labour market had been squeezed together like an accordion.

It is worth taking a closer look at some of these demographic patterns, because they suggest that if there are labour shortages on Canada's horizon, they won't occur for at least 15 years. This conclusion is based on a comparison of the relative sizes of age cohorts (10-year age groups) exiting and entering the labour force. In 1996 there were 1.2 million 55- to 64-year-olds in the labour force who are heading into retirement, compared with 3.8 million 15- to 24-year-olds who are starting their work lives. Assuming a 75 per cent participation rate (the current rate—it was 80 per cent in the 1980s), this potentially means 2.9 million entry-level workers. In 1996 there were over 3 million 45- to 54-year-olds in the labour force, among whom would be the front end of the baby-boom generation. Waiting in the wings is a much larger number (just under 4 million) of 5- to 14-year-olds who will be entering the labour force as the 45- to 54-year-olds move into retirement.[28] There were 4.2 million 35- to 44-year-olds in the labour force in 1996 who will be replaced by 1.9 million children under the age of 5 (and those born between 1997 and 2000)—the first time a retiring cohort will be numerically larger than the replacement generation.

These demographic projections do not indicate impending shortages, at least until those who were between 35 and 44 in 1996 enter their sixties in the decade starting in 2010. Of course there are unknown factors in this complex equation. Many of the 900,000 unemployed 25- to 54-year-olds form a ready pool of semi-skilled and, to a lesser extent, skilled labour. We also should seriously consider the possibility that older workers will remain in the labour market longer, reversing the trend towards earlier retirement that, after the mid-1980s, saw the retirement age drop to 62 in 1995.[29] Early-retirement incentives are being questioned as organizations recognize the loss of corporate memory and invaluable expertise they entail; at the same time some older workers may realize that they are unable to afford early retirement. Furthermore, the adult female labour-force participation rate levelled off in the early 1990s, so there is the potential for this rate to rise slightly. And immigration will continue to meet some labour demands, although levels could fluctuate. Broadly speaking, then, because participation rates have moved down a few notches, in the next five to ten years it appears unlikely that youth will be at the front of the job line as the demand for labour in Canada increases.

Work Attitudes and Behaviour

I've been talking loosely about 'youth', referring to those who were between the ages of 15 and 24 at any time since the early 1980s. Actually, though, the 1980s and 1990s encompass several distinct youth cohorts. Hence we need to think of each graduating high-school, college, or university class as facing a slightly different combination of economic circumstances from their predecessors. An important question, then, is how young people have adapted their work attitudes and behaviour to new economic, labour-market, and workplace conditions. There are two very different ways of answering this question. One approach is based on the belief that the old industrial order founded on bureaucracy, mass production, and mass consumption has given way to a new post-industrial (or postmodern) era—a change that can be seen in the greater diversity, uncertainty, and individualization of the paths that young people take into adulthood. The other approach rejects the idea that we're no longer influenced by all the workplace, educational, and social institutions that have come to define an industrial society. From this perspective, young people's experience of school–work transitions may be undergoing considerable change, but deep-rooted structures—social class, gender, race, geographic location—continue to limit or enhance opportunities along the way.[30]

I don't believe that our era is fundamentally different (or 'decoupled') from the decades prior to 1980. The proposition that educational, labour-market, and work structures matter less in the lives of young people than they did several decades ago seems untenable. These structures may well have been transformed, but I would suggest that they are even more important now in shaping the life chances of youth. Yet at the same time it is easy to find evidence suggesting that the norms governing the life course are changing. Take marriage, for example. In 1971 in Canada, only 56 per cent of people aged 20 to 24 had never been married. By 1996 the same could be said for 89 per cent, and growing numbers were opting for common-law relationships rather than marriage, which of course results in more births outside marriage.[31] And we have all seen examples of the 'cluttered nest', where 20-something singles prolong their departure from their parents' home. Most single 20- to 24-year-olds live with a parent, as do 44 per cent of men and 33 per cent of women aged 25 to 29.[32] These trends document a longer stage of dependence and, as a result, delayed entry into the adult roles that come with marriage (or its equivalent) and setting up one's own household.

Can we find evidence of new work norms and values being adopted by young people—or imposed on them by the dictates of the job market? National opinion polls by Ekos Research Associates document slightly higher levels of concern among younger workers, compared with workers over age 30, about growing social polarization and job loss, and a somewhat greater sense of powerlessness over their economic future.[33] A 1997 Angus Reid Group survey of youth and young adults (18 to 35) found an emphasis on job security, a desire for self-employment, and a strong work ethic. But only 35 per cent expected to have the multiple-career work experiences that many futurists are predicting. One indication of falling expectations is that fewer than half expected to meet or exceed their career goals.[34] Such polls are indicative of the current outlook among younger workers, including young adults in so-called Generation X, but they provide no way of judging whether things are different now than they were one or two decades ago. After comparing very similar samples of Edmonton grade 12 students in 1985 and in 1996, I can say that the basic work values had not changed over that period. In both cases, what high-school graduates wanted most of all is quality work—work that is interesting and challenging, has friendly and helpful co-workers, and provides a sense of accomplishment. In this respect, they were no different from the vast majority of Canadian workers that we looked at in Chapter 3. Despite the heightened job anxieties of the 1990s, the 1996 grads placed only slightly more priority on finding a job that is secure and pays well.[35]

School–Work Transitions

Work attitudes among youth, then, have altered little in more than a decade. But is the same true of actual school–work transition processes? I have suggested that the labour market is a far less hospitable place for younger workers in the 1990s than it was in the 1980s. But this conclusion is based on broad national trends. We won't know in detail how school–work transitions have been affected until we are able to document retrospectively how 1990s graduates fared in comparison with their counterparts of the 1980s. However, earlier research clearly shows that most 1980s secondary and post-secondary graduates eventually settled into stable employment, often by pursuing personalized strategies combining work experience, further education, and sometimes community volunteer work. The prognosis for high-school dropouts was far bleaker—a point to which I shall return. The crux of the matter is whether youth are able over time to launch fulfilling and productive lives as workers, citizens, and parents. Based on the experiences of 1985 high school and university graduates in Edmonton that my co-researcher Harvey Krahn and I followed for seven years, the answer, with important qualifications, is yes.[36]

In 1985, the high-school graduates in this study were in their late teens and the university graduates in their early twenties. When we surveyed them in 1992, many had achieved independent adulthood, formed partnerships, left their parents' homes, and started families. Yet compared to graduates in previous decades, their transition to adulthood took considerably longer. The process also required difficult choices and trade-offs about school and work. Young people who had stayed in school longer, for instance, were more likely to have postponed parenthood. The challenge of balancing work and family— one of the major pressure points today for workers of all ages—also begins to affect employment patterns. By 1992 part-time work had begun to replace full-time employment for many young women who had become parents. This trend was not evident among men, suggesting that traditional gender roles are reproduced within new forms of school–work transition.

Central to the experience of these '85 grads was continued participation in the educational system. For most of the 1985–92 period, the majority of high-school graduates were obtaining some kind of further education. Among the university graduates, about one in three obtained two additional years of university education after graduating in 1985, and roughly one in four obtained three to four years. More than one-third of the high-school sample and one-quarter of the university sample was still reporting educational activity in 1991–2.

The primary motives for pursuing further education were work-related. Clearly, these graduates understood the connection between ongoing education and survival (or, more optimistically, success) in the job market. This could predispose them to further involvement in the educational system, although the latter is only one way of engaging in lifelong learning. Many of these grads, for example, actively participated in informal and formal workplace learning, especially in rapidly advancing areas such as computers. If lifelong learning is indeed central to the new work world, it appears that many Canadian graduates are already headed in the right direction. Almost one in five in the high-school sample and one-third in the university sample exited and re-entered the educational system at some point in the seven years covered by our study.

Education and the Labour Market

Although the school–work transition has become more risky, uncertain, and individualized, there is no denying that post-secondary educational credentials increase one's chances of obtaining a good job. One year after graduating in 1985, for example, two-thirds of high-school graduates who had left the education system were employed in clerical, sales, or service occupations, mostly in lower-tier service industries. By contrast, more than two-thirds of the 1985 university graduates who had entered the labour market were in professional and managerial jobs, mainly in the upper tier of the service sector (business services, finance, communications, transportation, and distributive services, and the public sector).

By 1992, members of the sample were older and had accumulated more work experience. Most crucial, the advantages of higher education had become even more apparent. Seven years after receiving an undergraduate degree, over 80 per cent of the university grads held managerial or professional jobs. Those who had continued their education were especially successful in the labour market. But only one in ten high-school graduates who had not returned to school full-time at any point between 1985 and 1992 had obtained a managerial or professional job. Not all the better-educated '85 grads had obtained good jobs, however. Women had somewhat less success than men in this regard. Graduates of professional faculties (education and engineering) were more likely to have obtained the type of employment for which they had trained than were arts, science, or business graduates. Furthermore, the educational dividends were longer in coming. Those who experienced transition difficulties remained in unrewarding work until they eventually found a more challenging job that better matched their qualifications.

Part-time employment also declined during the seven-year study. When surveyed in 1992, only 13 per cent of the employed high-school respondents and 10 per cent of employed university respondents were still in part-time jobs, compared to 16 per cent of the Canadian labour force at the time. Continuing students were more likely to be working in part-time or temporary jobs. Considering only those who were not full-time students, about one in ten were in temporary jobs when surveyed in 1992. Eventually, it seems, most young workers do find their way into full-time and permanent jobs. What's changed since the 1960s or 1970s is that now it takes longer to attain that kind of work, and the journey is fraught with greater potential hazards.

Unemployment was all too familiar an experience for many members of the class of '85. A tough job market in the mid-'80s was the backdrop to the school–work transition patterns sketched above. The provincial unemployment rate when the Edmonton study began in 1985 was 10.6 per cent, and for 15- to 19-year-olds it was 20.1 per cent, making the job market at that time more competitive for youth than it was a decade later. The relatively large size of the youth cohort that was leaving school added to these problems. Still, university grads were half as likely as high-school grads to be unemployed when contacted in follow-up surveys (5 per cent, compared with 10 per cent). Even though another recession was under way in 1992, unemployment among the high-school grads, many of whom were now better educated, had dropped to 7 per cent. Yet short spells of unemployment were common. In the year after graduation, about three in ten members of both samples reported at least one period of unemployment. For most grads, at least one spell of unemployment was part of the transition process. In some countries, such as Britain, long-term youth unemployment became the norm in the 1980s, but this has not been the case in Canada—except among high-school dropouts.

A more common difficulty was various forms of underemployment. When surveyed in 1992, seven years after graduation, 31 per cent of the high-school graduates and 20 per cent of the university graduates reported feeling over-qualified for their jobs. Just over one-third (37 per cent) of employed high-school respondents and only one-half (52 per cent) of employed university sample members reported that they had the kind of job they had expected at this stage in their lives. Graduates of some faculties (arts, for example) were considerably more likely to feel overqualified than were education and engineering graduates. This kind of mismatch between educational credentials and job requirements not only reduces the quality of work life for a substantial number of well-educated young workers: from a broader societal perspective, it represents squandered human capital.

The key point is that a full-time job does not necessarily mean full utilization of a young person's human capital, even for university graduates. Employer downsizing, contracting-out, and increasing reliance on a low-paid, flexible workforce suggest a decline in job quality both in the upper-tier services and in the goods-producing industries. The polarization between skilled, challenging, and economically rewarding jobs on one hand and unskilled, low-wage, and insecure jobs on the other has come to define the service economy. Neither the negative 'McJobs' image nor the positive 'new economy', 'knowledge society' image accurately portrays this dualistic labour market. For young workers trying to find secure and rewarding work, the chances of obtaining a good job depend largely on the particular segment of the labour market they enter. The part-time, temporary, and seasonal jobs in the retail and consumer services (e.g., food and beverage, tourism, personal services) industries that form student labour markets offer low wages and unpredictable schedules. No doubt many students dislike these conditions, but they accept them because they realize that such work may be all that is available while they are concentrating on completing their education. The challenge is to move out of this student labour market into full-scale employment in the adult labour market. Given that the latter market has contracted and restructured, education assumes even greater importance in determining who gets the better jobs at the top end of the service economy.

Finally, a brief word about high-school dropouts. The Edmonton study does not tell us about high-school dropouts—a group that has been called a 'lost generation'.[37] Research on dropouts shows that even though they rejected the school system once—usually for a combination of personal, school, and family reasons—they have by no means given up on education altogether. In fact, Canadian dropouts may well be distinguished from those in other countries by their high levels of commitment to the value of education. Many eventually return to complete high school. According to Statistics Canada's School Leavers Follow-Up Survey, only 14 per cent of high-school dropouts aged 18 to 20 in 1991 had not completed their diploma or re-enrolled in high school by 1995. Soon to enter their mid-twenties, these particular young people tend to be male and from disadvantaged socio-economic backgrounds. Dropouts risk permanent marginalization in the job market.[38] Specifically, among this sample of 22- to 24-year-olds, 21 per cent of the dropouts were unemployed in 1995, compared with 13 per cent of those with a high-school diploma and no further education or training.

Labour-Market Polarization and Underemployment

This overview of school–work transitions in the 1980s and early 1990s poses several public-policy challenges. If education is the admission ticket to the game, those with the lowest credentials are sidelined, and those with no credentials at all—dropouts—can't even get in the stadium gate. In this respect, labour-market polarization is first and foremost a youth problem. This was true for the 1985 Edmonton grads portrayed above; today the same trends are even more evident. When the youth cohorts of the 1990s become adults, society will face the social, economic, and political consequences of their prolonged marginalization or outright exclusion. In the post-welfare-state era, those youth who falter in the transition process are more likely than at any time since the Second World War to be cast adrift economically.

Equally serious, from a human-resource perspective, is what appears to be the inability of the economy to generate enough skilled and rewarding jobs to accommodate the rising educational levels of workers. This problem of skill utilization is especially acute among young workers, who are attaining higher levels of education than any previous generation. This certainly was the case for the 1985 Edmonton grads. Given the prevalence of obtaining further education and training as a personal survival strategy, the situation is likely to become even worse for many, particularly the young.

Evidence that underemployment is pervasive among recent university graduates comes from the 1997 Alberta Graduate Survey (AGS), part of the

Government of Alberta's initiative to measure the performance of post-secondary institutions.[39] Two-and-a-half years after their graduation, the AGS surveyed over 6,000 1994 graduates from all programs at Alberta's four universities. At the time of the survey, early in 1997, the provincial economy was booming and unemployment had dipped to around 6 per cent. Thus it was not surprising that, on the whole, these graduates were doing quite well. Members of the class of '94 who were no longer in the educational system in 1997 experienced a fairly easy transition into the labour force, had above-average employment rates and incomes, below-average unemployment and part-time employment rates, and relatively high job satisfaction. Yet indications of underutilized potential were readily visible. Specifically, about two-thirds of those who had left the education system were in jobs requiring a university degree, and one-quarter reported feeling overqualified for their job, given their education, training, and experience.

Some of this overqualification reflects the difficulty that graduates from non-professional faculties (such as arts, science, business, physical education and recreation) have finding suitable, challenging jobs. Employers in the professions (engineering, nursing, teaching) seem to find it easier to slot young workers into jobs that fit with their training, a reflection of the closer integration of school and work in these professions. If the work relevance of general programs is questionable, then, this increases the chances that graduates of those programs will end up in clerical, sales, or service work, or in nonstandard jobs. In this case it is a labour-market mismatch that creates underemployment, but in other instances—for example, in management, administrative, and technical jobs—the root of the problem is the design of the job itself.

The situation is similar for other post-secondary graduates. Statistics Canada reports that in 1994, one in four community-college graduates under the age of 29 felt overqualified in a job.[40] This mismatch between young, well-educated workers and the requirements of their jobs suggests that the human-resource development approach to economic renewal is overly optimistic. As American critics of this approach argue, it has a 'field of dreams' element, implying that if educational and training programs produce capable workers, then high-quality employment will naturally follow.[41] Even though many members of Alberta's university class of '94 had well-paid, full-time jobs, their potential to contribute at higher levels was not fully tapped. This results in diminished quality of work life for individuals and loss to the economy in terms of productivity.

Conclusion

At this point in our discussion the past catches up with the future. Early research on the integration of technology and job design (called the 'socio-technical systems' approach) in the 1950s and 1960s, Scandinavian work-environment policies of 1970s, the North American quality-of-work-life movement in the same period, and current research on high-performance workplaces all indicate that a fundamental reorganization of work is required. At a time of rising educational levels, when all workers are being urged to engage in lifelong learning, underemployment and other forms of mismatch are becoming defining characteristics of new graduates' work experiences. Even more than in the 1970s, when North American youth were expressing a strong desire for higher-quality jobs, the crux of the youth employment problem today is job quality. Vestiges of the same rigidly bureaucratic, command-and-control employment systems that spurred the quality-of-work-life movement make it just as difficult to reform work now as when the baby-boomers were starting out.

This suggests that we need to rethink what it means to create work opportunities for recent high-school, college, or university graduates. A priority should be setting and achieving targets for high-quality entry-level job creation so that new grads can get a decent start in the work world. These jobs must be more than just alternatives to unemployment. As the OECD reminds us, though, youth unemployment is nested in the larger economic problem of high overall unemployment. Clearly, we need macro-economic and labour-market policies aimed at reducing overall unemployment by generating new jobs. It is equally important, however, to improve the quality of jobs so that fresh talent can be used and developed further. Reducing the national rate of unemployment and improving the overall quality of jobs by providing opportunities for skilled and personally rewarding work is the pathway towards a high-skill, high-wage economy that will benefit all generations.

Canada's Liberal government has tried to use the youth unemployment issue to political ends, knowing that public opinion supports action on this front. Its 1996 Task Force on Youth called on employers to bring down youth unemployment by providing 'first job opportunities' and urging the private sector (what about the public sector?) to think seriously about this obligation.[42] Corporate Canada did respond, led by one of the major banks, and has set up various programs based on stay-in-school initiatives, co-op and internship programs, and mentoring.[43] Ottawa's proposed Millennium Scholarship Fund attempts to address the affordability crisis in higher education and rising student debt loads. But this proposal came on the heels of the government's abdication of its role in training and of reduced transfer payments for post-secondary education. Both of these initiatives are constrained by conventional thinking about work, education, and youth. Faced with the limitations of such programs, we need to expand the discussion to consider innovative alternatives to the challenges of improving job quality, creating skilled jobs, reorganizing work, and providing more equitably distributed opportunities to earn a decent living.[44] Addressing the needs and aspirations of young workers today surely is the best way of ensuring a more rewarding working future for all Canadians.

Chapter 7

'Putting People First'

The phrase 'people are our most valued resource' rolls easily off the lips of business leaders these days. Similarly, politicians and policy pundits claim that upgrading the skills of the workforce will improve Canada's position in global markets. Meeting the challenges of competitiveness and productivity, whether in firms or in nations, has come to mean developing the skills and talents of people. To judge by the standard rhetoric in business and public-policy circles, the 1990s have been the decade of human-resource development, of 'putting people first'. But has it really? In fact, a fixation on cost-cutting prevents many employers from seeing how workers could contribute to longer-term productivity. 'My responsibility is the empowerment of people,' stated a Calgary-based NorTel manager, describing his firm's human-resource management philosophy.[1] It may well be the case that NorTel—one of Canada's best-known high-tech firms—indeed takes this challenge seriously. That would make it the exception, however, because the reality is that many firms do not nurture the talents and well-being of workers, and management's objectives of greater efficiency and productivity therefore remain unmet.

Calls to develop a nation's or a firm's human resources as a key to economic prosperity certainly have an appealing ring. Yet the dominant management strategies in the past decade have focused more on cost-cutting than on people development, contributing to an erosion of worker morale and loyalty. The serious gaps in employers' use of the education and skills already available in the workforce—documented in Chapter 5—reflect the fact that work structures prevent them from making optimal use of this talent. More generally, the view that human-resource development will contribute to economic prosperity is based on the faulty assumption that the demand for skilled labour will rise to absorb its increasing supply. It is because Canadians value education highly that so many individuals have acted on the belief that further education or training will help them in a risky and unpredictable labour market. But this response only serves to increase the supply of skills in the workforce. As a result, there is mounting pressure to reform traditional work structures and management systems. Failure to do so will prevent sizeable numbers of people from contributing the knowledge and skills acquired through their own educational efforts. In short, the missing piece of the human-resource development puzzle is workplace reform aimed at improving the quality of work.

Workers: Costs or Assets?

If business leaders and policy-makers are committed to putting people first, fostering continuous learning, and adopting human resource-based economic strategies, then they must bridge the chasm between people's abilities and the design of jobs and workplaces. Despite growing awareness among senior management of the importance of workers' knowledge, skills, and involvement in decision-making, the fact remains that traditional work structures, management control systems, and an overriding focus on costs and profits make it difficult to nurture these human qualities in workplaces. Resolving this contradiction is the most pressing issue on the human-resource policy agenda for the opening years of the twenty-first century.

When management does not treat its staff as a valued resource, employees may suffer, but so too may the organization, its shareholders, and the public. This issue was brought into sharp relief in the war of words between trade unions and financial market analysts over CN's announcement of a further 3,000 job cuts in the fall of 1998. Paul Tellier, the railway's CEO, justified the cuts by stating that CN was 'trying to become the most efficient railroad in North America'. Buzz Hargrove, president of the Canadian Auto Workers union (CAW), citing CN's recent profits, retorted: 'It's greed, just greed.'[2] Stock markets rewarded CN for its efficiency drive by boosting share prices. As one market analyst put it, summarizing the view of investors: 'They're definitely on the right track.'[3] Not long after, Tellier was named Canada's 'CEO of the Year' for his privatization of CN.[4]

There's more to this corporate downsizing episode than a people-versus-profits trade-off. Tellier argued that cost reduction, achieved mainly through new technologies, would make the railway more competitive against tough and lean American railways. And, he pointed out, workers would leave with generous severance payments. This round of downsizing brought the total number of jobs axed by CN since 1992 to 18,000—half of its workforce. Tellier warned workers to get used to continued job insecurity as long as the company was under intense competitive pressures from US rivals.[5] However, when mixed with workers' anger over the job cuts, this pall of insecurity could further erode CN's competitive position. As executives rush to reposition and rebalance their firms in their drive for competitiveness, it is worth reflecting on the true value of people. What role do workers play in charting the future course of a railway, or any organization for that matter? Are workers costs or assets?

If one accepts management's arguments about the imperatives of efficiency and productivity, then surely people matter even more. The fewer people there are in an organization, the more the contribution of each affects the bottom line. The cost–revenue ratio that CN's management hoped to lower by combining downsizing with technological change seems to have missed a key element in the efficiency equation. Any railway is operated by workers—and new technology depends even more than older technology did on their ingenuity and dedication. The enormously complex process of repositioning a corporation like CN can only benefit from the direct input of all its workers. By defining efficiency strictly in terms of balance sheets and cost–earnings ratios, management could reap the bitter harvest of deteriorating industrial relations and worker morale. Even if some of CN's human-resource managers sympathize with this argument (and they just might), their voices are likely muted—because in most corporate and government power structures, financial and line managers take priority over human-resource experts.

The Rhetoric

Employees matter more than ever before. This view is expressed in many quarters of the Canadian business community, even though actions like CN's are common. A leading management think-tank, the Conference Board of Canada, argues that economic globalization has unleashed 'unprecedented competition', forcing organizations to operate more efficiently and mobilize all their resources—especially people.[6] The NorTel manager quoted at the start of this chapter reflected this view in his reference to employee empowerment. Empowerment sounds progressive; but what does it mean? For the Conference Board, it means ensuring that employees can satisfy customers without asking permission to do so from their bosses. But what does this mean for employees? Does it pass control from managers to customers? Does it give customers licence to make demands that threaten the quality of work life, as is the case in those service industries where workers, especially women, experience harassment of various kinds? Maybe some workers stand a better chance of keeping their jobs if their firm does well. But as long as workplace innovation remains at this superficial level, there is little prospect of significant improvements in job quality. Too often, terms like 'employee empowerment' and 'participative management' are simply inserted into cost-reduction strategies aimed at boosting productivity and profits. Moreover, the term 'employee' has increasingly come to define a select group of full-time core workers, excluding the outer ring of individuals working on a part-time, temporary, or contract basis.

The Business Council on National Issues (BCNI), an influential corporate lobby, and the CAW union are powerful adversaries who have often squared off on economic issues. A decade ago, television debates over free trade with the US often pitted Bob White, then president of the CAW, against Thomas D'Aquino of the BCNI. However, these two opponents apparently agree on the need to treat workers as valued resources. In its 1993 working paper *Building a New Century Economy*, the BCNI placed treating employees as a company's 'greatest source of competitive strength' as the number-two priority, right after creating a culture of customer satisfaction and continuous improvement.[7] The BCNI explained that good employee–employer relations are central to a firm's 'competitive advantage' (a term that makes unionists wince). If the BCNI is serious about moving away from traditional top-down, command-and-control management styles, however, we need details on what model it advocates. Is it a workplace that is more flexible, non-bureaucratic, knowledge-based, participatory, and skill-intensive?

For its part, the CAW's view of work reorganization rests on a single principle: 'we want to use our experience, knowledge, and skills to produce good quality products and quality services in well-designed workplaces equipped with the proper tools and equipment. And we want to ensure that this production does not ignore our rights and entitlements.'[8] Experience has taught the union to be wary of management promises of a new cooperative partnership under the guise of increased competitiveness, because usually it does not mean sharing any control with workers. Rather, it suggests a treadmill programmed to gradually gain speed until the user simply can't keep up and is replaced by someone else eager for a job. The union's most basic concern is 'that management's agenda is not about surrendering its power, but about finding more sophisticated ways to extend it'. Is this a stalemate, or is there a common ground on which unions, workers, and management could meet?

In fact, the potential for such a meeting does exist. Terms like 'competitiveness', 'skill', 'empowerment', and 'flexibility' mean very different things for employees and employers, and consensus on mutually beneficial definitions for them could provide the common ground that is required. Quite possibly, the language of human-resource development could at least help to open a dialogue about how to achieve positive change: high-quality work performed in high-quality jobs. The difficulty, though, is that while the rhetoric of management has pointed this way during the past decade, in practice management's actions towards employees have tended to move in the opposite direction.

Efficiency, Competitiveness, and Downsizing

Downsizing was a dubious triumph of a short-term focus on costs over a sustained focus on people. The irony is that in the longer term, developing human resources inside firms will likely do more to reduce costs and improve efficiency than will the downsizer's blunt axe. Downsizing represents a mechanistic view of organizations in which workers' contributions are reduced to unit labour costs on a balance sheet. This view has its roots in the 'scientific' management thinking of the early twentieth century. Frederick Taylor, an American engineer who was one of the first successful management consultants, promoted industrial growth through a combination of technology and more efficient ways of organizing work.[9] The legacy of Taylor and other 'efficiency experts' of his era still thrives today. Indeed, scientific management has been called 'one of the most pervasive and invisible of the forces that have shaped modern society'.[10]

Taylor's ideas had considerable influence among major employers (including the railways) in the Canada of the early twentieth century. He advocated that jobs be based on a limited range of tasks following set procedures, tighter management controls on workers, and technological change. This three-pronged strategy would, he claimed, boost productivity.[11] Taylor thought money was the sole human motivation to work. He believed that jobs should be so simply designed that a trained gorilla could perform them. When Taylor's ideas were married with the mass-production assembly line technology pioneered by Henry Ford, a work system was created that defined human progress in terms of rising output, efficiency, and profits. In the management lexicon of the 1990s, this approach translates into competitiveness.

Despite the growing expertise of human-resource professionals in countering the most dehumanizing and alienating effects of this work system, it has been difficult to break free of the principles set down by Taylor and Ford. By the early 1990s, downsizing and cost-cutting through technological change had become the latest manifestations of the scientific-management philosophy. These were the business strategies of choice among Canadian private-sector firms.[12] A downsizing mindset pushes other, more people-oriented approaches well down on the management agenda. It's true that programs designed to help employees cope with workplace changes have become increasingly common— but they wouldn't be necessary if the human consequences of those changes had been considered in the first place.[13] A recent survey of CEOs discovered that employees didn't even make the list of their top nine priorities. Customers came first (at least people matter as consumers). And the number-two priority—cost competitiveness—could easily be interpreted as a reincarnation of Taylorism, which gives workers a low priority.[14] Despite several generations of management and organization theories that emphasize the importance of human resources, the idea that workers are the key to achieving all business goals remains a very hard sell.

Clashing Business Strategies

In 1998, Statistics Canada published the results of a workplace and employment survey that probed these issues from the perspectives of both managers and employees in the same establishments—a novel approach. While only pilot results are available, and therefore can't be taken as definitive, the findings are consistent with other research on the relationship between management strategies, working conditions, and human-resource development.[15] The study reveals a tension between two distinct kinds of business strategies: cost-based strategies such as downsizing and re-engineering, and those that promote human-resource development and product or service innovation.

Downsizing and re-engineering were the most common among a wide array of specific business strategies used by these establishments in the three years prior to the survey; indeed, one in four had downsized. Re-engineering, which involves the redesign of business processes to improve performance and cost, had been introduced by one in three of the establishments surveyed. By contrast, one in five viewed human-resource management strategies as very important or crucial to their overall business; such firms focused on developing workers' skills, involving them in decision-making, and improving labour–management relations. By contrast, fewer than one in eight said such employee-oriented strategies were of no importance at all; these typically were smaller employers in industries where wages and skills are relatively low.

What kinds of employers emphasize human-resource development in their overall business strategies? Larger firms tend to be more committed than smaller ones to developing their workers' skills. And we can only assume, in the absence of solid research, that the swelling ranks of the self-employed face many barriers to skill development, including cost, lack of information on what's available, and shortage of time. Employers who promoted skill development were also far more likely to provide flexible work arrangements, innovative ways of organizing work, and more training opportunities. For job quality to improve, organizational innovations such as team-based work, quality circles, and flexible job designs require the development of new skills through employer-provided training.[16]

Despite the synergy between people-centred work design and skill development, few employers have pursued this route. This highlights the gap between management rhetoric and action. The survey looked at changes ranging from employee suggestion programs, flexible job design, greater information-sharing, quality circles and problem-solving teams, and joint labour-management committees, to self-directed work groups. Some 44 per cent of the firms surveyed, mainly smaller establishments, reported no organizational changes[17] at all in the three years prior to the survey. A mere 7.2 per cent of establishments surveyed reported any of these changes, affecting 8.3 per cent of employees. Employee suggestion programs were the most common change— hardly a breakthrough.

To summarize, even among those establishments that see employees as a key business asset, few seem to be carrying this view into work designs that could significantly improve the quality of work. From a management perspective, this is surprising, given that the development of value-added products and services seems to go hand-in-hand with a knowledge-intensive work environment. There seem to be two quite distinct camps of employers: one committed to developing their businesses by developing their employees, and one that bases business decisions mainly on cost considerations. For employees, cost-focused establishments, with their reliance on downsizing, re-engineering, and flexible staffing in the form of part-time, temporary, and contract workers, would seem to be less desirable places to work. The employer of choice would be one that makes intensive use of human-resource management strategies, because it would also be likely to provide good benefits, such as pensions, and to be unionized—two indicators of high job quality. But how much better are actual working conditions in human-resource-intensive firms? Workers' expectations are raised by corporate pronouncements that they will 'own' their jobs in these more participative and flexible work settings. But reality can be disappointing for workers who run into subtly imposed constraints when they try to stretch the limits of their jobs.[18]

Worker Morale and Commitment

Downsizing is closely tied to two other favoured management tactics in large organizations: outsourcing work to smaller suppliers (or, in the public sector, privatization), and flexible staffing arrangements. These tactics lie behind a growing contingent labour force, accentuating divisions between core employees and a less privileged group of lower-paid temporary, casual, or contract workers. The underlying ethos of competitiveness and efficiency speaks volumes about management's priorities.

A sense of betrayal and demoralization among those employees who have survived the shakedowns and still form the core workforce, or who were restructured into the contingent workforce, is the major human consequence of downsizing and its sister strategies. This issue has been examined by Murray Axmith & Associates, one of Canada's leading career planning and transition consultants. Much of their recent business has consisted of 'outplacement', or assisting corporate and government clients in firing staff. In fall 1996, it surveyed 1,014 organizations across various sectors about hiring and dismissal practices.[19] The study addressed rebuilding after downsizing—undoubtedly a huge challenge, considering that 71 per cent of the employers surveyed had downsized or restructured since 1991. In most cases these initiatives resulted in improved costs and earnings. However, fewer than half of the firms increased their productivity, and fewer than one-third improved customer service. Worst of all was the impact of staff cuts or reorganization on the remaining staff, who showed noticeable declines in morale, loyalty, and job satisfaction.

Low morale and commitment can also be found in organizations that have not undergone wrenching staff cuts. Murray Axmith's report emphasizes the importance of hiring the most qualified workers, ensuring their commitment to organizational goals, and motivating them to excel in their jobs. However, over half of the employers responding to the survey found it more difficult to motivate workers and gain commitment than they had five years earlier. (It would be revealing to know how these employers gauged motivation and commitment, but very few studies offer this information.) Most firms had attempted to bolster sagging morale and commitment in the previous five years, mainly through what could be called minor preventative maintenance. But a big part of the problem is that firms can no longer offer the security of continuous employment. To compensate for this loss of security, some employers are attempting to improve communications, management skills, training opportunities, performance evaluation and compensation systems, and employee involvement in setting business plans. These initiatives are useful, but they fail to shore up increasingly fragile employment relationships.

The 1997 *Workplace 2000* survey, which the Angus Reid Group conducted on behalf of the Royal Bank, captured employees' views on how employment relationships are being redefined.[20] Assessing their findings, the Angus Reid Group concludes: 'Clearly, the dislocation caused by the recession, globalization, "right-skilling" and increased demands for productivity took its toll on workers in Canada.'[21] The report's message is mixed, though. On one hand, it detects rising optimism among employees, expressed as a greater sense of entrepreneurship (whatever that means). But it also identifies problems stemming from workplace pressures, including stress, overwork, difficulties in making ends meet, and longer work hours. Employers are advised that workers need to feel 'job ownership' and 'rewarded in a way than makes them feel . . . appreciated'.[22] A similar study of Canadian employees, by the human-resource management consultants Towers Perrin, offered much the same advice for regaining commitment: 'engage employees.'[23] According to these studies, providing high-quality work in a supportive and reasonably secure environment is paramount in renewing workers' morale and commitment.

For a start, jobs and organizations can be redesigned so that staff cuts are a last resort. In some cases, organizations may find staff reductions unavoidable if they are to survive. So it's helpful to learn from the experiences of employers with a strong human-resources emphasis that there are more humane ways of achieving reductions. I make this point with caution, being acutely aware of the potentially negative impact of any staff cuts on individuals and communities, and how they detract from the larger economic goal of job creation. Still, it must be said that reducing staff through attrition, attractive severance or early retirement plans, and career transition programs offering positive options to employees who are seeking career changes, is far better than simply issuing pink slips. Two leading Alberta-based corporations, Telus and Nova, have career transition programs that give employees who want to leave options such as partial salary to do voluntary community work for an extended period, support for further education, and assistance setting up a small business. Such programs rest on the belief that departing workers must be treated with dignity.[24] What's important in these examples is the centrality of humanistic values.

Even if the worst symptoms of 'survivor syndrome' are avoided among the remaining employees, a downsized organization's human resources will be depleted well beyond the number of jobs cut. The loss of experienced workers and their informal knowledge about how things really get done, the challenges of embarking on staff renewal, the stresses of overwork for remaining staff— these are the unintended consequences of downsizing. And as a former AT&T executive has suggested, downsizing may be especially traumatic for firms that have built strong employee loyalty.[25] He should know: the telecommunications giant became the target of a public backlash against corporate downsizing when it announced 40,000 layoffs. That executive made a good point, because the greater the sense of trust in a workplace, the more negative the impact when that trust is violated. Symptoms of survivor syndrome—guilt, betrayal, detachment, depression, risk aversion, need for information, low productivity—will be all the more acute.

Trust implies a mutual obligation among employees and employers to build working relationships on what is fair, just, and respectful. Trust is crucial for the effectiveness of any organization. Yet the direction of much organizational change in the 1990s has weakened the basis for trust. The implicit employment contract that emerged after the Second World War was based on job security, predictability, respect for workers' dignity and rights, and understanding of what constitutes fair effort and fair reward. Since the early 1980s employers have largely rewritten these ground rules in the course of restructuring, slashing public deficits, merging, and otherwise pruning costs.

The new employment rules are clearly evident in rising levels of executive compensation. This trend has not only accentuated workplace status and power differences; it has also revealed the hypocrisy of corporate cultures that emphasize common goals, teamwork, and shared values. Pay inequalities have long been part of the capitalist labour market. What's different in the past two decades is the spectacular rise in executive pay at a time when most workers have lost economic ground. One wonders how cynical employees can trust their employers to treat them fairly and be concerned about their interests. Even shareholders are beginning to openly ask how any single individual can contribute fifty times as much to the success of an organization as another. It's worth recalling that Adam Smith, the father of capitalist economics, considered a detailed division of labour to be a prerequisite for creating greater wealth.[26] Essentially, work is a social activity with a high degree of interdependence. Certainly strong and visionary leadership is worth rewarding—but let's give more credit to the contributions of everyone else in the organization too.

Until this happens, we will likely see employees' trust in employers slide further, which in turn will reduce loyalty and commitment. This decline is well under way. A *New York Times* survey, for example, found that almost two-thirds of respondents believed that workers were less loyal to their employers in 1995 than they had been 10 years earlier.[27] The American Management Association now talks about the 'value gap' that employees see between the values that organizations espouse and the actions of their management. This gap must be painfully obvious in firms whose mission statements emphasize valuing employees. That many rank-and-file employees, along with front-line supervisors and middle managers, no longer trust senior management has been singled out by human-resource professionals as a barrier to improved employee–employer relations.[28]

We should think carefully, then, about how to rekindle trust and loyalty. Frederick Reichheld, a management consultant with Bain & Company, argues that managers would like to have loyal employees, but don't want to invest the money or effort that would require. Reichheld suggests that managers know the cost of achieving loyalty, but do not appreciate its value. Through downsizing, he notes, 'a lot of companies today pursue policies that discourage or even destroy employee loyalty. Many observers have begun to wonder if we're not witnessing the death of corporate loyalty altogether.'[29]

Reichheld advocates 'loyalty-based management'. In his consulting work, he found many firms in which customer loyalty could not be improved without first addressing issues of loyalty on the part of employees and investors. This is impossible with a shortsighted view of profitability. Reichheld argues that loyalty, not profit, is the litmus test of corporate performance. He distinguishes between virtuous and destructive profits—the former deriving from the human assets of the organization, the latter from exploiting assets ('profiteering') rather than adding value. Business schools teach about profits from the perspective of shareholder value. Reichheld counters with a different slant on profits, one grounded in human resources. Loyal employees learn ways to cut costs and improve quality, increasing customer value and productivity. This sets in motion a feedback loop in which better compensation, resources, training, and productivity promote loyalty.

'New Paradigms'

New approaches such as loyalty-based management move in the direction of high-quality work by truly valuing workers, but they haven't taken root in corporate North America. More generally, the widely sought paradigm shift remains a mirage. The call for revolutionary new management ideas goes back to the early 1980s, with the publication of Tom Peters and Robert Waterman's best-seller *In Search of Excellence*.[30] For all the rebellions against traditional thinking, we have yet to see any revolutionary new approaches to management at either the theoretical or the practical level. New management techniques are much like fireworks, generating lots of noise and flash, but soon fizzling out. When management gurus wax eloquent about a new paradigm, sceptics respond with questions about who actually will implement the new approach and how organizational inertia will be swept aside. A paradigm doesn't emerge on its own: it is the product of actions and reactions by key players in the drama of the workplace.

Actual workplace change gets bogged down in the contradictory positions staked out in academic and popular management literature. The conflict can be seen in recent public-sector management thinking. Despite different cultures and goals, the private and public sectors came to share one dominant strategy in the 1990s: downsizing. The job cuts in public administration (central government at all levels, from municipal to federal) were the deepest, shrinking this sector more than any other industry in the 1990s. The 1996 Census marked the first drop in the number of federal and provincial government employees since 1901. Federal government employment dropped by 15 per cent between 1991 and 1996. In Alberta, employment in public administration declined 27 per cent between 1989 and 1997, when in all private-sector industries it was increasing.[31] Some of this downsizing was achieved through layoffs. The rest was accomplished by attrition, speeded up by massive early-retirement programs.

Along with shrinking the public sector came attempts at a total makeover. David Osborne and Ted Gaebler's 1993 *Reinventing Government* was received as a handbook for injecting private-sector entrepreneurship and flexibility into lumbering government bureaucracy. Implicit in one passage that was widely cited as a justification for less government though downsizing and privatization is what I interpret rather as a call for improved job quality. Osborne and Gaebler write: 'Many employees in bureaucratic governments feel trapped. Tied down by rules and regulations, numbed by monotonous tasks, assigned jobs they know could be accomplished in half the time if they were only allowed to use their minds, they live lives of quiet desperation.'[32] Among the solutions they propose are reduction of red tape, clearer missions, and more 'entrepreneurial' forms of leadership that will 'return control to those who work down where the rubber meets the road'.[33] Entrepreneurial leaders encourage participatory management and teamwork, and ensure that employees have the skills and morale needed to rise to their expanded responsibilities. Of course, critics of this business-style of government are correct to point out that solutions such as contracting-out and privatization invariably reduce overall job quality.[34]

To what extent has public-service reform addressed the quality of jobs and the work environment? The government of Canada tried to incorporate some job-quality improvements in its PS2000 initiative, a massive effort to simultaneously reduce and remake the federal civil service. But like Osborne and Gaebler, the federal government mixed the objectives of teams, worker empowerment, a learning environment, and flexible work arrangements with the reality of job cuts and wage freezes. Combining these incompatible policies scuttled any chance to gain the cooperation of public-sector unions in workplace renewal. However, the government's handbook advising managers how to empower workers could, at least in theory, lead to major improvements in job quality: 'Empowerment is a set of practices, attitudes and behaviours that frees people up—that *enables* them to make full use of their knowledge, energies, and judgement to provide better service.'[35]

Why hasn't this kind of thinking caught on? Perhaps it is understandable that government managers, especially in the middle ranks, view it with trepidation. Their limited authority and reluctance to buck the status quo make change difficult. There are few models from the private sector that can serve as guides, and the good examples that do exist have not been widely communicated. And, as in the corporate world, middle managers frequently resist any reallocation of authority downward. Osborne and Gaebler point out that opposition to flattening organizational pyramids is greater from the middle ranks of managers than from unions. In the 1990s, as for the last century, managers are their own worst enemies. Frederick Taylor said as much when he denounced intransigent foremen and middle managers as blocking the path of progress. Those vested with some limited power in a bureaucracy seem most intent on clinging to the little they have.

It is not surprising, then, that management gurus accuse actual managers (presumably not those who read their books) of not really knowing what they're doing. Take Michael Hammer and James Champy's influential *Reengineering the Corporation* (1993).[36] They admonish managers to unlearn everything they have learned about how a business should be run and 'throw it away'. A few years after this book was published, many converts to re-engineering were throwing this idea away too.[37] Re-engineering was one of those 1990s management bandwagons that raced down the main street of corporate North America amidst great fanfare. Claiming to radically redesign a firm's processes, structure, and culture, it produced results that were far less dramatic than promised. Nonetheless, Hammer and Champy struck a chord when they argued that the major problem businesses face is heading into the twenty-first century with organizations designed for the nineteenth. Outmoded ways of organizing work based on managerial controls, hierarchy, and a detailed division of labour do need to be eliminated; these vestiges of the industrial revolution are encumbrances on true reform in workplaces. That much is not news. Yet while re-engineering's basic diagnosis was accurate in this respect, its lack of attention to the human side of workplaces made it ineffective as a cure. This is often the case with new management prescriptions.

The foregoing discussion highlights the difficulty of changing workplaces so that they put people first. Whether the goal is to make a government department more entrepreneurial or to re-engineer a manufacturing firm, humanistic values tend to give way to economic ones. What will it take to achieve the kind of change that shifts power downward to employees and redesigns jobs so they are more skill- and knowledge-intensive? The philosopher of science Thomas

Kuhn theorized that in the world of science, a paradigm shift required the ascendance of a radically new way of thinking about the entire scientific enterprise.[38] The same is true in workplaces. As emerging paradigms compete with established ones, old assumptions are questioned. We seem to be in the 'questioning' phase now, although as I suggest below, there are signs of consensus about what the new paradigm looks like. Getting there is slow and painful, because a true transformation in the way an organization operates affects all areas of activity, takes several years to implement, and, above all, is a process in which all stakeholders must collaborate.[39]

Workplace Innovation

What qualifies as 'innovative' when it comes to workplaces and jobs? We can speak of innovation with respect to organizational strategies, structures, human-resource management practices, and technology. These are the major types of change that directly affect the quality of workers' jobs. In all these areas, change can be perceived as threatening by specific groups, whether managers or workers, or by unions. These groups have their own concerns about loss of entitlements, recasting of power relations, and threats to job security. However, thinking on the part of both management and academics has converged around a new model of organization that has the potential to benefit all three groups. This model pictures an organization that is innovative in a number of ways: it is flexible and adaptable to change; it has few formal levels of hierarchy; it is responsive to its environment; it is concerned about all its stakeholders; it empowers people; it rewards them; and it helps them gain new skills. This kind of workplace is often called 'high performance'. That model applies mainly to large-scale organizations, however. Far less attention has been paid to innovative work organization and human-resource management in smaller firms.[40] As for the self-employed, we can only surmise that quality is an issue for them, although the fact that more than two out of five say they entered this form of work in order to gain greater independence suggests that their previous employment was lacking in that respect.[41]

The research on new work systems rejects the idea—first proposed by Frederick Taylor almost a century ago—that there is 'one best way' to organize and manage work. Taylor dressed up ideology as science, arguing that there was only one efficient way to do any job or produce any product. This rigidity in management systems, at least at the rhetorical level, has become pervasive. However, the details of what constitute effective work practices vary depending on who is asked—executives, middle managers, workers, or customers. Equally important, effectiveness will vary with an organization's industry, size, workforce composition, and national location. Common to all successful approaches, however, is a people-focused strategy for innovation.[42] Regardless of the contingencies, there still is a common denominator: valuing people.

So far, research on workplace innovation has focused on what have become known as 'high-performance' work systems. In *The New American Workplace* Eileen Appelbaum and Rosemary Batt link high-performance systems to higher wages and higher skills in the economy overall.[43] Gordon Betcherman and his colleagues make similar arguments in their important study *The Canadian Workplace in Transition*. Yet both studies caution that the prevailing business and political environments provide little encouragement for this kind of workplace innovation.

What are the benefits of the new model? For employers, they include improvements in productivity, quality, customer satisfaction, market share, profitability, and employee relations. For workers, innovations that improve job quality often require extensive changes, ranging from the way jobs are designed, to responsibility and decision-making scope, to training, compensation, and security, to power relations and a role for unions. Any of these changes could have advantages or disadvantages for workers, depending on the details. Because few organizations have introduced a full-scale high-performance model, the question of benefits for both employers and employees remains difficult to answer. However, new research suggests that work reorganization along the lines just described, coupled with a more humanistic management orientation, are prerequisites for a more skills-based, learning-intensive work environment.[44]

Some critics claim that 'high performance' is a loaded term. Given that increased performance or commitment may or may not result from this approach, they argue that it would be more accurate to talk about 'high involvement'. But what does 'involvement' mean? One team of researchers has explained it this way: 'Without power to make decisions, employee participation is superficial. . . . High involvement is a property of organizational systems, not solely of individual organizational members. It is reflected in the way the organization is structured and managed, not simply in the perceptions, attitudes, and beliefs of employees.'[45] In the end, regardless of how we define 'high-performance work system', 'workplace innovation', or 'best practice' in terms of human-resource management, what may matter most is giving workers a stronger voice and more opportunity to use and develop their abilities.

To make our discussion more concrete, I want to mention one recent effort to address these issues of workplace innovation. The next chapter presents many more examples, but for now I want to illustrate two points. First, workplace innovation leading towards high-quality work is only on the margins of the public-policy agenda in Canada today. Second, the changes being proposed have yet to get at the heart of the human problems in workplaces. Let's consider the federal government's 1997 *Collective Reflection on the Changing Workplace*, a report from the Minister of Labour's Advisory Committee on the Changing Workplace.[46] The Committee's mandate covered a wide range of issues related to the changing nature of work, new employment relationships, workplace innovation, the information highway, and the workplace of the future.

Its report reiterates what is fast becoming the standard policy line of government: adapting to breathtaking global economic change by investing in the development of people. As the report concludes: 'Investing in human capital is key to the smooth functioning of the new labour market and the high-performance workplace.'[47] Such a conclusion calls for a culture of lifelong learning and training, full employment so people can put their skills to use, and a wider spectrum of work options so that personal and family circumstances can be better accommodated. All these are ingredients of high-quality work. However, nothing is said about what happens within a workplace, especially how work is designed and organized. Like so many other recent pronouncements on the future of work, this report does not reckon with the contexts in which workers cultivate and apply their knowledge and skills. With representatives of both business and labour on the Committee, perhaps consensus was achieved only at the expense of dealing with these tough issues.

How Do Organizations Learn?

Learning is central to workplace change, to human-resource development and organizational innovation. Public policy in the 1990s has also promoted the concept of lifelong learning as a means of ensuring that workers' skills are regularly updated and expanded. In 1996, the ministers of education for the OECD nations endorsed lifelong learning for all citizens as an important national goal.[48] Behind this goal is the assumption that national economic prosperity depends on the growth of knowledge-based industries and jobs, which requires better-trained and -educated workers. The Conference Board of Canada provides an employer's perspective on lifelong learning, encouraging workers to continually hone their 'employability skills'. As the Board puts it: 'Well educated people who are committed to excellence and to lifelong learning are the key to the social and economic well-being of our country; they are critical to the survival and growth of Canadian business.'[49]

We saw in Chapter 5 that lifelong learning requires shifting the emphasis in formal education from front-end loading—getting one's schooling when young—to a more open and flexible system that provides opportunities to obtain education throughout one's adult life. More and more, this can be done without actually returning to school. Internet-based instruction and virtual classrooms make it easier to access learning opportunities—provided you can afford a computer and the tuition fees. But lifelong learning means more than this. It also means creating organizational environments in which knowledge is highly valued and ongoing learning activities are encouraged. These activities include informal learning that is built into a job, structured in-house training programs, or off-site education and training supported by the employer.

We've already seen how actively Canadian workers participate in all types of formal and informal learning. Many younger workers seem to have embraced the ethic of lifelong learning, if only from economic necessity. However, it is difficult to imagine workers engaging in effective lifelong learning unless they are in work environments that make this possible. Advocates of lifelong learning, oddly enough, have little to say on this point. As the educational activities of individuals are gradually shifting in the direction of lifelong learning, work organizations are creating roadblocks. Ironically, the reason many workers launch into training programs or return to school is to find an escape route from a job that restricts opportunities for personal development. If progressive employers and public-policy experts are committed to promoting ongoing learning, they must address the question of how work environments can encourage such activity.

The central blind-spot in discussions of lifelong learning and learning organizations is the failure to recognize that many workplaces are not designed to promote learning as part of a job. Nor do they stimulate the use of newly acquired skills. Instead, many organizations and jobs have been designed precisely to regulate the amount of discretion a worker can exercise—a recipe for discouraging learning. Thus adult education and training policies intended to promote lifelong learning can have at best limited success—unless, of course, they provide incentives for employers to upgrade job skill requirements and to give workers more latitude to acquire and apply new knowledge in their jobs. Two organizational learning consultants with the firm Arthur D. Little Inc. have explained the paradox of little change amidst lots of rhetoric about change in this way: 'The wholesale adoption of new management ideas, packaged into universal panaceas and applied in predefined, precise steps, has been a principal reason for the failure of many TQM [Total Quality Management] and Reengineering programs. It's likely to be a reason for the failure of prepackaged Learning Organization programs as well.'[50]

Even so, the concept of the learning organization has the potential to address quality-of-work issues. Peter Senge, whose name is synonymous with the learning-organization concept, uses the example of a basketball team to illustrate the importance of developing collective potential in any organization:[51] a few star players won't make much difference if the team as a whole is not drawing on the full potential of every player. Another example is Tafelmusik, the widely acclaimed baroque orchestra based in Toronto. It operates as a collective, creating organizational conditions through consensus decision-making and revenue-sharing. Each member is able to contribute her utmost to the orchestra while growing personally as an artist.[52] From the rarified worlds of professional sports and music comes a general lesson. Attempts at workplace innovation often fall flat because they do not encourage workers to learn and contribute their expertise in all aspects of their daily work.

Senge also is harshly critical of management's preoccupation with costs, profits, and shareholder value.[53] These bottom-line priorities give only secondary importance to the creation of knowledge and good ideas. 'Can there be little wonder,' Senge asks, 'that people in such organizations are uncommitted, that they view their jobs as mundane and uninspiring, and that they lack any deep sense of loyalty to the organization?'[54] This rhetorical question hints at the vital link between learning organizations and job quality—a link that Senge and other learning organization champions don't explore. Implicit in these discussions, however, is the point that learning-based organizations must necessarily develop each worker's potential.

Of course, 'organizational learning' is just a metaphor. Organizations learn only through the learning activities of their members. In a true learning environment, change comes to be seen as a natural and healthy process, not something to be feared. Managers in learning organizations must accept that workers need to exercise 'mastery and determination', which is another way of saying they must be empowered to make decisions about how they do their jobs.[55] Such empowerment requires changes not just in a workplace's structures, but in its culture as well. According to Edgar Schein, an expert on organizational culture, the information age demands workplace learning cultures based on a core belief in active learning and problem-solving.[56]

No consensus exists so far on how best to move organizations towards a learning model. Some experts, especially those promoting a high-performance workplace, suggest that dramatic transformations in work structures and cultures are needed.[57] Others view organizational learning as another tool for improving corporate performance.[58] Neither perspective is adequate. Instead, I would argue that an organization's capacity to promote learning is directly related to the skill content of jobs, the distribution of decision-making authority, and the thrust of management strategies. If a workplace is going to sever its ties with Taylorist job design and rigid bureaucratic hierarchy, then the change process itself must be an active learning experience for all workers.

Learning also requires a longer-term perspective on human-resource development. A learning culture does more than provide employees with extra training courses. If business and political leaders are serious about developing people's skills and knowledge through continuous learning inside and outside workplaces, then the quality of work itself becomes a central issue. A study by Gordon Betcherman, Kathryn McMullen, and Katie Davidman, *Training for the New Economy*, shows that successful training requires organizational contexts and jobs designed to foster learning. They explain: 'Firms can only benefit from the skills employees gain from training where the organization of work allows them to apply these skills in practice. Flexible job designs that encourage employee initiative and innovation are a key condition for effective training programs. Where these are in place, employers can build on the capabilities of a well-trained labour force by instituting challenging and flexible job designs that have been shown to improve productivity and quality.'[59] In short, a skill-intensive job design—which in turn promotes more learning—can enable a skilled workforce to help employers in devising competitive strategies.

Conclusion

Workplaces in the 1990s have changed dramatically. Yet all too often these changes have not moved in the direction suggested by the rhetoric of 'people development'. Instead, the latest cost-cutting or restructuring tactics are adopted, usually with negative effects on employee morale, confidence, and productivity. By contrast, improving the quality of work can benefit not only workers and managers but those shareholders who are willing to look beyond the next quarter's returns, and, in the case of government services, the public. The key is to stake out a common ground. In fact, restoring a human dimension to corporate and government management agendas may well be a critical step towards ensuring future national economic prosperity.

Certainly there is general agreement that a new paradigm for organizing and managing work is long overdue. And, as the examples in the next chapter will show, workplace innovation is possible. There is always the risk, of course, that some firms may go too far too fast in this regard. Some of the leading information technology firms, for instance, are legendary for overloading some of their workers with job stimuli and demands. As Douglas McKenna, senior director of human resources at Microsoft, said in 1997, 'We take capable people and we throw them into a job that's over their head.'[60]

Realistically (fortunately, some would say), the vast majority of firms can never hope to emulate Microsoft's relentless drive for market dominance through ceaseless product innovation, and the mind-stretching work that this demands. At a more basic level, what remains to be seen is who will champion innovative approaches to work in any particular workplace. To improve the overall quality of work it is essential that the interests of workers and employers are equally served. That's why it is also crucial for workers, their unions, and professional associations to play an active role in the innovation process. We can't assume that employers and governments always know best.

Chapter 8

Workplace Innovation

'I operate a 5 (or 10) million dollar machine,' complained an operator in a Sarnia, Ontario, chemical plant, 'but have to obtain approval from the foreman for an overtime meal when I am asked to stay at work beyond my usual departure time.'[1] The frustration expressed by this operator goes to the heart of the reasons it is so important to create high-quality work. This worker's union and company together reached the conclusion that it was in everyone's interests to give operators more responsibility and control in a brand-new plant they would jointly plan. Unfortunately for the dissatisfied operator, part of the union–management deal was that the status quo would remain undisturbed in the old plant, where he worked.

At a recent workshop I ran for senior managers in a medium-sized service-sector firm, we were discussing how to achieve the 'high-performance workplace' model outlined in Chapter 7. A manager candidly urged colleagues to 'critically reflect' on what the high-performance concept really means, noting that it implies everyone has to work at '110 per cent'. If people are already working flat out, he wondered aloud, is it healthy to squeeze more productivity from them? The discussion then moved to a related topic: how managers 'get in the way' of meaningful change, and the need to be guided in any change strategy by the core values of the organization. In the end, everybody present seemed to agree on the need for change, but no one harboured any illusions about the hurdles standing in the way.

These two illustrations exemplify the promises and pitfalls of workplace reform. If high-quality work is a realistic goal, as I believe it is, then we need to know more about the conditions under which some employers have moved successfully in this direction. This chapter will explore the frontier of workplace innovation—a place where relatively few firms in Canada have ventured. Yet it is on this frontier that we find progress towards the goal of high-quality work.

Canadian organizations have chalked up some impressive successes in this area, and the combined efforts of managers, workers, and, frequently, unions have extended the frontier farther than many people think. While there is no one-size-fits-all approach to creating people-centred workplaces, there is sound evidence that this general goal is both realistic and beneficial. As I will show, there are convincing signs that in large organizations these payoffs include better use of people's talents, greater personal work rewards, and increased potential to achieve economic prosperity in ways consistent with Canadians' work values. But the story is still unfolding. We simply don't know enough about the causes, consequences, and complexities of the kind of workplace reform that can improve the quality of work. So this chapter is a call for further research, directed at the limitations of the case studies it presents. There is a need for more solid and extensive evidence that can make a 'business case' for high-quality work, a case that hinges on the link between the quality of work life and organizational productivity. Also useful would be action-oriented research designed to find out how the same positive results achieved by the large corporate and government employers described in this chapter could be achieved by small workplaces, low-skill, low-wage areas of work, and occupations employing individuals who do not have a college diploma or university degree.

Valuing Workers

Our point of departure is the idea that a workplace, like a society, can be democratic. Here I turn to the seminal Canadian study of workplace democracy, conducted by Queen's University business professor Donald Nightingale almost two decades ago.[2] Nightingale's view of a democratic workplace contains elements of what I've been calling high-quality work. As citizens of a democratic society, he observes, Canadians have a moral right to participate in the political process. Yet that principle has not been applied to workplaces. Disenfranchised at work, individuals are less loyal, less satisfied, less fulfilled, and less productive than they would be under more democratic conditions. A democratic workplace gives workers a say in policies that affect their work life and provides wide scope for decision-making within jobs. It does so by reducing hierarchy within the organization and redistributing power downwards. Today's management gurus call this empowerment.

Workers reap tangible benefits when they have more decision-making power. In the democratic workplaces that Nightingale studied, workers' job satisfaction and commitment to the organization were higher and they felt less alienated from their work than their counterparts elsewhere. If their working conditions included increased job autonomy, responsibility, and variety, then workers' satisfaction was even greater. Employers also benefit when workers participate in decision-making, because those workers expect more from their jobs, which in turn encourages them to seek out ways of contributing more knowledge and skill. While Nightingale didn't directly measure the impact of workplace democracy on a firm's productivity, the link is clear. That's because organizing work democratically frees up the 'human talent and ingenuity' now stifled by rigid, authoritarian work regimes.[3] As Nightingale explains: 'Workplace democracy overcomes [the] puzzling anomaly of the contemporary workplace: those most experienced with the daily details of the work are prohibited from contributing to its improvement.'[4]

Surprisingly enough, a similar conclusion was reached by the federal auditor general in the 1980s. Although it was quickly relegated to the dusty shelves reserved for so many government reports, this one deserves careful reading. It is a remarkably insightful look into what makes public-sector organizations effective in meeting their goals. Auditors general are best known to the public for ferreting out the waste and mismanagement of public funds. Logically, one would expect this mandate to include examining how a government deploys its staff; yet governments are rarely held accountable for their people management. In any case, as the nation's largest single employer, surely the federal government should have a keen interest in effective people management.

After compiling a list of eight different federal organizations that were widely viewed by senior government managers as doing an excellent job, the auditor general's research team looked for the common ingredients in their success. The criteria for being a 'well-performing organization' included service quality and timeliness, responsiveness, cost-effectiveness, and employee satisfaction. 'The most striking attribute of these eight organizations,' the auditor general concluded, 'is the emphasis they place on their people. People are challenged, encouraged and developed. They are given power to act and to use their judgement. There is a "caring" attitude in these organizations, based on the belief that, in the long run, high performance is a product of people who care rather than of systems that constrain.'[5]

In practical terms, these classic studies show beyond any doubt that innovative change is possible. Furthermore, coming from a business professor and an auditor general, they should allay fears among managers that calls for democratization, participation, or empowerment are somehow revolutionary. What's changed between the time these studies were conducted and the present is that the pressure to improve the quality of work is far more intense now. And the social and economic consequences of not finding better ways of working are much greater too.

Pressures for Work Reform

Nightingale's book came at the end of the humanistic 'quality of work life' era. The 1970s were a time of hope that more humanistic values could help to improve work life. It was also a time of growing unease about the dehumanizing effects of the mass-production system that underpinned post-1945 industrialization. The economic turmoil brought on by the 1981–2 recession buried these concerns, and since then issues of work quality have remained on the sidelines in public-policy debates. In the throes of what was widely perceived as an unprecedented economic crisis, and facing fierce competition from Japan and the rising economic powers of Asia, North American management retrenched. A lean and mean business mentality was encouraged by the prevailing political climate of conservatism (or more accurately, neo-liberalism). Thatcherism and Reaganomics, mimicked in Canada by a Conservative government under Prime Minister Brian Mulroney, marked the ideological triumph of market forces in public policy. Hence the single-minded preoccupation among business élites with lower costs, bottom lines, and economic survival. The economic creed of the 1980s celebrated personal wealth and success. Individuals who struggled to survive in an inhospitable labour market bore the full responsibility for their failure. This winner-take-all mentality, especially in the higher corporate and government echelons, left no room to cultivate humanistic values in workplaces.

Today, public-sector cutbacks and wholesale corporate downsizing appear to be tapering off, and the negative impact of these actions on human resources is becoming a new concern. Thus the present may be the most opportune time since the late 1970s to carefully consider the benefits of workplace reform. Worker empowerment—or involvement, or participation, or democracy—is a way of bringing workplaces in line with individuals' values and aspirations. If done comprehensively, in tandem with job redesign enhancing learning opportunities and skill development, the payoffs will be substantial, both for the individual organization and for the economy. Such reforms have the potential to revive the morale and commitment of workers shell-shocked by a decade of economic uncertainty.

As a first step, the management values that justified downsizing and the general erosion of job security must be held up to public scrutiny. Never has the need for participatory and personally involving work been greater. Evidence is easy to find. For example, in 1997, when Edmonton teachers voted overwhelmingly to strike, the flashpoint was an early-retirement incentive plan sought by an aging workforce that felt unappreciated, overworked, and on the verge of burning out. The Ontario Ombudsman's annual report for the same year expressed alarm at the pervasive demoralization and overwork in the province's public sector. And private-sector consulting firms have documented in no uncertain terms that corporate downsizing had disappointing economic results and negative human consequences.

Work Reform in Canada

How does an organization actually plan and implement work innovations? What factors contribute to the success of these changes? It is difficult, even under ideal conditions, to ensure that the goals of various work reorganization and job redesign schemes are actually met. One impediment to workplace innovation is the lack of useful information about what is and isn't effective. Often, in response to a crisis, organizational leaders grasp at the first solution that comes to mind, or what they heard at a recent management seminar or from a consultant. Plans are often hatched in a hurry and with incomplete information. Employers and workers can't be expected to dream up solutions on their own. Better diffusion of what has been effective elsewhere is therefore essential.

For an overview of the current innovative practices in Canada, I rely on four major sources: a large database of workplace innovations negotiated into collective agreements and a number of case studies of workplace innovation sponsored by the Workplace Information Directorate at Human Resources Development Canada (HRDC); HRDC's 'Lessons Learned on the Innovative Workplace', a study conducted by Ekos Research Associates and the Canadian Labour Market and Productivity Centre; the Human Resource Management Practices Survey; and the Working with Technology Survey. Together, these diverse studies constitute a rich source of practical insights about how and under what conditions a workplace reform agenda is successful, and the difficulties that may be encountered along the way.

Naturally there are limitations to such case studies and surveys. Most of them document successes, even though it would be very useful to know why some innovations failed. Furthermore, there is an almost exclusive focus on large workplaces, most of which are unionized; hence the interests of employees were more likely to be considered than would be the case in non-unionized settings. Information on the innovation process in non-union workplaces, particularly small firms—the source of most job creation these days—is lacking. In fact, we know very little about work practices and human-resource issues in the small-business sector. This is a black box that researchers must venture to open up.

Negotiated Workplace Innovation

Since 1994 the federal government, through Human Resources Development Canada's Workplace Information Directorate, has tracked innovations in collective agreements. This database includes only agreements covering 500 or more unionized workers, so the insights that emerge apply only to large workplaces.[6] In 1996 there were 350 settlements covering about three-quarters of a million workers, or less than five per cent of all workers in Canada. The first interesting point is that just over one-third of these agreements included wage rollbacks or freezes, even though there had been no sign of recession for several years. It should be no surprise, then, that economic security remains a major concern for unionized workers. For their part, managers want to achieve more flexibility in how their firms operate. Security and flexibility are often at odds, but there are small patches of common ground where innovation can be cultivated.

There is no consensus on what makes a particular organizational change innovative. The federal study looked for five kinds of change negotiated by unions and management—industrial relations, work organization, compensation and working conditions, training, and employee participation. Anything that went beyond a traditional approach in these areas was deemed to be innovative. However, this list has clear limitations. For example, 'work organization' measures only how work is distributed among workers, 'working conditions' do not include health and safety or other work environment features, 'training' does not include opportunities for continuous on-the-job learning, and 'employee participation' is restricted to joint union–management committees. Even so, tracking these negotiated changes can help us appreciate how, in large organizations, union–management relations are adapting to rapidly changing business environments.

Some sixty per cent of these unionized workplaces reported at least one innovative practice in 1996. Some of these represent only minor advances, but they cover a wide range of real changes. For example, innovative industrial relations include the extension of collective agreements beyond the usual 36 months. Somewhat bolder initiatives were found in British Columbia's education sector, where joint employer–employee committees were to resolve contentious issues such as workloads and class size, both of which affect work quality. Work reorganization was addressed by one in four of the collective agreements, but mostly through minor improvements. For example, major supermarkets in western Canada now have cross-training, which facilitates the movement of clerks across all areas in a store. This minor improvement will create more flexibility for the employer and give workers new opportunities for more task variety.

Flexibility—a major objective in new approaches to organizing work—raises concerns among workers about job security. The Canadian Auto Workers Union, following its 1996 strike at General Motors, achieved a milestone breakthrough on the contentious issue of contracting-out. GM can continue contracting out the production of certain auto components, but for every job lost in this way it will create a new in-plant job. This arrangement preserves what the union calls 'job ownership' for GM workers, providing some protection against the negative impact of the company's flexibility strategy. Other major employers, such as INCO and Quebec Telephones, have negotiated the introduction of multi-skilled, self-directed work teams as the route to flexibility. Such teams go further in the direction of improving work quality. Other innovations that are creating more flexibility for both employees and employers mainly involve moving away from rigid work schedules by using flex-time (variable start and end times for the work day), compressed workweeks, and, in one public-sector organization in Quebec, a four-day workweek of 32 hours.

Training and staff development are also areas of change, although only one in three collective agreements had specifically addressed these issues. Options that encourage educational leave are becoming more common. Both Bell Canada and the CBC have set up joint union–management committees to devise new approaches to link training to an employee's career development. (Yet whatever positive reputation either employer had in the past has been tarnished by recent staff cuts and, in Bell's case, resistance to pay equity for some female workers.) Canadian Pacific Hotels and Resorts and one of its unions have tried to put into practice the concept of lifelong learning. What's notable about this example is that it comes from the hospitality industry, an area of the economy better known for low skills and wages than people development. If anything, the CP initiative underscores the importance of encouraging more consumer-service firms to seek ways of improving the skill content of jobs, which could have all-round benefits for workers, firms, and customers.

Contrary to the public perception that worker–management relations in unionized workplaces are too adversarial, the most common form of innovation is the adoption of joint committees to explore new ways of doing things or to solve mutually identified problems. Roughly sixty per cent of agreements in 1996 included some form of joint committee, typically dealing with compensation and working conditions. Less often, such committees addressed areas of work organization, even though evidence presented below shows that when unions and management work in concert there is good potential to come up with new and more effective ways of doing work. As the United Steel Workers of America states in its policy on work reorganization: 'worker empowerment means increasing the influence of workers and their local unions over decisions in the workplace, including decisions over job design, training and technology. It is not "all or nothing". Local unions can extend their influence gradually in any number of areas.'[7] I will pursue this point in the next chapter, arguing that the future of the labour movement may well depend on unions' finding creative ways to exert this very kind of influence.

Innovation and Transformation

Will the workplace innovations described above open the door to more sweeping transformations? Not if the approach is restricted to altering just one part of an entire work system. Here it's useful to distinguish between piecemeal and comprehensive innovation.[8] Superficial intervention leaves intact old ways of working and the organizational culture that supports them. However, integrating several innovations into a more comprehensive program of change increases the odds that change will transform the way work is organized and carried out.

Ekos Research Associates has examined union–management workplace innovations in depth.[9] Using the same HRDC collective-agreement database, it considered practices to be innovative if they were found in less than 25 per cent of agreements and were considered by the union and management negotiators to be innovative. This more rigorous definition helps to distinguish piecemeal change from transformation, identifying the characteristics of innovation that lead to the latter.

Ekos researchers focused on tracking the move to greater workplace flexibility. In terms of work reorganization, this was achieved through contracting-out—a flashpoint for unions. More beneficial for workers, no doubt, was flexibility gained through loosening work rules, reducing layers of bureaucracy, expanding job descriptions to encompass more responsibilities, job rotation, multi-skilling (training a worker to do several skilled jobs), and teamwork. Human-resource management practices can also foster more functional (what workers do) and numerical (how many workers are required) flexibility. Innovations in this area include training, employee participation schemes, job security provisions, and alternative ways of arranging when, where, and how work gets done.

The Ekos research makes it clear that workplace change is a sporadic and complex process punctuated with unexpected twists and turns. There is no easy ten-step path, contrary to the brash claims made by some business writers and management consultants. Change doesn't happen overnight; it is a halting and incremental process that may take years. Moreover, it needs to be customized to suit the unique features of each workplace. Innovations that seem effective in one firm may backfire in another. Because organizations have different starting-points, what may be considered innovative in one setting is old-hat in another. Teams are a good example. Engineering firms make extensive use of project-based teams. So do leading computer hardware and software firms, where products with short life cycles are designed by multi-disciplinary teams. Workplaces in the booming hospitality sector, however, are less likely to use a team approach. So a new teamwork strategy in an engineering consulting or software firm will be quite a different look from a team strategy introduced in a tourist resort, where the very idea seems novel.

The Ekos study also shows that without strong support from top management, change strategies will be stillborn. Managers and employees stand to lose and gain different things, and this can lead to conflicts unless acceptable compromises are reached. Everyone involved in a change process must have full information at every stage. In this respect in particular, the sharing of information can help to even out some power differences. Any change project needs clear and realistic goals. Such goals are the basis for shared expectations, and make it easier to evaluate progress along the way. They can't be carved in stone, because the unexpected inevitably happens, and needs to be incorporated into the process. Creativity may be unleashed; on the other hand, a market downturn could force the rethinking of the overall corporate strategy. In short, the goals must be adaptable.

Innovation: Who Benefits?

Who benefits from workplace innovation? The answer comes with many qualifications. We don't have enough long-term, in-depth research on these initiatives to permit hard and fast generalizations. But there is accumulating evidence that the changes described above have a good chance of improving productivity and efficiency, boosting satisfaction among workers and managers, fostering more cooperative labour relations, reducing absenteeism, and enhancing the quality of customer service. This list is a mixture of management and worker objectives. A major challenge, then, is to give the same priority to improvements in work quality as to improvements in productivity, making these two goals complementary.

Workers and managers have different perspectives on workplace change. For workers, a key realization is that workplace change can be negotiated. It doesn't have to be imposed by management—in fact, it is less likely to be successful if it is imposed from above. Change programs completely controlled by management are not going to yield the results that managers themselves want, because meaningful worker input is crucial for success. Managers in organizations that have launched successful workplace innovations recognize the collaborative nature of the process, which may require training so that employees have the information and soft skills (problem-solving, teamwork, dispute resolution, etc.) required to fully participate in planning, implementing, and monitoring change.

Nine case studies in both unionized and non-unionized workplaces, conducted by the Workplace Information Directorate at HRDC, identify a range of specific benefits of 'high performance workplace practices': lower quit rates; fewer layoffs, accidents, and grievances; higher worker morale and job satisfaction; lower absenteeism and stress; and productivity gains.[10] Of course, no single change project will yield all of these benefits: the outcomes are as diverse as the approaches taken. Moreover, the use of different change and outcome measures makes it difficult to compare across cases; and any benefits can't necessarily be attributed to innovative work practices alone. Nevertheless, some tangible results have been found.

At the Canadian Imperial Bank of Commerce, for example, the results included improved employee morale and job satisfaction and lowered absenteeism resulting from flexible work arrangements and a family-friendly environment. There were signs of increased employee and customer satisfaction and some production efficiencies when self-directed work teams were introduced at an NCR factory. Following extensive work restructuring at one of Stelco's mills, fewer workers were able to turn out more steel, and received higher wages for doing so. A joint union–management committee at Canada Post identified ways to create more jobs, generate more business, and enhance workers' skills.

The above examples show gains for both management and workers, although in some cases the trade-off was a loss of jobs. In other cases, the end results have done a lot more for productivity than for the quality of work or job security. For instance, the main effects of the introduction of participative management at a Quebec building-product manufacturer were increased production and reduced costs. Similarly, one paper plant used high-performance work practices to cut production costs and increase customer satisfaction. On the plus side for workers, however, labour relations improved in both firms. This result could benefit workers by cutting down on the number of formal grievances and making it easier to find informal solutions to problems.

Greater information-sharing and training were also common. In most cases, teams presided over the restructuring process. An essential ingredient is a high level of trust between workers and managers, but this may be difficult to obtain if recent relations have been marked by conflict, or if downsizing still casts a pall. In unionized settings, local unions must be treated by management as legitimate partners—much easier said than done. In many instances, innovation is best described as creative crisis management, with senior managers initiating the process.

Realistically, there are many barriers to successful innovation.[11] Middle managers may be reluctant to embrace change for fear that in the process they will lose their authority or become dispensable. Workers may resist change because of worries about job security, lack of trust in management, or a simple preference for the familiarity of the status quo. Firms with highly adversarial labour relations will find it difficult to develop joint initiatives of any kind. The change strategy itself may be flawed, especially if it focuses on only one aspect of an organization. And often it takes a serious threat to an organization's very survival to kick-start major change. For a process of innovation to spread, however, it must take root in an economically healthy organization—and in such a workplace there may be no incentive to consider any change at all.

No discussion of workplace innovation in Canada can be complete without reference to regional variations. Here, as in other areas, Quebec is quite distinct. Over the last decade, the province's three central labour federations have taken a proactive stance on workplace change, actively promoting the objectives of democratization and innovation. No doubt a major motivation has been job creation and preservation. As Clément Godbout, president of the Fédération des travailleurs et travailleuses du Québec (FTQ) explained: 'Without a plant, there is no union; we have become more attentive to the problems of the industry.'[12] A number of factors make Quebec labour unusually sympathetic to employers. For one thing, because of their high membership levels and tradition of militancy, unions in Quebec operate from a stronger position than their counterparts in most other provinces. For another, the specific cultural milieu and political climate of Quebec encourage employers and unions to work together on common economic problems.

Nevertheless, according to the limited number of case studies available it appears that in Quebec, as in other provinces, the most common impetus for innovation is a crisis such as an imminent plant closure. The introduction of new technology is also a strong incentive in documented Quebec cases. Typically, despite Quebec labour's stated intention of being proactive, management takes the lead. Once launched, however, the change process is more likely than elsewhere in Canada to be orchestrated by joint union–management committees. Although management tends to claim that the motivation for change is to make the firm productive or competitive, in fact these goals appear secondary to simple survival. Whatever the reason for it, innovation is clearly in the interests of workers as well as employers. Among the results are reductions in the numbers and layers of managers, more teamwork, increased job responsibilities for workers, better labour relations, and increased productivity and quality.[13]

Balancing Interests

Is it possible to strike a balance between humanistic and economic objectives in the process of workplace innovation? Does a new work system just give management a slightly sharper tool for extracting more effort and compliance from workers? Or do successful innovation projects reflect a genuine spirit of social and economic betterment? According to the American industrial-relations experts Thomas Kochan and Paul Osterman, this is the case with what they call the 'mutual gains enterprise', which links workplace reform and democracy with a sustainable economic future.[14] In Canada, there are several examples of balanced and comprehensive workplace innovation offering mutual gains.

Long the flagship of the Canadian work-reform movement, Shell's Sarnia chemical plant was built from the ground up in the late 1970s using 'socio-technical' design principals. Management and the union (now the Communications, Energy, and Paperworkers Union) forged a new partnership aimed at creating a post-bureaucratic organization that would enhance the quality of work life in a high-tech industrial setting. The main characteristics of the Shell plan were self-managing teams, pay based on skill development, a flat organization with only three levels, and high trust between the employer and workers. But even this workplace change project was fragile: despite the path-breaking innovations incorporated into the plant's design, a recent shuffle in top management brought a reversion to more traditional work methods.[15]

The New Brunswick Telephone Company (NB Tel) used a similar socio-technical approach to confront the constant change and uncertainty of the communications industry. Although the company was financially healthy, management realized that a 'What-do-I-do-now-boss?' approach wasn't viable in the volatile environment of a deregulated telecommunications industry.[16] The union (the same one involved in designing the Shell Sarnia plant) saw an opportunity to provide workers with greater input and to improve job quality.

The union and company formed a joint committee on organizational change, guided by a written agreement called 'A New Partnership in the Workplace'. Design teams made up of employees from specific areas recommended changes in work design and set out action plans. The organization shifted to a team-based approach that integrated previously separate functions (e.g., customer service, sales, and repairs). Teams took over many management functions, including budgeting, scheduling work, defining and meeting training needs, health and safety issues, the daily allocation of work, and performance review systems.

While it's too early to tell how NB Tel's team approach will affect the firm's performance, it's evident that employees are benefiting from more challenging work over which they feel greater ownership. Even so, there is some dissatisfaction among workers, because the compensation system has not been changed to reflect their increased contributions. Furthermore, stress levels have risen, underscoring the importance of an integrated change strategy that includes a healthy work environment. If the new system is indeed worker-centred, then presumably the teams have the discretion to remedy these problems, although to address compensation would mean challenging the traditional prerogatives of management. This may be the ultimate test of the new team-based system.

Having a union play an active role probably helps to promote workers' interests, because it increases the possibility of worker consultation, information-sharing, and power redistribution. I'm not suggesting that unionization is a prerequisite for successful workplace innovation; if it were, non-union workers would by definition be excluded from the benefits of workplace innovations. For another, not all unions—or managers—are receptive to collaborative arrangements. Unions often have little success recruiting workers in firms with well-developed high performance workplace practices, because such practices can be used by management as a substitute for union representation. Naturally, they tend to be defensive whenever they face these initiatives.

To be sure, unions have cause to be sceptical. Employers put their own interests first, whether the issue is teamwork, employee involvement schemes, or profit-sharing. Foremost among these interests is the goal of achieving greater employee compliance without having to sacrifice too much control. In the conventional management thinking, a union is an 'outside third party', even though its involvement reflects the employees' choice and it is run by democratically elected members. Keeping unions at bay is frequently the goal, either implicit or explicit, of 'new' human-resource management practices. This tendency reflects the paternalistic assumption that if employees are treated well, they won't 'need' a union.

Broader Innovation Trends

While the above case studies are rich in detail, three surveys, conducted between 1993 and 1995, point to wider trends.[17] One examined human-resource practices in 714 firms with 40 or more employees in manufacturing and business services nationally. Another investigated workplace training in a national sample of 2,584 establishments of all sizes representative of the private sector, excluding agriculture. The third, which also looked at human-resource management issues, examined 1,277 organizations with 20 or more employees in all industries across Atlantic Canada.

The most important finding from the first study was that 70 per cent of the firms responding to the survey clung to traditional methods of organizing and managing work. In the 30 per cent of cases where change had occurred, most initiatives focused on reducing costs, especially labour costs. The authors' conclusion doesn't mince words: 'our evidence indicates that the large major-ity of Canadian firms still follow traditional approaches to human resource management. Despite the environmental pressures, these organizations are maintaining Taylorist job designs, making low investments in employee train-ing, not integrating human resources into strategic planning, not involving employees, and not responding to their employees' needs for more family-friendly policies.'[18]

One in five of the firms surveyed had attempted to increase employee partic-ipation through approaches such as teamwork, job redesign, and employee involvement schemes. Changes of this kind would go the furthest towards improving work quality by giving workers greater say and making jobs more personally rewarding. A smaller cluster of firms, mostly large corporations in the business services sector, had implemented new compensation systems basing pay on a worker's skill and knowledge or offering forms of profit- or gain-sharing. These are the two most common routes, at least in the early 1990s, that Canadian firms are taking towards the high-performance workplace model described in the preceding chapter. The least innovative firms are smaller ones in older industries, whose business strategies focus on cost-reduction. Large firms with business strategies revolving around people devel-opment were the most innovative. This finding is yet another indication of the growing inequity in working conditions—in addition to pay and benefits—between small and large employers.

The second survey was primarily interested in technological change in work-places. It found that more than one-quarter of the firms surveyed used profit-sharing or some form of variable compensation. Such schemes have gained popularity among managers in the 1990s as a way of encouraging greater employee commitment and effort. Roughly half the firms in the sample reported employee involvement, such as joint committees and quality circles. About the same proportion used work teams, and two-thirds had mechanisms for communications and information-sharing with employees. Larger firms, technologically advanced firms, those competing internationally, and those with business strategies emphasizing people development were the most likely to report such workplace innovations. In both surveys, the firms with these schemes in place had better performance, as reported by managers, than did firms operating in a more traditional mode.

Missing from most recent research on workplace innovation is a comprehensive assessment of the advantages or disadvantages of innovative schemes for employees. The first study outlined above attempted to explore this question but was unable to find any clear effects. However, the third study, conducted in Atlantic Canada, discovered that an organization's culture and overall philosophy exerts a powerful influence on the quality of the work experience as well as on productivity.[19] Sharing information and involving workers in decision-making were strongly related to higher employee satisfaction, better employer–employee relations, and improved economic performance. The effects of culture and philosophy were far more important than those of any specific innovation initiatives such as work teams, incentive pay, job sharing, or job enrichment.

What this smorgasbord of research tells us, then, is that innovation requires more than a new 'program'. It means transforming the culture and values of an organization—doubtless the most difficult areas in which to bring about real change. The goal of achieving high-quality work must be rooted in organizational culture and values. It is at this deeper level that workers and managers build a sense of shared commitment to putting people first, understanding the need for change, and building the mutual trust required for this venture. Workers' social and psychological needs and human potential must be strongly valued, elevated to the same level as profits, productivity, and competitiveness. All these factors are organically connected. [20]

Innovation and Power

Most of the above studies assume that workplace innovations will improve productivity as long as opportunities for skill development and employee input are increased. This view represents an incomplete understanding of the daily realities of worker–management relations. As a counterbalance, it is important to consider the power structures and potential conflicts that underlie these relations. A clearer perspective on the pitfalls of workplace innovation can be obtained from three case studies of state-of-the-art 'lean production' manufacturing facilities. Unlike the studies examined above, which viewed change from the top down, these studies offer a bottom-up view.

The balance of power in workplaces has always tilted towards top management. Even in the collective agreements negotiated by the largest and most militant unions, 'management's rights' clauses continue to protect the customary prerogatives: to hire and fire, close down the business, relocate, introduce new technology, or restructure the organization. Non-union workplaces leave workers entirely subject to the will of management. Unions give workers greater scope to negotiate, but they must still operate within the economic and political environment of a particular organization. When unions collaborate with management in workplace reform, management can see itself as obliged to give something up. In fact, many managers view consultation and collaboration as instances of power loss, not power sharing.

We must break free of this thinking if we are to achieve real workplace reform. As a start, it's helpful to be aware of the power dynamics at play when workers and managers enter into collaboration on change. It is also necessary to understand that a more equitable distribution of power will bring more substantial improvements in work quality. Otherwise, the rhetoric of empowerment and innovation will remain just that: rhetoric. Without direct employee input, high-performance work systems can lead to stress and work intensification, realizing critics' fears that 'high performance' means little more than people working faster.[21] The likelihood that this will be the case is greatest when management controls the change process.

Although employers who insist on maintaining control miss out on the full expertise that workers have to offer, for some employers this is an acceptable trade-off. To better grasp these tensions, let's consider three examples of employers who implemented workplace reforms similar to those discussed above, but with the intent of closely regulating the entire work process.

When Goodyear Tire shut down its 70-year-old factory on the outskirts of Toronto in 1987, over 1,500 jobs were lost, many of them well-paying unionized production jobs.[22] A year later, amidst disputes over pensions and severance pay owed to these workers, the Ohio-based multinational announced construction of 'the world's most modern tire plant' in Napanee, a small town in eastern Ontario. A state-of-the-art facility, the new plant would employ approximately one-third as many workers as the old factory had, would have no union, and would pay lower wages. As Goodyear's blimp, 'The America', floated over Napanee, the town was welcomed into the Goodyear family.

Goodyear's idea of a corporate family is rooted in a traditional, paternalistic approach to people management. Its corporate philosophy is 'People are our Most Important Asset'. Personnel experts recruited the plant's workforce on the basis of 'attitude', screening applicants through a series of intensive interviews. Skills were far less important, and the company did not recognize apprenticeship programs—usually the hallmark of a skilled manual worker. The plant operated around the clock, with 21 rotating teams. 'Team members'—Goodyear's term for employees—were expected to show up for unpaid team meetings before the start of a shift. Computers would monitor all aspects of production, while the plant's newspaper and 24-hour FM radio station would reinforce the virtues of team productivity. This workplace was to be tightly controlled, technically and psychologically.

The Goodyear Napanee plant is what's called a 'greenfield' site, because work systems were integrated into its design. Introducing the latest in production and people-management technologies is easier in a brand new facility than in an existing one. The Napanee plant resembles other production facilities in Canada that use a system of 'lean production': what managers see as an ideal combination of (adapted) Japanese management techniques, just-in-time inventory control, re-engineered production processes, and rigorous quality controls, with a smattering of the latest North American human-resource management practices emphasizing the recruitment and training of workers who will 'fit in' and function as team players. Workers in lean-production facilities, however, often experience this work system as 'management by stress'. Every work minute is engineered to have 60 seconds of maximum productivity.

The Canadian Auto Workers Union's study of CAMI, a General Motors-Suzuki joint production facility for small sports utility vehicles in Ingersoll, Ontario, is testament to the human costs of lean production.[23] Japanese manufacturing is renowned for quality and responsiveness to fast-changing consumer markets. These achievements are rooted in production systems built around robots, sophisticated information technology, and teamwork. Yet the essential ingredient is the worker, not the technology. CAMI carefully selected 2,300 recruits from 43,000 applicants, then trained them in its values of empowerment, open communications, continuous improvement, and teamwork.

Initially, workers were enthusiastic. Union–management relations were cooperative and harmonious, and a spirit of high worker commitment and mutual trust prevailed. In practice, though, teamwork and continuous improvement (referred to by its Japanese term, *kaizen*) fell short of workers' expectations. Flexible use of labour came to mean using the fewest workers possible; multiskilling (acquiring a range of skills through training and performing a variety of tasks over time) became multitasking (doing several tasks at once). Job rotation became a way of having team members cover for absent or injured co-workers by doubling up on jobs. Repetitive strain injuries became a frequent symptom of work speed-ups in pursuit of reduced production costs. For CAMI workers, hopes of having a say in making their jobs more interesting evaporated. As one team leader, put it, beyond the language of a new work philosophy, workers came to view CAMI as 'just another auto plant'.[24]

It was no surprise, then, when, in the fall of 1992, CAMI workers launched the first strike ever at a Japanese plant in Canada. While wages and benefits were also issues, it was the plant's work organization that led 98 per cent of workers there to endorse the strike. After five weeks, workers negotiated changes in team organization and work pace, more say in health and safety, and provision of relief workers. The CAW researchers concluded that while the strike at CAMI made it unique among Japanese transplants in North America, its working conditions were quite typical. The resolution of the strike points to the crucial role that workers play in designing new work systems. When management controls the design of these lean-production facilities, it tends to concentrate on computerized control systems and social engineering principles without taking into account how workers will experience this environment.

Another example of lean production at a greenfield facility can be seen in the Alberta Newsprint Company's mill in Whitecourt, Alberta.[25] With its highly sophisticated papermaking technology, the ANC mill has become one of the most efficient and productive in North America since it opened in 1990. The mill is designed to achieve a high level of labour flexibility through a team-based system. With only one giant papermaking machine, dubbed 'Wild Rose 1' by the workers, there is a constant awareness of the need to keep it operating at peak output. The open layout of the plant encourages communications among workers, who are expected to acquire a wide range of skills so they can perform many tasks in a fluid team setting, not just one narrowly defined job. Cooperation and continuous improvement are central to the work philosophy, and pay is knowledge-based. These innovations break down the traditional system based on seniority and clear demarcations among production workers, maintenance workers, and technical skilled trades, a system that ANC's management viewed as rigidly inefficient.

Not only did ANC rapidly achieve its production and financial goals, but employee surveys have documented that the plant is a satisfying and challenging place to work. More than 90 per cent of workers surveyed by a team of university researchers reported being extremely or quite satisfied, and more than 84 per cent agreed that working in the mill was always challenging. Control over one's work and involvement in decisions were both reported to be high. All these are signs of good working conditions. However, almost three in five workers found their work repetitive, and there were some complaints from workers about the difficulty of accessing training and education facilities, given the mill's distance from urban centres—a problem that, because of the pay-for-knowledge system, resulted in pay inequities.

Part of the explanation for the high levels of satisfaction at ANC lies in the management's recruitment practices. As at other new lean-production sites, considerable resources were invested in recruiting the right kind of worker, which above all meant a worker with the right kind of attitude. Recruiters attached far less importance to skills and experience—few former pulp and paper workers were hired—than to personal qualities: 'honesty, reliability, a good work ethic, trustworthiness, and self reliance'.[26] It is not surprising that workers recruited for these qualities would share the management's philosophy and adapt easily to the conditions at ANC.

Conclusion

Stepping back from these details, we should bear in mind that Goodyear, CAMI, and ANC are not typical Canadian workplaces. These plants were built from scratch, combining high-tech production with the newest 'soft technology' of people management. On one hand, they demonstrate the productivity payoffs of new approaches to work organization. On the other, they reveal a number of drawbacks for workers: work environments are closely regulated, management's philosophy demands unwavering compliance or 'buy-in', and the promise of teamwork often falls short of the mark. Would these plants sacrifice production standards by giving workers more say in shaping the daily work environment? Would they run even more efficiently if workers had been consulted in the initial design of the plants? We have no answers to these questions. In all three cases, management was so intent on writing the script for workplace innovation, on achieving control over all aspects of production activity, that the chance of its involving workers as trusted partners was indeed remote.

These studies also raise broader questions about the how workers respond to workplace change. While ANC would appear to be the model team-based, high-tech workplace, even there workers expressed some dissatisfaction. This raises the possibility that some jobs are inherently repetitive, and that, even with the latest hard and soft technologies, there are limits to how interesting and challenging they can be made. Or perhaps some workers—again this could apply to the sorts of workers recruited at ANC and Goodyear or to some of the unionized workers involved in earlier examples—place more value on their weekly paycheque than on the psychological rewards of work or the existence of a 'trust relationship' between them and their boss.

In other words, 'high-quality work' may mean different things for different groups of workers. This is not inconsistent with the overall trends outlined in Chapter 3. When dealing with trends and averages, it is important not to lose sight of the diverse views that workers may hold, depending on their social and demographic characteristics. An even knottier problem is how to improve the quality of work in the least skilled, most mundane and boring jobs. So far, there are no case studies or surveys that get at these bottom layers of the labour market, where workers would surely benefit from even modest quality improvements.

Chapter 9

Unions and the Quality Agenda

Today's uncertain economic environment has generated a barrage of speculations and contradictory images of the future. To use the metaphors of management gurus, 'constant whitewater' is creating a need to 'thrive on chaos', to 'teach the elephant to dance', or, less dramatically, to recognize a paradigm shift. In Chapter 1, I sorted the work futurists into three broad camps: champions, doomsayers, and tinkerers. Among the champions is Nuala Beck, who predicts that, since cheap silicon chips and educated workers fuel the new economy, industries with high levels of both will prosper.[1] As for work organizations, Joseph Boyett confidently predicts a 'meltdown of the barrier between the leader and follower, the manager and worker. Bosses, in the traditional sense, will all but disappear.'[2] In the high-tech future of these optimists, old work structures will be eclipsed, enabling many people to become mini-entrepreneurs and knowledge workers.

The dark visions of the doomsayers are a stark contrast. Richard Barnet pronounces that 'The global job crisis is so profound and its interrelated causes are so little understood that the best of the currently fashionable strategies for creating jobs just nibble at the problem; others are likely to make it worse.'[3] David Noble argues that information technology has been used 'to deskill, discipline, and displace human labour in a global speed-up of unprecedented proportions'.[4] These pessimists tend to share a deterministic view of technology as inevitably dehumanizing, manipulated by management solely to boost productivity.

Few futurists of any stripe, however, see unions as central to the process of economic transformation. So what is the role of unions in shaping the future of work? For most futurists, the answer is simple: unions are vestiges of an obsolete industrial system. William Bridges chastises unions for being 'wedded to the archaic job world. . . . Job descriptions became their sacred texts.'[5] Jeremy Rifkin simply encourages them to actively promote a shorter workweek, quoting Lynn Williams, a former Canadian leader of the United Steel Workers of America, on this point.[6]

Canadian unions have been reinventing themselves for decades. Today, though, they must do so with even greater ingenuity, vision, and speed. One central component of this challenge is to effectively address workers' concerns about job quality.

The International Labour Organization documents that union members declined as a percentage of the country's wage and salary earners between 1985 and 1995 in the US, the United Kingdom, most of continental Europe, Australia, and New Zealand. Bucking this trend, Canadian unions actually made slight membership gains, showing resilience in tough economic times.[7] More recently, Canadian unions have scored organizing breakthroughs at a Wal-Mart store and a McDonald's restaurant—the first locations in either corporate empire anywhere in North America to become unionized—and at Starbucks, the trendy coffee-shop chain. Offering retail and fast-food employees an opportunity to exercise their right to a collective voice is a costly, uphill battle for unions, but it is necessary for their sustainability. As the ILO cautions, however, membership numbers are only part of the global challenge faced by unions.[8]

An even more fundamental challenge is to respond to the mounting pressures for reform within workplaces. Unions that fail to champion a quality-work agenda will be missing a crucial opportunity to address the needs and aspirations of large sections of the workforce. Yet, as we saw in the last chapter, in recent years most collective agreements have only begun to address the quality issues embedded in the content and organization of work and the general work environment.

Many of the pressures for workplace change are more difficult for unions to address than the traditional bread-and-butter items of wages and benefits. Working people, including union members, often find that their daily work experiences do not meet their expectations for personally rewarding and meaningful work. This gap between work values and workplace reality is not only a human-resource management problem for employers. To remain relevant, unions too must adjust their goals and strategies to address work-quality issues head-on. The presence of a union is a good indicator of above-average job quality in economic terms (pay, benefits, security). In future, however, the quality criteria must be expanded to include the kinds of human-resource issues—ranging from a healthy work environment and flexible work arrangements to opportunities for learning and decision-making—that so far have been either overlooked or kept under the tight control of management.

Unions and the Future of Work

At one level, today's debates about the changing nature of work have a familiar ring for union officials and activists. Employers' tactics and economic trends that threaten union survival, the need to launch new organizing drives and devise new collective bargaining strategies that reflect the needs of a better educated and more diverse workforce—these are pressures that unions have faced before. The late 1960s and early 1970s was also a time of upheaval in the Canadian labour movement. When the Canadian Labour Congress (CLC) launched its million-dollar white-collar organizing drive over 25 years ago, there were doubts about the chances of success for a movement rooted in traditional blue-collar, male-dominated industries. And major setbacks did occur, notably the demise of the Association of Commercial and Technical Employees (ACTE) and the subsequent failure of bank unionization.

Even so, the Canadian labour movement has adapted to an increasingly white-collar, skilled, and female workforce in a service-based economy. A quarter-century ago, the typical union member was a blue-collar male with some high-school education working in a factory, mine, or mill. This lunch-bucket image of the union member no longer fits. Of the 3,590,000 Canadian union members in 1998, 73 per cent worked in the service sector; 67 per cent were in white-collar occupations; 59 per cent had a post-secondary diploma or degree; and 46 per cent were women.[9] Sceptics counter that until the late 1980s the membership gains that saved Canadian unions from American-style decline came from the public sector—and were later reversed with deficit-reducing job cuts. Yet even this setback has not signalled the imminent demise of Canada's labour movement.

What are the implications of current debates about the future of work for unions? To survive, unions must first base their strategies on a thorough understanding of the trends that are increasingly pushing work-quality concerns into the spotlight. The big question is how unions can respond in ways that will invigorate the labour movement for the twenty-first century. If unions seize the challenges presented by the current pressures for change on workplaces, they will defy their critics by demonstrating their evolving role in a democratic society. In an era when the balance of workplace power has tilted even more in the direction of employers, unions have a vital role to play in promoting issues of concern to workers.

A Quality Agenda for Unions

Unions have been slow to engage management in discussions about prominent themes in the enormous how-to literature aimed at managers, despite the direct relevance for union members' working conditions. Although a bewildering array of approaches is being peddled, advocates and critics alike have focused on the new approach to human-resources management, with its emphasis on people.[11] Learning and empowerment are the mantras of the 1990s, central to the discourse on productivity, innovation, and competitiveness. Economic policy now assumes that human-resource development will make organizations more innovative, adaptable, and flexible. I've emphasized high-performance work systems and related workplace innovations as the means to these ends. Yet research on high-performance work systems suggests that few Canadian employers have implemented these changes as a comprehensive package.[12] Most firms, especially those of medium and small size, have narrow job designs; practice command-and-control decision-making, without employee participation; provide little training; and are not family-friendly.[13] The opportunity for unions to develop a worker-centred approach to workplace innovation is clear. True, collaboration with management on work reorganization can threaten the viability of unions.[14] Having said that, I also want to stir up the debate by encouraging unions to examine why high-performance work systems often appeal to workers and then ask how they can better address these quality needs.

Although high-performance work systems still exist more in theory than in practice today, lean production now dominates the automotive sector.[15] The fact that the North American auto industry is highly unionized means that unions can draw on their experiences there—both negative and positive—to influence the debates about the workplace of the future by proposing clear alternatives. Similarly, how work will be organized and managed in future will be determined by discussions and negotiations in which unions can play a vital role. For now, it would be beneficial to enlarge what has been a fairly one-sided discussion by introducing various union perspectives (recognizing that unions don't always agree) on the work environment, job design, and human-resource development.

A worker-centred response to issues such as the number of jobs available, the quality of this work, the distribution of work time, the impact of technology on the quality of work, opportunities for skill use and development, and participatory decision-making is emerging from organized labour. Examples include the Canadian Auto Workers' statement on work reorganization, the union-directed Technology Adjustment Research Program on technological change, and the Ontario Federation of Labour's support of training.[16] Among the other issues that unions should address are the profound contradictions in the lives of many workers today. Many are putting in longer hours at a time in their lives when they want to work less, but have no economic choice. Yet 1.3 million are jobless and hundreds of thousands who want to work full-time can only find part-time jobs. Despite the growing emphasis on people-centred organizations, downsizing has been the dominant management strategy even for profitable firms. Survivor syndrome, stress, and burnout have become commonplace in the 1990s. Yet the majority of workers place high value on work environments that promote good psychological and physical health. A sizeable number of workers do accept the doomsayers' 'end of work' scenario, with computer-induced mass unemployment, but they are outnumbered by those who think their jobs have improved because of computers. While workers find the notion of a learning organization consistent with their own goals, they can see that inadequate and unequal access to training opportunities accentuates economic insecurity and polarization. And despite their heightened concern about unemployment and job security, many workers also want more flexible and challenging work. These clashing trends suggest a rather different image of the future from those presented by futurists, offering concrete quality issues for unions to reflect on as they devise organizing and collective bargaining strategies for the twenty-first century.

Unions and Labour-Market Trends

I now want to sketch the main features of emerging work arrangements in Canada today that most directly affect the future of union membership. The de-jobbed economy of William Bridges and others does not stand up to scrutiny. In 1994, one-third of all workers were engaged in nonstandard work, which includes part-time and temporary work, multiple-job holding, and own-account self-employment.[17] That this represented a 5 per cent increase since 1989 is surely cause for concern. But the largest component of nonstandard work is part-time work, which began creeping up in the 1970s and then stabilized in the early 1990s. According to Statistics Canada's new definition (referring to people whose main job is less than 30 hours per week, even if they have other jobs that raise their total hours worked to more than 30), 12.5 per cent of all workers were part-time in 1976, a figure that increased to 18.8 per cent by 1994.[18]

Much of this increase can be explained by youth employment. More than a quarter of all part-timers are teenagers, mainly students.[19] The part-time employment rate for workers 25 years and older increased relatively slowly, from 9.5 per cent to 13.9 per cent between the mid-1970s and the early 1990s. But for employed 15- to 24-year-olds, the rate jumped from 21 per cent to 45 per cent in the same period. (Young people are also over-represented in the ranks of temporary workers, holding one in six in temporary positions.[20]) Part-time work among adult women has remained fairly stable—accounting for roughly 20 per cent of the total female labour force—for two decades. What's most striking in the part-time employment trend is the leap in involuntary part-timers, from 11 per cent to 35 per cent of all part-timers between 1975 and 1993.[21]

Self-employment is another touchstone of the so-called new economy, having strong ideological appeal in a neo-liberal era that promotes entrepreneurship and self-reliance. Now accounting for one in six workers (up from one in ten in 1981), self-employment is an area that unions should watch closely, since every self-employed person represents a loss from the pool of potential union members. Even more startling, self-employment accounted for much of the job growth in Canada in the 1990s.[22] Most of these new jobs represent own-account (solo) self-employment. These workers, who now comprise 11 per cent of all workers, have so far fallen outside the scope of the union movement. Whereas part-timers can be brought into existing bargaining units and collective agreements, this isn't the case with the self-employed. Those who own and operate businesses aren't eligible for union membership, particularly if they employ others. And an entirely different approach to union representation is required for the solo self-employed, whose businesses are not incorporated and do not employ others.

The restructuring of the labour market has contributed to greater polarization in incomes and job rewards, although less so in Canada than in the US.[23] The increase in nonstandard work is a factor, because the quality of these jobs is inferior. On average they pay less, provide fewer intrinsic rewards, few or no benefits, and little security.[24] But it would be wrong to tar all nonstandard jobs with the same McJobs brush. Increasingly, temporary, part-time, and contract work is found across the economy, involving professionals and other knowledge workers, especially in government, social services, and some areas of health care. It is also important to recognize that substantial numbers of nonstandard workers are already part of the union movement. Unions represent 25 per cent of part-timers, compared with 35 per cent of employees in full-time jobs.[25] Similarly, 27 per cent of workers in temporary jobs (many of whom are also part-timers) are unionized, compared with 36 per cent in permanent jobs. A strong selling point for unions, then, is that unionized temps tend to earn more than their non-unionized counterparts (the difference in 1991 was $4.75 an hour). This is a much greater union wage advantage than found among permanent employees, where the average differential was $2.75 per hour in 1991.[26] Too often, especially in the labour movement, it is assumed that full-time continuous work is the hallmark of a high-quality job. While this is generally the case, for some groups—notably women (or men) with child-care responsibilities, individuals pursuing their education, and older workers phasing out of full-time work—flexibility is an important consideration. Where unions can play a role is in ensuring that achieving this flexibility does not mean sacrificing other features associated with high-quality work, such as skill, learning, pay, and rights.

Central to any discussion of nonstandard work are the issues of increasing economic inequality and declining living standards. Both are evident in Canada. From a public-policy perspective, it is important to recognize that the more polarized distribution of income in the past 15 years is largely the result of an unequal distribution of work hours. As unemployment has risen, so too has the number of individuals working 50 or more hours weekly (now 11 per cent of the workforce). This fact certainly lends weight to proposals for redistributing work time. A related issue is overtime compensation, which seems to be more the exception that the rule; of the two million individuals who worked overtime in 1997, 53.5 per cent were not paid for their extra effort.[27] Given that collective bargaining covers work hours and schedules, it should be possible for unions to demonstrate leadership on this issue.

One way that unions may be able to influence the quality of work is by engaging—as some already are—in the debate over redistribution of work time as a means of alleviating unemployment. The North American labour movement was encouraged to give this idea serious consideration by the outcome of the 1993 IG Metall union's strike at Volkswagen in Germany: a 29-hour workweek with only modest pay reductions, creating 30,000 new jobs. Efforts to redistribute work time will require greater flexibility in work arrangements. It will be difficult to find common ground with employers who have seen labour flexibility as a cost-reduction tool rather than a means of either creating more jobs or improving work quality.[10] Unions will have to rethink their approaches to overtime, job descriptions, and work schedules. By even seriously considering these issues, however, unions have begun contributing to a reshaping of work.

Job Gains and Losses

Union planning for the future will also require analysis of where job gains and losses have occurred. Between 1946 and 1995, the service sector mushroomed from 1.9 million workers to 9.9 million, or from 40 per cent of the labour force to 75 per cent. The number of workers in the goods-producing sector doubled, growing to 2.7 million, but employment in the primary sector was halved, from 1.4 million to 700,000 today—only 5 per cent of the total labour force.[28] In recent years, most job creation has been in services: between 1990 and 1997, employment in the service sector grew by 8.7 per cent, while in the goods-producing sector it decreased by 1.1 per cent.[29]

It is true that managerial, professional, scientific, and technical jobs in the upper-tier service industries have been increasing faster than other jobs; the biggest increases were in business services, such as computer and related services, architectural and engineering services, scientific and other technical services, and accounting and bookkeeping services. Yet business services account for only about 13 per cent of all employment, and obviously not all of these jobs fall into the professional or management categories. The 'lower-tier' retail and consumer service industries are much larger, accounting for over 26 per cent of total employment.[30] In short, the service sector has highly stratified job conditions and rewards. When absolute size is considered along with growth rates, it seems unlikely that upper-tier, knowledge-based services will overtake lower-tier services. Health care, education, social services, public administration—the broad public sector—make up the largest share of upper-tier services, accounting for about 23 per cent of total employment in 1996. But while the public sector is highly unionized, downsizing and deficit-reduction policies have been slowly shrinking membership numbers.

As for occupational trends, since the early 1980s, growth has been high in occupations associated with a post-industrial economy: management, administration, social sciences, natural sciences, and engineering. Such jobs have traditionally been either ineligible for unionization or difficult to organize. However, they account for only about one in five jobs; their numbers are overshadowed by those in clerical, sales, and service occupations, which are well down the hierarchy in terms of skill and rewards. While the proportion of employment that these three occupations represent fell between 1981 and 1996, they still account for just under two in five jobs in Canada.[31]

Interwoven with these changes in employment patterns are important continuities. For example, clerical work has been the largest occupation for decades, and has been adapting constantly to technological change. When planning new organizing, unions should be guided as much by what has been happening in the recent past as by anticipated future changes. Predictions of a labour force populated by knowledge workers, or of masses of marginalized contingent workers, are not supported by the evidence.

Future Labour Demand

Predicting future job losses and gains is a crucial issue for unions. The Canadian Occupational Projection System (COPS) is perhaps the best method available—albeit a flawed one—for projecting future labour demand in Canada.[32] COPS projects a 16 per cent expansion in the demand for labour between 1998 and 2008, or approximately 1.6 per cent growth in labour demand annually. The three industries expected to show the highest overall growth rates in this 10-year period (between 23 and 25 per cent) are sales and personal services, professional services, and construction. This would translate into just over half-a-million new jobs in sales and personal services, some 342,000 in professional services, and 178,000 jobs in construction. While growth rates in business services and durable-goods manufacturing are projected to be close to the labour-force average, both sectors will also account for substantial numbers of new jobs. These projections suggest that polarization will be accentuated as jobs are created at the top and bottom of the labour market. Notable from the labour movement's perspective are the large numbers of jobs expected in sales and personal services, manufacturing, and construction—all areas with good potential for recruiting new members.

Turning to specific occupations, COPS also projects well-above-average growth rates (all over 22 per cent) in the following areas: management; business and finance; natural and applied science (engineering); assisting occupations in health services; sales and service occupations; and professions in arts and culture. COPS projects that approximately 2.27 million new jobs will be added to the economy between 1998 and 2008. The largest absolute gains are expected to be in management (over 357,000 jobs) and in sales and service occupations, both semi-skilled (274,000 jobs) and skilled (203,000 jobs). By contrast, very few new clerical jobs are expected. The numerical increases projected for low-skilled sales and service jobs; job installing, operating, and maintaining transportation and equipment; and assembly and machine-operating jobs in manufacturing far outweigh the expected demand for professionals.

These projections don't take into account such key factors as the changing character of the labour supply, demographics, sudden changes in global markets, or the rate of technological change. Nor does COPS say anything about the changes documented above in work arrangements and the resulting labour-market polarization. In any event, forecasts by the US Bureau of Labour Statistics (BLS) paint a similar picture. Most of the occupational growth it projects until 2005 is in low-paying service positions, and the fastest growth rates are expected in small specialized areas in health care and computers.[33] According to BLS projections, at the turn of the century 70 per cent of all jobs in the US would not require post-secondary education.[34] This point is worth emphasizing, because the public can often be misled by projections of the educational requirements in rapidly growing (often numerically small) occupations when these are not balanced by reference to the overall skill and educational requirements of the labour force, which are considerably lower.

Union Membership Patterns

While there has been some discussion of the forces shaping the future of unions in Canada, we lack a systematic analysis of future union membership trends.[35] In the US, researchers have projected further shrinkage in private-sector union membership[36] To maintain their membership levels, public-service unions will need to expand their horizons beyond government into the non-profit sector and privatized services. And occupations in lower-tier services (retail, personal services) will be the greatest potential source of new recruits.

As for recent membership trends, the profile of Canadian union membership was stable in the 1980s, showing little change with respect to either industries or occupations. And the overall unionization rate has hovered around one-third of all paid employees for the past three decades.[37] For details of industrial and occupational patterns in union membership, I've relied on Statistics Canada's 1994 General Social Survey.[38] The four occupations with the largest numbers of unorganized workers are manufacturing and processing (35 per cent unionized, but 1.08 million unorganized); clerical (still the largest occupational group, in which 30 per cent are organized but 1.3 million are not); services (a diverse category, comprising fire-fighting, security, police; food catering, preparing, serving; service jobs in hotels and motels, tourism, cleaning, and hair care: 26 per cent organized but just under 1 million unorganized); and sales (only 7 per cent unionized; slightly more than 800,000 unorganized).

Three industrial sectors with below-average unionization rates each have over one million unorganized workers: manufacturing, retail sales, and consumer services. Only manufacturing has a current union density approaching the national average. Retail workers will likely be somewhat difficult to organize, if past experience is any indication. Thus manufacturing and service workers will likely comprise most of the new union recruits well into the next century. Even in a service economy, then, manufacturing workers are central to the future of unions. When we look at actual job creation in the 1990s, manufacturing (durable and non-durable) had a net gain of 61,500 jobs, despite shrinkage in goods-producing industries overall.[39] As John Myles has argued, 'manufacturing matters' in a post-industrial economy.[40]

Also important are the kinds of organizations creating or eliminating jobs. Firm size is particularly relevant, because it has direct bearing on the recruitment and retention of union members and, ultimately, the future prospects for union organization. Small firms have accounted for a disproportionate share of employment growth since the late 1970s,[41] a trend that in part reflects the rise in self-employment. At the same time big business and large public-sector institutions have been shedding labour through downsizing, re-engineering, technological efficiencies, and the like. Hence the chance that the restructuring of large workplaces will eliminate unionized jobs is very high, whereas the chance that new jobs will be located in unionized settings is very low.

As evidence, consider these figures. In 1994, just 6 per cent of employees in firms with fewer than 20 workers were unionized, yet these firms employed 23 per cent of all wage and salary workers.[42] Workers in firms with between 20 and 99 employees were 19 per cent unionized, and accounted for about 17 per cent of the workforce. The next tier, firms with 100 and 249 workers, is far more unionized—37 per cent—but accounts for only 9 per cent of the workforce. In the largest firms, with 1,000 or more workers, about half the workers are unionized; these account for 37 per cent of the workforce. In absolute numbers, there are over 3.5 million unorganized workers in workplaces with fewer than 100 workers, and they tend to be under the age of 25. These smaller workplaces are also clustered in the consumer services and retail sectors. The presence of young workers could be an advantage for unions, if they can effectively appeal to the work values and concerns of this age group. But small firms have always posed barriers to unionization, not the least of which is the impossibility of achieving the economies of scale on which some unions depend to stretch their scarce resources.

Labour-Force Demographics

Shifts in the characteristics of the workforce will have a direct impact on the future of unionization. The labour-market projections we looked at earlier indicate only the expected demand for certain occupations—not the kinds of workers likely to be filling those jobs. There is a broad consensus that workplaces are being reshaped by three demographic forces: the feminization of the workforce; aging, especially of the huge baby-boom generation; and increasing cultural diversity as visible minorities and Aboriginal people make up a growing share of the labour force.

I will focus here on feminization and aging, which are especially fundamental to future union membership growth. This is not to say that workforce diversity isn't important in its own right. In many respects, though, unions are already addressing this issue. The Canadian Labour Congress's 1996 task force on racism is an example of the steps being taken to promote a more inclusive unionism.

The feminization of the workforce has had profound consequences for employers, unions, and society as a whole. Women's labour-force participation rates have risen steadily in the past four decades, levelling off at over 57 per cent by 1995.[43] As a result, women have been joining unions at a faster rate than men, changing the face of unions in the process. Dual-earner families comprise over 60 per cent of all two-parent families. And 15 per cent of all mothers in the workforce are single parents, many struggling in low-wage jobs. The largest share of female employment growth has been among mothers of young children. The participation rates for women with at least one child under the age of six at home jumped from 48 per cent to 66 per cent between 1981 and 1991. Because these changes occurred at a time of declining real incomes and greater work intensity and insecurity, work–family conflicts and stresses have become major problems.

Despite the fact that women now make up 45 per cent of the labour force, the domestic division of labour, especially child-care responsibilities, still recalls an earlier, less egalitarian era.[44] The demands of the 'second shift' of unpaid domestic work and child-care are creating high levels of stress for employed mothers. In one national study by Statistics Canada, severe 'time-crunch' stress was reported by almost one in four women in dual-earner families.[45] Men too experience work–family tensions: 16 per cent of all dual-earner men also reported severe time-crunch stress. In a survey jointly conducted by the Alberta government and the Alberta Union of Provincial Employees, roughly half of both women and men reported that work–family conflicts were stressful for them.[46] Furthermore, female and male baby-boomers are increasingly taking on elder-care responsibilities—another source of work–family tension.[47]

Numerous studies have arrived at the same three conclusions: job–family tension is pervasive, especially among parents of pre-school children; it is not the individual's problem, given that workload and other job demands are often at the root of it; and it is not just a women's issue.[48] The fact that employers are beginning to address work–family conflicts reflects the impact that such conflicts have on productivity, notably rising absenteeism among women with child-care responsibilities.[49] There is also a growing need for greater flexibility in work schedules and hours. For example, the National Child Care Study found that mothers with some flexibility in their hours of employment reported significantly lower levels of job–family tension than did those without it.[50] Yet less than 25 per cent of workers have flexible schedules, and these seem to be available mostly to core workers who tend to put in longer than average hours in any case.[51]

Clearly, workers want to strike a better balance between paid work and personal and community life. Thus creating family-friendly work environments should be a high priority for unions. Among the possibilities are cafeteria-style benefit programs, employer-supported educational leave, work-sharing, and self-funded sabbaticals. At the moment, very few unionized employees have the option of job- or work-sharing, and less than 20 per cent have the opportunity to take job-related educational leave.[52]

In short, I'd suggest that unions use to their own advantage employers' rhetoric of family-friendly workplaces. The challenge will be to achieve flexibility that benefits not only workers but employers, by contributing to improved productivity through reduced absenteeism, turnover, and stress. This will not be an easy process, as the experience of the Alberta Union of Public Employees shows. In some Alberta government departments, a bureaucratic and controlling management culture blocked family-friendly policies, although in some areas flexible work schedules were implemented and broader awareness of the issue was created.[53]

Another trend with major implications for union membership is the aging of the workforce. The relative size of the cohort aged 15 to 24 had shrunk from 26.4 per cent of the working-age population in 1971 to 17.7 per cent by the early 1990s.[54] The aging of the baby-boomers, the oldest of whom are now in their early fifties, has pushed the issues of retirement and pensions into the public spotlight. It has also raised the problem of renewal within union ranks. By the early 1990s, there were 835,000 fewer workers between 15 and 24 than in 1980, when the size of the youth labour force peaked: this means that unions must work even harder to recruit youth if they are to maintain their membership levels.

Against this background, it is important to examine the demographic patterns of union membership. Unionization rates among 15- to 24-year-olds declined from 16 per cent to 13 per cent between 1989 and 1994.[55] There also was a very slight drop (27 per cent to 26 per cent) in the next cohort (25 to 34) in the same period. Unionization rates actually increased slightly in the 35–54 group, but declined from 31 per cent to 27 per cent among workers aged 55 to 64.

The contradictory demographic characteristics of young workers can either inhibit or facilitate the work of union organizers. On one hand, workers in their teens and twenties tend to be transient, with a much higher rate of job-changing than older ones. Workers under the age of 25 are concentrated (and increasing) in jobs with below-average unionization levels, such as service (mainly food and beverage preparation and lodging and accommodation) and sales occupations. The 1994 unionization rates in these occupations were 25.5 per cent and 7.4 per cent respectively, compared with a total labour-force rate of 32.5 per cent.[56] And, as we know, such jobs tend to be in smaller firms, which traditionally have been union-resistant. On the other hand, young people entering the labour market during the 1980s and 1990s have generally borne the brunt of economic hard times. Unemployment, declining wages, and nonstandard employment have been far more pronounced among workers under 25 than among older workers. At the same time, the rising educational attainment of 'Generation X', which is largely a response to the tight job market, is fuelling disillusionment. Unlike previous generations, youth entering the labour market since the early 1980s can't count on achieving a better living standard than their parents.

That these economic experiences could heighten young people's interest in unions is evident in my longitudinal study of school–work transitions in Edmonton, Toronto, and Sudbury between 1985 and 1989.[57] Some 28 per cent of employed high-school and university graduates in this three-city study were union members four years after graduation, in 1989. And among non-members, 38 per cent were willing to join a union. The good news for unions is that this support for union representation is highest among those who have been union members in the past: approximately 53 per cent of those who had been union members when surveyed in 1986 or 1987 would have joined again in 1989. Consistent with the rapid increase in female union membership in the labour force overall, young women in non-union jobs were more likely than their male counterparts to be interested in joining a union (41 per cent and 34 per cent, respectively). The fact that organizations such as the CLC and the CAW have recently begun to address the challenges of organizing young workers signals the shift in emphasis that is needed to rejuvenate the labour movement.

Workers in Transition

The concept of transitions is increasingly common in discussions of workers' experiences in the labour market. Recently there have been calls for labour-market policies that will help to minimize the disruptions caused for workers of all ages making transitions in and out of jobs.[58] And how many times have you heard that the next generation of workers can expect five to seven job or career changes in their working lives? Such claims are not based on any research, but they reflect a heightened awareness that work transitions have become more risky for individuals. Labour-market experts have indeed documented 'enormous flux' in the labour market, with approximately half of the working-age population (15–64 years) either leaving or entering the labour market, switching jobs, or becoming jobless, roughly every seven months. [59] But are there more transitions, or job changes, now than several decades ago? To take a sceptical view, a booming economy also generates job changes, and the smattering of evidence available suggests that labour-market mobility may actually be no greater now than in the 1970s.[60]

From labour's perspective, however, these are important issues because organizing strategies and union structures must be able to accommodate the transitions that workers experience. Job changes have an obvious impact on union membership. For union organizers, it is useful to think in terms of workers being mobile rather than stationary. It's relevant to know that approximately half of 25- to 44-year-old union members in 1994 were also union members in their first job.[61] This means that there are approximately 550,000 workers who belonged to unions in their first job but no longer do. Even accounting for some who have moved into jobs outside the scope of bargaining units, or who harbour negative feelings about their union experiences, there is still a large potential pool of support. This suggests that it is important to see how union membership could be made more portable, especially for workers changing jobs within the same occupation or industry. Among the issues that unions should explore are occupational-based membership, different membership categories, and a broad range of employment-related services—from pension and health benefits plans to career counselling—that workers could carry with them as they change jobs. [62]

A Human-Resource Development Agenda for Unions

Another pressing concern for workers is achieving higher-quality work through improvements in their work environment and job content. Chapter 3 showed that challenging, interesting work that provides opportunities for self-direction and self-development has long been a priority for most workers. With constantly rising educational levels, jobs must become more skilled and knowledge-intensive if they are to meet this need. As I've heard a number of union officials complain, many managers expect workers to 'park their brains at the door' when they enter the workplace. Obviously, individuals should take some responsibility for the 'lifelong' learning that government and employers tell us is the way of the future; indeed, numerous employed Canadians are actively pursuing their own educational upgrading.[63] And young workers, in particular, may be on the leading edge of the lifelong-learning trend, continuing to acquire employment-relevant education long after graduation.[64] All this should encourage unions to go much further in developing a worker-centred perspective on human-resource development.

If Canada is becoming a knowledge society, it is mainly as a result of workers' own educational initiatives. We rank among the best-educated nations in the world, with more than two in every five workers possessing a university degree or other post-secondary credential. Yet large numbers of employees perform work that is low-skilled and requires less education than they have. More than 20 per cent of employees feel overqualified for their jobs, a problem that is somewhat more common among non-union workers than union members.[65]

However, this problem of underemployment is overshadowed by business criticisms of workers' job-readiness. Business has mounted various attempts to influence the educational curriculum to make it more work-relevant; the Conference Board of Canada, with its employability skills profile and its active promotion of school–business partnerships, has been at the forefront of this trend.[66] As employers extend their efforts to win the minds of workers into the educational system, it is important for unions to balance the business agenda for education. At the community level, unions too can be important partners in linking classrooms with the work world. Young people should leave school with an understanding of what unions can offer them. It is essential that schools develop partnerships with the full range of community organizations, not just corporations. And when employers complain about the deficiencies of the education system, or imply that workers lack some crucial qualifications, they need to be reminded that their recruitment processes and work systems are making insufficient use of the talents of a significant segment of the workforce.

There is a common fear that the information technology revolution, coupled with economic globalization, means Canada will lose out to foreign competitors unless workers become better skilled. This idea does not stand up to scrutiny. For instance, there is a surplus of computer literacy in this country. In 1994, over two-thirds (68 per cent) of the employed were computer-literate, but only half of all employees (and even fewer self-employed people) actually used a computer in their work.[67] More generally, job structures often deprive workers of opportunities to use their education and talents. So another compelling reason for unions to address human-resource development issues is that 'dumb jobs' are a source of worker dissatisfaction and stress. No wonder many workers welcome the upgrading promised by high-performance work systems. An emphasis on improving the quality of work could make unions more appealing, especially to young workers with high expectations of obtaining skilled and interesting work.

When unions address quality issues they tread on traditional management prerogatives. Yet it was management that placed the issue on the collective bargaining agenda by trumpeting the virtues of the learning organization, the high-performance workplace, employability skills, and human-resource development. Given that most workers want to use their brains in their jobs, unions could help to devise strategies to that end. There is considerable evidence that workers who exercise job control and have opportunities to develop their skills and abilities will be more innovative and adaptable, healthier physically and mentally, and more involved in their workplace and community.[68] This evidence makes a powerful argument for massive work reform, an area in which unions could play an important role.

Consider, as well, how high-quality training and ongoing learning enhance workers' employability should they have to, or want to, seek other employment. As a team of leading American industrial relations scholars have argued, perhaps the greatest employment security a firm can offer is 'continuous training and development opportunities' to increase external employability.[69] However, providing this security may require fresh approaches to union–management relations. Union educator D'Arcy Martin cites an example from NorTel. When the Communications, Energy, and Paperworkers Union was asked to create a partnership with NorTel management, a local union official quipped that now that the door was open, the union 'should do more than just barge in and speak our minds. We should first remove the wall that holds the door in place.'[70] This bold comment suggests a desire to broaden the scope of what unions negotiate to include a range of job-quality issues.

Conclusion

This chapter has laid out a number of issues for unions to consider as they plan for the future. I've talked about the importance of part-time and temporary workers among future unionists, about the urgency of the need to recruit young workers and address the human-resource development issues that management has already placed on the change agenda. Job content, ongoing learning, and balancing work and family all must become core issues for unions, along with improving the quality of work for the sizeable numbers of workers who feel undervalued and underutilized. In short, an emphasis on quality work may well be crucial to the sustainability of the labour movement.

But let's not lose sight of the fact—all too often overlooked—that unions themselves are employers who operate many workplaces across Canada. I would urge unions to be very attentive to their own human resources. Union workers, to modify a common management maxim, are the labour movement's most valuable asset. As my 1990 study of workload among Canadian Union of Public Employees (CUPE) staff revealed, nearly three-quarters of union representatives and office staff had heavy workloads, which frequently resulted in symptoms of stress and burnout.[71] CUPE's response was to hire more staff (including a human-resource professional), create a full-time staff development and training position, and establish procedures to deal with workload complaints—a good start. But now some unions face declining revenues, even when their memberships are rising. Clearly this makes it difficult for them to follow CUPE's lead in addressing workload problems.

Nonetheless, unions must consider doing things differently. Innovative and flexible approaches to providing members with benefits and services, a trend that began in the mid-1980s with the AFL-CIO's report on the changing situation of workers and their unions, must be pursued.[72] The threat to unions posed by the new human-resource management and high-performance work systems can be reduced if unions counter with a clear vision of their own. More broadly, the public debate about the future of work is up for grabs. Unions can articulate the concerns of those workers who now lack a collective voice, balancing the dominant voice of management.

Two themes have run through this chapter. The shape of the future is visible today. And the kind of workplace that will emerge tomorrow depends on the decisions and actions taken today. In both respects, the quality of jobs and the work environment is central. So, to quote Peter Drucker, the dean of management gurus: 'surely this is a time to make the future—precisely because everything is in flux'.[73] The message for unions is clear: they can play an important role in the future of work, especially if quality becomes the centrepiece in their future agenda.

Chapter 10

Creating a Higher Quality of Work

The daily experiences of Canadians in many different jobs and work settings provide ample reason to make the goal of higher-quality work a national priority. Improving the quality of work will mean addressing issues from rights and security to skills and fulfilment. To guide the way, I am proposing a 'people-centred' agenda for work reform. This agenda is motivated by two beliefs: that work activity is fundamental to developing our potential as humans, and that individuals can shape the future of work to meet their needs and aspirations. At the same time, this focus on people coincides with employers' goals for their organizations. A work environment that encourages employees to make the fullest possible use of their skills is vital to organizational success—which in turn contributes to national prosperity and quality of life. What we need are public discussions about the quality of work: how to improve it; the benefits of such reform for workers and employers alike; and how workers, employers, unions and professional associations, governments, and other organizations with a stake in the future of work could jointly develop action plans.

The task of improving the quality of work is particularly urgent today, after almost two decades of wrenching economic change. Many workers have felt the steel edge of workplace restructuring. Even some of those who have not been caught in the downsizing process feel demoralized, overworked, or underemployed. There is a pervasive sense that the work and non-work parts of our lives are clashing, to the detriment of both, instead of integrating in complementary ways. And if the negative current trends—among them a growing contingent workforce, increasingly polarized work hours and earnings, and a single-minded pursuit of lower costs and more efficiency on the part of employers—continue, the country's economic prosperity will be further undermined.

A disaffected workforce performing below its full potential is surely cause for concern, especially at a time when government policy-makers, business leaders, and educators are all promoting continuous learning as a way of building a knowledge economy. Following their logic, all workers will have to actively learn and apply their knowledge in the course of their work. But individual employees can't do this alone. New employment norms can be shaped only by collaboration among workers, employers, and governments. The goal of higher-quality work could be the rallying point for a national project to create work conditions that more accurately reflect Canadians' values. Achieving that goal means nurturing a higher-skilled, better-paid, and more secure workforce whose well-being is enhanced by their work environment.

There is no shortage of good ideas about how to improve the quality of work. The issue has been on the fringes of governments' and employers' workplace policies for decades. Some fifty years ago, the International Labour Organization's declaration of workers' rights committed all signatories, including Canada, to full employment and rising living standards; opportunities for individuals to make meaningful contributions and develop their potential through their work; just work rewards; a healthy and safe work environment; a living wage; labour-management cooperation; and recognition of collective bargaining rights. In short, it recognized that high-quality working conditions are fundamental to a democratic society. Several decades later, the movements for quality of work life and workplace democracy brought similar issues to the forefront. These ideas are just as relevant today, when economic prosperity more than ever requires that working conditions encourage the development of human potential.

Similarly, learning and knowledge are concepts that for decades have been linked with economic development. The communications scholar Marshall McLuhan identified lifelong learning as a bellwether trend in the 1960s: 'The future of work consists of learning a living in the automation age.'[1] At the same time, the management expert Peter Drucker talked about the rise of knowledge-based industries as signalling a shift in the basic resources of capitalism, away from physical assets towards information.[2] Neither McLuhan nor Drucker, however, addressed the question of how the shift to a learning-based organization run by knowledge workers might actually come about—let alone how a knowledge economy would be created. The latter in particular remains an open question. In 1999, the federal government proclaimed: 'To ensure Canada has a leading knowledge-based economy in the 21st Century, the government will work with its partners to help Canadians increase their skills and knowledge.'[3] Like most discussions of how to create a knowledge-based economy, this one is long on generalities and short on specifics.

To develop a specific plan we need to set two goals: creating more jobs of decent quality and enhancing the quality of existing work. Despite the drop in the unemployment rate in 1999, job creation clearly must remain a major national objective. But it is equally important that the jobs we create provide work that is meaningful and fulfilling. Even among full-time workers in relatively secure jobs, there are many who long for greater challenge, more opportunities for self-development, the choices required to achieve a more balanced and integrated life, or even just a change in their work routine. Ideally, at the beginning of our work shift we want to look forward to our day (or night), and at the end of it we want to feel a sense of personal accomplishment. The vast majority of people prefer a job that offers more than just a pay cheque. That's why beneath the veneer of job satisfaction we find an undercurrent of discontent with issues such as decision-making, authority, skill requirements, workload, and security.

It's convenient to think that by talking about change we're actually making it. The language of empowerment, gain-sharing, teamwork, consultation, and learning ends up reinforcing the status quo. Consultants sell managers new terminology, and with it the illusion that they have reinvented their firms. A more constructive approach would be to use Canadians' work values as the template for designing the future workplace.

The Basic Principles of Higher-Quality Work

The quality of work that Canadians want rests on four pillars. One is the opportunity to engage in tasks that are fulfilling and meaningful to workers personally. The second is a decent standard of living—not just a reasonable wage, but a sense of economic security. And because ensuring that security may mean changing employers, better supports are required to ease people through job transitions. In addition, regardless of their duration, employment relationships must be based on mutual trust. The third pillar consists of health, well-being, and support for family life, or life outside work generally. In themselves, these are crucial determinants of overall quality of life, but they also directly affect people's ability to be productive in their jobs. Thus workers, employers, and governments all have a stake in finding ways to improve working conditions in these respects. Finally, the fourth pillar consists of rights. In a knowledge-based economy, worker participation in decision-making ought to be a basic right.

A checklist of eight goals based on these four pillars is presented on page 175. This checklist can be used to assess overall work trends, employers' practices, government policies, and the agendas of unions and professional associations. Above all, these points are intended to generate discussion and debate.

Work today is defined by many troubling and often contradictory forces. This checklist of goals can help to focus discussions on how work trends could be redirected to better serve the larger public good. For example, the problems of too much work for some and not enough for others could be addressed if specific employers acted on their responsibility to provide a decent living standard and economic security by recruiting recent graduates and reallocating to them the (often unpaid) overtime work that older workers currently do, with the latter serving as mentors. For many organizations, this would have the

A checklist of goals

1. A basic right to work that provides a decent living standard and economic security.
2. Mutual trust among employers and workers.
3. Opportunities for all workers to constructively participate in decision making on how, when, and under what conditions they do their work.
4. A culture of openness regarding information about the business and provision of the resources workers need to use this information effectively.
5. Healthy and safe work environments, developed through collaboration between workers and employers.
6. Work environments supportive of a balanced life, so that family and personal goals can be achieved alongside work goals.
7. Encouragement of innovation based on workers' initiative and creativity.
8. Opportunities to use and further develop skills, knowledge, and abilities in the course of doing one's job.

added benefit of helping to prepare the next generation of workers to move quickly into positions of greater responsibility. To expand the opportunities for individuals to use and develop their skills, governments' labour policy-makers and employers' human-resource managers would have to recognize underemployment for the serious problem it is; this seems only reasonable at a time when the productivity gains of technology investments depend on making the best possible use of workers' skills and knowledge. The idea that no human resources should go untapped is especially important in light of management's growing concerns about recruiting and retaining workers. To create work environments supportive of a balanced life, workers, unions, and community organizations will have to educate employers about the need for, and benefits of, such policies. In time, if these reforms are achieved, our understanding of 'flexibility' will change: no longer will the term refer to low-cost staffing policies, but rather to individuals' ability to make choices about when and where they do their work.

Of course, reinventing work in these directions will not be easy. One major barrier is workers' distrust of large corporations, unions, and government.[4] Any top-down change initiatives orchestrated by the élites of these institutions will be met with scepticism by rank-and-file workers. Although executives, union officials, and senior government policy advisers must take leadership roles, the change process has to be participatory. Individual workers in their workplaces, voluntary organizations, and communities must become actively engaged in rethinking how they do their work. Governments are slowly responding to pressures for both greater accountability and increased public input by creating opportunities for 'citizen engagement' (for example, through town-hall meetings, community consultations, and the Internet). The same idea can be adapted to the work world: 'worker engagement' in designing and implementing change strategies in their workplaces, professions, or industries is a way of ensuring that all points of view are considered.

In fact, there are signs of grassroots involvement in workplace renewal. A number of advocacy groups, including unions, have recommended voluntary redistribution of work hours to help reduce unemployment. Community pressure on governments to support various child-care options is increasing. There have been renewed calls for a universal basic income. Environmentally sustainable economic development is a growing concern. On these and other work-related topics, discussion groups and forums have been sponsored by non-profit and voluntary organizations such as social planning councils, religious organizations, unions, environmental groups, and community-based coalitions. Another approach can be seen in the Canadian Policy Research Networks' community-run public dialogue groups on 'The Society We Want'.[5] These groups develop grassroots visions and progress indicators in the areas of work, health, and family. The point is that the principles of quality work—specifically, learning and direct participation—must be built into workplace change strategies.

What Governments Can Do

Ever since the Second World War, governments have influenced the quality of work through minimum wage rates, employment standards, occupational health and safety regulations, training provisions, and labour legislation. In particular, employment standards laws (which set conditions such as minimum wages, hours of work, length of the workweek, overtime, and notice of termination) protect the rights of workers. However, recent examples suggest contradictory trends. Whereas Saskatchewan requires that employers provide part-time workers with 50 per cent of the benefits coverage received by full-time staff, Ontario has proposed cutting 'red tape' in employment standards legislation by, among other things, lengthening the legal workweek, reducing severance pay requirements when firms shut down, and easing overtime restrictions.[6] And British Columbia is changing its Employment Standards Act to exempt high-tech professionals from provisions regarding hours of work, overtime, and statutory holidays, to give firms the flexibility they claim they need in order to grow.[7] If a higher quality of work is to become a centrepiece of public policy, employment standards legislation must be bolstered to raise the floor for those workers in the weakest bargaining positions—those who are neither union members nor well-educated knowledge workers. Such a move would reinforce the principle that a decent quality of work is a basic right.

Promoting opportunities for people to use their skills and abilities is another area where governments can be helpful. The discontinuity between available skills and their actual use and development belies the corporate claim that 'people are our most important resource'. The rhetoric of 'people development', 'the learning organization', and the 'knowledge economy' has set the stage for action. As one senior government official observed after a presentation I gave on this topic: 'We know what the problems are, we just lack the collective resolve to act on them.' Indeed, small numbers of employers in both the private and public sectors have made some progress in this direction. For that progress to continue, more employers must share information about their successes (and failures). In addition, industry associations and governments should encourage and support joint employer–employee or employer–union efforts to link improved working conditions with improved quality in the products or services created.

Until the empirical evidence is truly overwhelming, however—and in such cases it rarely is—it's unlikely that many Canadian employers will readily acknowledge the connection between working conditions, including skill requirements, and firm performance. A more integrated approach to economic and social policy would be useful in this regard. For example, Human Resources Development Canada—the federal department responsible for work issues—recently identified two goals for labour policy in the new millennium: to promote workplace productivity and to improve the quality of working life.[8] It did not, however, point out the link between the two. Policy-makers need to show more clearly the extent to which productivity depends on what happens inside workplaces. In short, improving the quality of work needs to be seen simply as good business practice.

The federal government and some of its provincial counterparts have sponsored research on innovative work organization and human-resource management practices. This information must be more widely communicated. Far more could be done by the federal and provincial governments, municipalities, and local economic development authorities to support workplace change that benefits all stakeholders. Creating forums in which business, labour, non-union employees, and contingent workers could discuss these ideas would be helpful. As employers, governments should set an example for the private sector by improving their own work practices, and facilitate the adoption of similar practices by other employers. There are many creative ways to do this: by running pilot projects to create learning organizations; promoting better coordinated and more accessible training for workers; offering awards or tax incentives to encourage employers to invest in healthy work environments, skill development, and programs supportive of workers' family responsibilities; mounting educational campaigns; sponsoring research documenting the social and economic benefits of higher-quality work; and, finally, ensuring that legislation (employment standards, labour relations, occupational health and safety, employment insurance) is consistent with the policy goals of 'learning', 'skills', and a 'knowledge economy'.

Governments could also promote partnerships with industry, workers and their organizations, educational and training institutions, and other labour-market stakeholders. In this respect we can learn a lot from European examples.[9] In Europe, employers, workers, unions, and governments tend to see one another as 'social partners'. Within many enterprises, workers are consulted on issues affecting them; the 'works councils' in which such consultations take place are becoming common across Europe. There has also been substantial progress on workers' rights, with a 1989 Charter of Fundamental Social Rights providing community-wide standards for working conditions and worker involvement in workplace decisions that affect them. Because unions are widely seen as central players in economic and workplace policy formation, downsizing is less common than in North America, and the productivity benefits of new technologies are more likely to be shared with workers. As a result, levels of mutual trust between workers and employers are generally higher than in the US or Canada.

North American critics assert that this more worker-friendly environment has costs, among them reduced flexibility, overstaffing, and generous social security benefits that hamstring European industries and keep unemployment high. But such critics overlook the way the organization of work in Europe is changing: bureaucratic restrictions are being eased and new technologies introduced; the use of self-managing work teams is increasing; there is greater flexibility in work assignments; job responsiblities are expanding; training opportunities are improving; and business information is being shared more openly with workers.[10] The most recent initiative by the European Commission (EC), *Partnership for a New Organisation of Work*, is a 'green paper' intended to stimulate public debate about alternatives for organizing work. To achieve the EC's goal of a 'productive, learning and participative organisation of work',[11] old forms of work organization must be swept away. Hierarchy, top-down chains of command, task specialization, and repetitive work are all considered unsuited to a post-industrial, knowledge-intensive economy. This approach is more collaborative and worker-centred than most workplace innovations currently under way in North America.

By contrast, the US provides an example of a future scenario that Canadians would be wise to avoid. The American Worker at the Crossroads Project, a Republican-led subcommittee of the US Congress, has taken aim at any federal regulation, program, or labour law deemed to stifle 'flexible' workplace practices. A core assumption is that workers lack the adaptability and skills needed to handle new technologies, higher skill demands, and globalization. The committee's solution is to get rid of antiquated laws and regulations and let workers fend for themselves.[12] This ideologically conservative, free-market scenario reflects the 'boot-strap' individualism that has been central to

American culture.[13] If the US adopts these recommendations, the winners will be a small group of well-educated workers with sophisticated technological skills; the losers will be the large majority, who will face greater insecurity, fewer protections, and at best modest opportunities to use their skills.

What Employers Can Do

As important as government action is, the main impetus for workplace reform must still come from employers—and to provide that impetus, they must recognize the benefits of change. Ideally, firms of all sizes and in all sectors should see a high quality of work as their corporate responsibility to shareholders as well as to employees and the community at large. One way of encouraging this perception might be for independent researchers and journalists to follow the example of the influential *Report on Business Magazine* in its annual rankings of Canada's top 1,000 companies.[14] The *ROB*'s list of '50 Top Employers' is based on firms' productivity (revenues and profits) per employee. But what are these 50 firms like as places to work? How much does each invest in employee training? Do they actively support family life and employee wellness? How good are the wages and job security? Are high skills required of workers? Do the firms put sound human-resource management practices at the core of their business strategies? Is the corporate culture based on trust and respect? Including quality indicators along with revenue and profit figures would go a long way towards persuading employers of the link between work quality and productivity.

Employers who are motivated by the imperatives of productivity, competitiveness, flexibility, and efficiency need to be made aware of the mounting evidence that work quality—skill, discretion, autonomy, consultation, a healthy work environment—contributes directly to the achievement of their goals. At a time when market globalization has raised the competitive bar, the Conference Board of Canada has pointed out—and some leading employers agree—that 'one of the biggest wastes' in organizations is that of 'human potential'.[15] A reform agenda based on the quality of work would help to prevent such waste.

We should not underestimate the problems that employers face. Overcoming organizational inertia is difficult, and many employers are trapped in old ways of thinking about people issues in the workplace. However, concerns about the quality of work cut across all levels of an organization—including management. Managers have been under intense pressures from rising workloads, longer work hours, and the need to deal with ever greater uncertainty. The 'winners' who have enjoyed big pay increases and can look forward to bright career prospects may not see any need for change, but they can't work in isolation; they are part of work systems, many of which require reform if they are to operate effectively. Besides, even among those high-flyers are some who would appreciate a less demanding work pace and more family and personal time themselves. The common ground does exist, then, for a shared manager-employee agenda to improve the quality of work.

Canadian businesses concerned about their competitiveness in global markets should take heed of the Organization for Economic Cooperation and Development's suggestions for workplace change. Having compared developments in all the major industrialized nations, the OECD advocates a 'high trust, high-skills'—in other words, 'high performance'—workplace. This model, which has been discussed in Canada since the mid-1990s, can have positive outcomes for both employers (improved organizational performance) and workers (better working conditions and more skilled work). What's interesting is the connection the OECD makes between economic productivity and work reform. Specifically, the organization's image of an innovative workplace includes many of the hallmarks of higher-quality work: complex jobs with a wide range of skills and tasks; ongoing opportunities for workplace training; a flatter organizational structure; distribution of responsibility across all levels; and high trust between workers and the employer. The OECD's contribution to policy discussions of workplace reform also signals that governments have an important role to play in promoting internal workplace changes—an area typically left to employers or (less frequently) union–management negotiations.

Of course, if only a few organizations implement the sorts of reforms suggested by the OECD, there is the risk that the divide between 'good' and 'bad' jobs will widen further. Because workplace change requires resources, larger organizations will be in the best position to move forward. If they develop quality-work objectives in order to recruit and retain the best available workers, changes that should serve the larger public interest will merely become another source of division and inequality. We need to think of a knowledge-based economy as including all workers, not just the relatively small group of educated technical, professional, and managerial workers. All workers should have a chance to make fuller use of their knowledge, experience, skills, education, and mental and physical potential. This is a more democratic interpretation of the knowledge economy than is commonly found in official policy discussions today.

Finally, left out of these discussions altogether are small-business employees, solo self-employed or contract workers, and home-based workers. These individuals have many of the same work aspirations and needs as employees. But without resources and rights—training, child-care support for working parents, employment standards, occupational health and safety protections, and a pension system that does not discriminate against those with multiple employers—improving the quality of their work will be difficult. Thus it is imperative that small firms, the self-employed, and other contingent workers not attached to a single employer find ways to engage more fully in training and skill development, the use of advanced information technology, and innovative forms of work organization. This will require active assistance from governments, post-secondary institutions, local economic development boards, and industry and professional associations.

Current debates about the future of work go back to the 1960s and 1970s. Along the way, as we have seen, many opportunities to set a new workplace agenda have been lost. The 1990s can be seen as a bridge between the old and the new economic eras. Amid contradictory and confusing future-of-work images, there is a guiding beacon: the importance for individuals, employers, and society of improving the quality of work. This people-centred agenda for workplace change has the potential to contribute to economic prosperity and a better quality of life. It places the future of work in our hands.

Notes

Introduction

1   *Globe and Mail*, 'Work forces' series (20, 22–6 April 1996); ' Work in progress' series (28, 30, 31 Dec. 1996, 1–3 Jan. 1997).

2   Victor Keegan, 'Steady jobs in a free fall', *Edmonton Journal* (18 Aug. 1996): E4; 'A world without bosses—or workers', *Globe and Mail* (24 Aug. 1996): D4. This is the same article under different titles; the original article was published in *The Guardian* (19 Jan. 1996).

3   *Globe and Mail* (11 July 1998): A1.

4   Joseph F. Coates, 'Reworking work: tough times ahead', *Annals of the American Academy of Political and Social Science (Special Issue on Impacts of Changing Employment: If the Good Jobs Go Away)* 544 (March 1996): 155.

5   International Labour Organization, *World Employment 1996/97: National Policies in a Global Context* (Geneva: ILO, 1996).

6   *Globe and Mail* (20 Apr. 1996): A8

7   Nuala Beck, *Shifting Gears: Thriving in the New Economy* (Toronto: HarperCollins, 1992): 2.

8   Harvey Krahn and Graham S. Lowe, *Work, Industry, and Canadian Society*, 3rd edn (Scarborough: ITP Nelson, 1998): 26.

9   Economic Policy Institute, *The State of Working America 1989–99* < http://epinet.org/books/swa.html >.

10 Michael E. Porter and Monitor Company, *Canada at the Crossroads: The Reality of a New Competitive Environment* (Business Council on National Issues and the Government of Canada, 1991): 89.

11 Kenneth E. Boulding, 'Introduction', in Elsie Boulding and Kenneth E. Boulding, eds, *The Future: Images and Processes* (Thousand Oaks: Sage, 1995): 1

12 Cited in *Globe and Mail* (11 Aug. 1992): B20.

13 Fred Best, 'Introduction', in Fred Best, ed., *The Future of Work* (Englewood Cliffs: Prentice-Hall, 1973): 2.

Chapter I: The Future of Work

1   *The Economist* (16 Dec. 1995): 6.

2   William Bridges, *JobShift: How to Prosper in a Workplace Without Jobs* (Don Mills: Addison-Wesley, 1994): viii.

3   Jeremy Rifkin, *The End of Work: The Decline of the Global Labor Force and the Dawn of the Post-Market Era* (New York: Putnam, 1995): xv.

4   Human Resources Development Canada [HRDC], *Report of the Advisory Committee on Working Time and the Distribution of Work* (Ottawa: Supply and Services Canada, 1994).

5   The term was first used analytically by the philosopher of science Thomas Kuhn in his 1962 book, *The Structure of Scientific Revolutions*, 2nd edn (Chicago: University of Chicago Press, 1970), which presented a theory of how entire approaches to scientific research shift historically.

6   The two databases searched were the *Canadian Periodical Index* and the *Canadian Research Index*. The key words used were automation, alienation, employment, future/ forecasts, hours of work, job satisfaction, leisure, leisure society, quality of work, technological unemployment, work.

7   Abraham M. Maslow, *Motivation and Personality*, 3rd edn (New York: Harper and Row, 1987).

8   Jeremy Seabrook, *The Leisure Society* (Oxford: Basil Blackwell, 1988): 182. See also Otto Newman, 'The coming of a leisure society?' *Leisure Studies* 2 (1983): 97–109; A.J. Veal, *Leisure and the Future* (London: Allen & Unwin, 1987); Clive Jenkins and Sherman Barrie, *The Leisure Shock* (London: Eyre Methuen, 1981).

9   Charles Handy, *Future of Work* (Oxford: Basil Blackwell, 1984).

10   André Gorz, *Paths to Paradise: On the Liberation From Work* (London: Pluto Press, 1985): 32.

11   The European Assizes against unemployment, job insecurity and social exclusion, Brussels, 19 April 1998; see web site < www.mygale.org/02/ras/marches >.

12   Donald G. Reid and Roger C. Mannell, 'The globalization of the economy and potential new roles for work and leisure', *Society and Leisure* 17, 1 (1994): 251–66.

13   HRDC, *Report*.

14   Sally Lerner, 'Basic Income: Sowing the Seeds, Ensuring the Harvest', keynote address to the *New Zealand Universal Basic Income Conference*, Wellington (March 1998): 8.

15   Daniel Bell, *The Coming of Post-Industrial Society* (New York: Basic Books, 1973). This point is made by Newman in 'The coming of a leisure society?': 103.

16   Judson Gooding, *The Job Revolution* (New York: Walker and Co., 1972), 7. The book is based on articles originally published in *Fortune Magazine*.

17   Ibid.: 20–1.

18   This is the title to the epilogue in Louis E. Davis and Albert B. Cherns, eds, *The Quality of Working Life: Vol. I: Problems, Prospects and the State of the Art* (New York: Free Press, 1975).

19   Neil Q. Herrick and Michael Maccoby, 'Humanizing work: a Priority Goal of the 1970s', in Davis and Cherns, eds, *The Quality of Working Life*: 64.

20   Canadian Council on Social Development. *New Concepts of Work* (proceedings of a conference sponsored by the CCSD [March 1973]): xvii.

21   *The Angus Reid Report* (January–February 1996): 1

22   Edmonton Social Planning Council, *Listen to Me: The Final Report of the Quality of Life Commission* (Edmonton, 1997). Available on the ESPC web site < www.compusmart.ab.ca/ espc/qofl1.html >.

23   Tom Wayman, 'To be free full-time: the challenge of work', *Labour/Le Travail* 35 (Spring 1995): 223.

24   *Report on Business Magazine* (July 1998): 88. In 1997, the typical Canadian CEO earned an average of US $440,886.

25   See for example, Peter F. Drucker, *Post-Capitalist Society* (New York: HarperBusiness, 1993).

26 *The Alberta Workforce to the Year 2000* (Edmonton: Advanced Education and Career Development, 1990).

27 MaryAnn McLaughlin, *Employability Skills Profile* (Ottawa: Conference Board of Canada, 1992): 3.

28 Robert B. Reich, *The Work of Nations: Preparing Ourselves for 21st Century Capitalism* (New York: Alfred A. Knopf, 1991).

29 *Globe and Mail* (12 Jan. 1997): B19.

30 Grant Schellenberg, 'Good work if you can get it?' *Perception* 17, 4 (1994): 4–6.

31 Michael J. Piore and Charles F. Sabel, *The Second Industrial Divide: Possibilities for Prosperity* (New York: Basic Books, 1984).

32 Available on the ILO web site: <http://www.ilo.org/public/english/overview/decphil.htm>.

33 Lars Osberg, Fred Wein, and Jan Grude, *Vanishing Jobs: Canada's Changing Workplaces* (Toronto: James Lorimer, 1995).

34 Juhani Lonnroth, 'Global employment issues in the year 2000', *Monthly Labor Review* (September 1994): 5–6.

35 Ibid.: 8.

36 Economic Council of Canada, *Good Jobs, Bad Jobs: Employment in the Service Economy* (Ottawa: Supply and Services Canada, 1990).

37 *Unemployment and the Future of Work: An Enquiry for the Churches* (London: Council of Churches for Britain and Ireland, 1997).

38 *The Downsizing of America* (New York: Times Books, 1996).

39 Ibid.: 294–5.

40 Wellford W. Wilms, *Restoring Prosperity: How Workers and Managers Are Forging a New Culture of Cooperation* (New York: Times Business, 1996).

41 Ibid.: 260.

42 Gordon Betcherman, 'Workplace transformation in Canada: policies and practices', in Bryan Downie and Mary Lou Coates, eds, *Managing Human Resources in the 1990s and Beyond* (Kingston: IRC Press, Queen's University, 1995).

43 The Canada Labour Code regulates collective bargaining and working conditions for all federal public-sector workers as well as those in federally regulated industries such as transportation, communications, and finance.

44 *Seeking a Balance: Canada Labour Code Part 1, Review* (Ottawa: Supply and Services Canada, 1995): 23.

45 Ibid.: 32.

46 Alan Wolfe, 'The moral meanings of work', *The American Prospect* 34 (September–October 1997): 82–90.

47 Ibid.: 6.

48 *Globe and Mail* (6 Sept. 1994): B14.

Chapter 2: The Crisis in Work

1 Angus Reid, *Shakedown: How the New Economy is Changing Our Lives* (Toronto: Doubleday Canada, 1996).

2 *Maclean's* (29 Dec. 1997–5 Jan. 1998).

3 Michael Adams, *Sex in the Snow: Canadian Social Values at the End of the Millennium* (Toronto: Viking, 1997): 33; Ekos Research Associates Inc., *Rethinking Government III: Final Report* (Ottawa, 15 Aug. 1997).

4   William Thorsell, 'Get over it', *Report on Business Magazine* (January 1998): 10.

5   *Maclean's* (29 Dec. 1997–5 Jan. 1998).

6   *Maclean's* (7 Jan. 1985).

7   Peter C. Newman, 'A confident nation speaks up', *Maclean's* (7 Jan. 1985): 10.

8   The 1992 poll asked respondents their views on the most important things that governments should do now. From a list of options, 57 per cent chose investing in education and training, even if that meant increasing the debt, while 41 per cent chose reducing the debt, even if that meant cuts to services; *Maclean's* (4 Jan. 1993): 16–17.

9   Deirdre McMurdy, 'Falling expectations', *Maclean's* (4 Jan. 1993): 34, 36.

10 Robert Marshall, 'The nation's pulse', *Maclean's* (3 Jan. 1994): 24.

11 *Maclean's* (2 Jan. 1995): 12. When asked 'has your personal financial situation worsened over the past 10 years?' 31 per cent said it had worsened, 33 per cent said it had improved, and 36 per cent said it had stayed the same.

12 Joe Chidley, 'Reduced expectations.' *Maclean's* (30 Dec. 1996–6 Jan. 1997): 23.

13 Allen Gregg, 'A post-deficit agenda', *Maclean's* (30 Dec. 1996–6 Jan. 1997); 'A confident nation', *Maclean's* (29 Dec. 1997–5 Jan. 1998).

14 Gregg, 'A post-deficit agenda': 44.

15 Most respondents (63 per cent) stated a preference for self-employment over working for a firm. In terms of firm size, 41 per cent preferred to work in a firm with about 10 people and 31 per cent in a firm of about 100 workers; Gregg, 'A confident nation': 32.

16 Gregg, 'A post-deficit agenda': 45.

17 *The Angus Reid Report*, 'The public agenda over 1996' (November–December 1996): 27.

18 *The Angus Reid Report*, 'Government cutbacks and their impact' (January–February 1996): 31–45.

19 Ekos Research Associates Inc., *Rethinking Government IV: Final Report* (Ottawa, September 1998): 61.

20 39 per cent of respondents considered the scenario likely and 32 per cent considered it unlikely.

21 Ekos Research Associates Inc., *Rethinking Government III: Final Report* (Ottawa, 15 August 1997); 71 per cent said differences in income and wealth were dividing Canadian society 'to a great extent', compared with 70 who chose the same response for French-English differences.

22 In response to the same question, 43 per cent said that they would 'focus on other pursuits and never work another day'.

23 *The Angus Reid Report* (November–December 1996): 6.

24 *The Angus Reid Report*, 'Views on the education system' (January–February 1996): 27. The same poll found that in October 1995, 40 per cent of respondents felt that the nation's public school system was providing a worse education than 25 years ago, compared with 36 per cent who gave the same response to the same question in 1986. In 1993, when the economy was in worse shape, 46 per cent replied 'worse'.

25 Ekos Research Associates, *Reskilling Society (Phase II): Worker Perspectives* (Ottawa, 31 August 1994). Based on a stratified random sample of 2,580 working Canadians, conducted in March–April 1994.

26 Ibid.: vii.

27 On the latter point, see Gordon Betcherman, Norm Leckie, and Kathryn McMullen, *Developing Skills in the Canadian Workplace: The Results of the Ekos Workplace Training Survey*, CPRN Study No. W 02 (Ottawa: Canadian Policy Research Networks Inc., 1997). Based on surveys of firms conducted in 1993 and again in 1995, the incidence of formal

training over this two-year period decreased, although it is more difficult to say if this short time period reflects a longer-term trend. Training incidence seems to have increased overall since the 1980s, however.

28   Ekos Research Associates Inc., *Rethinking Government III*: 81. Respondents were presented with a list of 13 issues to rank, ranging from the four mentioned to debt and deficit, crime and justice, environment, culture and identity, and immigration.

Chapter 3: What Canadians Want from Work

1   *Edmonton Journal* (22 Dec. 1997): A1.

2   Angus Reid, *Shakedown: How the New Economy is Changing Our Lives* (Toronto: Doubleday Canada, 1996): 270.

3   Ekos Research Associates Inc., *Rethinking Government III: Final Report* (Ottawa, 15 Aug. 1997): 44–5. On a 7-point scale, where 1 = not at all important and 7 = extremely important, the combined responses of 5, 6, and 7 were 93 per cent for responses personal growth and development, 90 per cent for salary and benefits, and 85 per cent for job security.

4   Matthew Fox, *The Reinvention of Work: A New Vision of Livelihood for Our Times* (New York: HarperCollins, 1994).

5   Edmund F. Byrne, *Work Inc.: A Philosophical Inquiry* (Philadelphia: Temple University Press, 1990): 13.

6   Adam Smith, *An Inquiry into the Nature and Causes of the Wealth of Nations* (New York: Modern Library, 1937) [originally published 1776]: 734.

7   The term 'social contract' entered the public lexicon in the mid-1990s, when Bob Rae's NDP government in Ontario was attempting to gain union and employer support for massive public-sector restructuring and wage cuts. This effort was a dismal failure and a bad example of how to renew the social contract, which has deep roots in liberal political theory going back to Hobbes, Locke, and Rousseau. A social contract, in more philosophical terms, is an implicit and voluntary understanding of the rights, responsibilities, and obligations of citizens, government, and economic institutions in a society.

8   Peter F. Drucker, *Post-Capitalist Society* (New York: HarperBusiness, 1993).

9   M. Burstein, N. Tienharra, P. Hewson, and B. Warrander, *Canadian Work Values: Findings of a Work Ethic Survey and a Job Satisfaction Survey* (Ottawa: Information Canada, 1975). A survey of job satisfaction was conducted in late 1973, based on a randomized national sample of just over 1,000 members of the working population aged 15 and older. The work ethic survey was conducted in early 1974 with a nationally representative sample of 1,978 adults between the ages of 16 and 60.

10   *Maclean's* (7 Jan. 1985): 15.

11   *The Gallup Report* (14 March 1988).

12   Burstein et al., *Canadian Work Values*: 29.

13   Based on a nationally representative sample of 1,165 individuals 18 years or older who were working full-time or part-time in the labour force; Rona Maynard, 'How do you like your job?' *Report on Business Magazine* (November 1987).

14   Ibid.: 114, 117.

15   David Olive, 'The new hardline', *Report on Business Magazine* (October 1991): 15.

16   Angus Reid Group and the Royal Bank, *Workplace 2000: Working Toward the Millennium: A Portrait of Working Canadians* (Fall 1997); based on a representative

sample of 1,000 Canadians who were full-time or part-time employees or self-employed, and conducted in August–September 1997; an earlier *Workplace 2000* survey (1996) used a smaller sample.

17 Angus Reid Group and the Royal Bank, *Workplace 2000*: 2.

18 A 1996 poll, which yielded the same result, also found that 39 per cent of these underemployed workers expected to be in the same situation in several years time; *The Angus Reid Report*, 'Focus on Canadians and the workplace' (November–December 1996): 17.

19 Statistics Canada's 1994 Adult Education and Training Survey indicates that 23 per cent of all employees received employer-sponsored training in the year prior to the survey. A review of all major studies of workplace training in Canada estimates that about half of all firms provide their employees with training, and between one-fifth and one-third of employees receive formal training (informal training is more widespread but less well documented). See Gordon Betcherman, Norm Leckie and Kathryn McMullen, *Developing Skills in the Canadian Workplace: The Results of the Ekos Workplace Training Survey*, CPRN Study No. W 02 (Ottawa: Canadian Policy Research Networks Inc., 1997): 4.

20 *The Angus Reid Report*, 'Focus on Canadians and the workplace' (January–February 1996): 21.

21 See our Web site < www.ualberta.ca/ ~ glowe/transition >. See also Graham S. Lowe and Harvey Krahn, 'Work aspirations and attitudes in an era of labour market restructuring: a comparison of two Canadian cohorts', *Work, Employment & Society* 14, 1 (2000): 1–22.

22 *The Towers Perrin Workplace Index: How Canadian Employees Really Feel About their Work* (November 1995). Based on a spring 1995 survey of 587 employees (18 years of age and over) working in private-sector firms with 300 or more employees.

23 Ibid.: 2.

24 Ibid.

25 *Focus* [Towers Perrin newsletter] (Winter 1996): 3.

26 *The 1997 Towers Perrin Workplace Index: Great Expectations in the High Performance Workplace* (1997). While this report presents findings from the TP American survey, the framework and the arguments are similar to those used in the 1995 Canadian Workplace Index.

27 *The Towers Perrin Workplace Index: How Canadian Employees Really Feel*: 11.

Chapter 4: The 'New Economy'

1 Economic Council of Canada, *Good Jobs, Bad Jobs: Employment in the Service Economy* (Ottawa: Economic Council of Canada, 1990).

2 Statistics Canada, *The Daily* (17 March 1998); data are from the 1996 Census.

3 *Canadian Oxford Dictionary* (Don Mills: Oxford University Press, 1998).

4 On the dehumanizing effects of unemployment see Marie Jahoda, *Employment and Unemployment: A Social-Psychological Approach* (Cambridge: Cambridge University Press, 1982); Patrick Burman, *Killing Time, Losing Ground: Experiences of Unemployment* (Toronto: Wall & Thompson, 1988).

5 Statistics Canada, *Labour Force Update: A New Perspective on Wages* 2, 3 (1998): 19.

6 George Butlin and Gillian Oderkirk, 'Educational attainment—a key to autonomy and authority in the workplace', *Education Quarterly Review* 4, 1 (1997): 32–52.

7   The Adult Education and Training Survey, conducted by Statistics Canada in 1994, found that in 1993, 27 per cent of the working population participated in job-related training. Training includes all structured credit and non-credit courses and training on or off the job. See Patrice de Broucker, 'Job-related education and training—who has access?' *Education Quarterly Review* 4, 1 (1997): 10–31.

8   Harvey Krahn, *Quality of Work in the Service Sector*, General Social Survey Analysis Series 6 (Ottawa: Statistics Canada, 1992).

9   Christopher Clark, *Public Sector Downsizing: The Impact on Job Quality in Canada* (Ottawa: Canadian Council on Social Development, 1997): 2.

10   Marie Drolet and René Morissette, *Recent Canadian Evidence on Job Quality by Firm Size*, No. 128, Research Paper Series, Analytic Studies Branch (Ottawa: Statistics Canada, 1998). Small firms employ fewer than 20 people, medium-sized firms 20–499, large firms 500 or more.

11   Christopher Jencks, Lauri Perman, and Lee Rainwater, 'What is a good job? A new measure of labour market success', *American Journal of Sociology* 93, 6 (1988): 1322–57.

12   Andrew Jackson and Pradeep Kumar, *Measuring and Monitoring the Quality of Jobs and the Work Environment in Canada,* paper prepared for the Centre for the Study of Living Standards Conference on the State of Living Standards and Quality of Life in Canada (Ottawa: 30–1 October 1998): 2.

13   Randy Hodson, 'Dignity in the workplace under participative management: *Alienation and Freedom* revisited', *American Sociological Review* 61, 5 (1996): 722.

14   G. Picot, Z. Lin, and W. Pyper, 'An overview of permanent layoffs', *Canadian Economic Observer* (February 1997): 3.1–3.14; A. Heisz and S. Côté, 'Are jobs less stable in the services sector?' *Canadian Economic Observer* (May 1998): 3.1–3.11.

15   Andrew Heisz, 'Changes in job tenure in Canada', *Canadian Economic Observer* January (1996): 3.1–3.9.

16   The annual unemployment rate ranged between 11.3 in 1992 and 9.2 per cent in 1997; *Canadian Social Trends* (Spring 1998): 26.

17   Zhengxi Lin, 'Employment insurance in Canada: policy changes', *Perspectives on Labour and Income* 10, 2 (1998): 42.

18   Centre for the Study of Living Standards. 'The Rise of Involuntary Part-Time Employment in Canada' (September 1997): 5.

19   *Globe and Mail* (8 Oct. 1996): B13.

20   Harvey Krahn and Graham S. Lowe, *Work, Industry and Canadian Society* 3rd edn (Scarborough: ITP Nelson, 1998): 85.

21   Data are from Statistics Canada's Survey of Work Arrangements. See Dominique Pérusse, 'Regional disparities and non-permanent employment', *Canadian Economic Observer* (January 1998): 3.1–3.10.

22   Statistics Canada, *The Daily* (2 Dec. 1998).

23   Data are for 1995; Mark Reesor and Brenda Lipsett, 'Employer-sponsored pension plans—who benefits?' (Draft paper, Applied Research Branch, Human Resources Development Canada, 1997).

24   Statistics Canada, *Labour Force Update: Canada—US Labour Market Comparison* 2, 4 (1998) (Ottawa: Statistics Canada).

25   Data are from Karen D. Hughes, *Gender and Self-employment in Canada: Assessing Trends and Policy Implications* (Ottawa: Canadian Policy Research Networks Inc.,

1999) and Statistics Canada, *Labour Force Update: The Self-Employed* 1, 3 (1997) (Ottawa: Statistics Canada).

26 Ibid.: 32.

27 Statistics Canada, *Labour Force Update: Hours of Work* 1, 2 (1997) (Ottawa: Statistics Canada).

28 Luke Pelot, 'A profile of small business across Canada', *Insights On* [Statistics Canada] 2, 3 (1998): 1–5.

29 Statistics Canada, *The Daily* (17 March 1998).

30 Ibid. (26 Aug. 1997).

31 Ibid. (12 May 1998). Statistics Canada's low-income cut-off line is the income below which people spend more than 55 per cent of income on basics like food, shelter, and clothing, making them worse off than average. Statistics Canada cautions that this LICO is not a poverty line, although in practice many social analysts interpret it as such.

32 National Council of Welfare, *Poverty Profile 1996* (Ottawa: National Council of Welfare, 1998).

33 National Council of Welfare, *Welfare Incomes 1996* (Ottawa: National Council of Welfare, 1997).

34 Ross Finnie, 'Differences in earnings inequality by province, 1982–94', *Canadian Economic Observer* (February 1998): 3.1–3.12.

35 Marc V. Levine, 'Public policies, social institutions, and earnings inequality: Canada and the United States, 1970-1995', *American Review of Canadian Studies* 26, 3 (1996): 315–39. See also Peter Gottschalk and Timothy M. Smeeding, 'Cross-national comparisons of earnings and income inequality', *Journal of Economic Literature* xxxv, (June 1997): 633–87; Armine Yalnizyan, *The Growing Gap: A Report on the Growing Inequality Between the Rich and Poor in Canada* (Toronto: Centre for Social Justice, 1998).

36 Garnett Picot, 'What is happening to earnings inequality and youth wages in the 1990s?' *Canadian Economic Observer* (September 1998): 3.1–3.18. Between 1989 and 1997 the participation rate dropped 2.7 per cent for those 15 and older; Statistics Canada, *Labour Force Update: An Overview of the 1997 Labour Market* 2, 1 (1998): 46.

37 Ibid.

38 Statistics Canada, *Labour Force Update: A New Perspective on Wages* 2, 3 (1998).

39 Jeremy Rifkin, *The End of Work: The Decline of the Global Labor Force and the Dawn of the Post-Market Era* (New York: Putnam, 1995); David Noble, *Progress without People: New Technology, Unemployment, and the Message of Resistance* (Toronto: Between the Lines, 1995); Heather Menzies, *Whose Brave New World? The Information Highway and the New Economy* (Toronto: Between the Lines, 1996).

40 B. Lafleur and B. Lok, *Jobs in the Knowledge-Based Economy: Information Technology and the Impact on Employment,* Report 197-97 (Ottawa: Conference Board of Canada, 1997): 16.

41 Beverly H. Burris, 'Computerization of the workplace', *Annual Review of Sociology* 24 (1998): 154.

42 See, for example, Kathryn McMullen, *Skill and Employment Effects of Computer-Based Technology: The Results of the Working with Technology Survey III* (Ottawa: Canadian Policy Research Networks Inc., 1996).

43 Lafleur and Lok, *Jobs in the Knowledge-Based Economy*: 16.

44 *Globe and Mail* (30 April 1998): B12.

45 Joe Chidley, 'Reduced expectations', *Maclean's* (30 Dec. 1996–6 Jan. 1997): 22–5; *Angus Reid Report* 'Canadians' perspectives on work and workplaces' (May/June 1996): 22–34.

46 Graham S. Lowe, 'Computers in the workplace', *Perspectives on Labour and Income* 9, 2 (1997): 29–36.

47 Shoshana Zuboff, *In the Age of the Smart Machine: The Future of Work and Power* (New York: Basic Books, 1988).

48 Canadian Information Highway Advisory Council [CIHAC], *Building the Information Society: Moving Canada into the 21st Century* (Ottawa: Industry Canada, 1995) < http://info.ic.gc.ca/info-highway/ >.

49 Paul Dickinson and George Sciadas, *Access to the Information Highway: The Sequel*, Analytic Paper Series number 13 (Ottawa: Science and Technology Redesign Project and Services Division, Statistics Canada, 1997).

50 CIHAC, *Building the Information Society: Moving Canada into the 21st Century*, rec. 14.1.

51 International Labour Organization, *World Labour Report (Geneva:* ILO, 1993): 65.

52 *Globe and Mail* (20 Oct. 1998): B12.

53 Summary Statement from the 1998 National Leadership Roundtable on Employee Health, Institute for Work & Health (Toronto, 28–9 April 1998).

54 Institute for Work & Health, 'How the workplace can influence employee illness and injury', Background Paper, National Leadership Roundtable on Employee Health. See also Kathryn Wilkins and Marie P. Beaudet, 'Work stress and health', *Health Reports* 10, 3 (1998): 47–62; Michael F. D. Polanyi et al., 'Creating healthier work environments', *Canada Health Action: Building on the Legacy*, Vol. 3, *Issues and Settings* (Ottawa: National Forum on Health, 1998): 94.

55 *Globe and Mail* (21 Sept. 1998): B13.

56 Juliet Shor, *The Overworked American: The Unexpected Decline of Leisure* (New York: Basic Books, 1991).

57 P. Kumar, M. Coates, and D. Arrowsmith, *The Current Industrial Relations Scene in Canada* (Kingston: Queen's University, Industrial Relations Centre, 1987): 15–17.

58 Business Council of British Columbia, *Industrial Relations Bulletin* 26, 6 (17 June 1997).

59 See *Better Times*, the newsletter of 32 HOURS: Action for Full Employment and the Shorter Work Time Network of Canada.

60 Hélène Paris, *The Corporate Response to Workers with Family Responsibilities* (Ottawa: Conference Board of Canada, 1989).

61 Conference Board of Canada, 'Work-life Balance Still Out of Kilter', press release (Ottawa, 13 July 1999).

62 Gordon Betcherman, Kathryn McMullen, Norm Leckie, and Christina Caron, *The Canadian Workplace in Transition* (Kingston: IRC Press, 1994); Paul Osterman, 'Work/family progams and the employment relationship', *Administrative Science Quarterly* 40 (1995): 681-700.

63 After widespread public opposition to this change, backed by clear evidence that the reforms especially penalized women, as of mid-1999 the federal government was planning to loosen the eligibility for parental and adoption leave (*Globe and Mail*, 5 July 1999: A4).

64   Judith A. Frederick, *As Time Goes By . . . Time Use of Canadians* (Ottawa: Statistics Canada 1995).

65   Statistics Canada, *Labour Force Update: Hours of Work* 1, 2 (1997).

66   Statistics Canada, 1994 General Social Survey, microdata file. The reference period was the 12 months prior to the survey; 35 per cent of females and 34.4 per cent of males reported excess worry and stress as a result of too many demands or too many hours.

67   Roberta L. Jamieson, 'Burning out in Ontario's public service', *Globe and Mail* (4 June 1998): A23.

68   Marie Drolet and René Morissette, *Working More? Working Less? What Do Canadian Workers Prefer?* No. 104, Research Paper Series, Analytic Studies Branch (Ottawa: Statistics Canada, 1997).

69   Brenda Lipsett and Mark Reesor, 'Flexible Work Arrangements', in Paul-André Lapoint, Anthony E. Smith, and Diane Veilleux, eds, *The Changing Nature of Work, Employment and Workplace Relations. Selected Papers From the xxxiv Annual CIRA Conference* (Canadian Industrial Relations Association, 1998): 33–5.

70   Ibid.

71   Statistics Canada, *The Daily* (24 Aug. 1998).

Chapter 5: Education, Skills, and the Knowledge Economy

1   *San Francisco Examiner* (24 Oct. 1998). Levine's website, where *Disgruntled* is published on-line, is < www.disgruntled.com >.

2   Economic Council of Canada. *People and Jobs: A Study of the Canadian Labour Market* (Ottawa: Information Canada, 1976): 32.

3   Ibid.: 185.

4   David R. McCamus, 'Why Xerox spends so much on employee education', *Issues* (April 1991).

5   Human Resources Development Canada, 'Emerging employment patterns and their implications for labour policy', presentation to the Canadian Association of Labour Law Administrators (Summerside, PEI, 23 Sept. 1998).

6   D.W. Livingstone, *The Education–Jobs Gap: Underemployment or Economic Democracy* (Boulder: Westview Press, 1998): 3.

7   National Centre on Education and the Economy, *America's Choice: High Skills or Low Wages! Report of the Commission on the Skills of the American Workforce* (Rochester: National Centre on Education and the Economy, 1990).

8   Ibid.: 3.

9   A survey of its members by the Canadian Federation of Independent Business found that enthusiasm and willingness to learn are more important than formal education when recruiting young workers; *Globe and Mail* (1 Oct. 1998: B13).

10   *Globe and Mail* (8 Oct. 1998): C1. See also Bruce Livesey, 'Making nice', *Report on Business Magazine* (March 1998): 96–104.

11   Statistics Canada, *The Daily* (10 Dec. 1998).

12   *Canadian Advanced Technology Association / Angus Reid Group*, press release 'Skills Shortage Survey' (4 June 1997). An e-mail survey gathered the data, and of the 2,400 CATA members with an e-mail address, 220 responded.

13 Don DeVoretz and Samuel A. Laryea, *Canadian Human Capital Transfer: The United States and Beyond* (Toronto: C.D. Howe Institute, 1998). The brain drain problem is hotly debated. For example, the Chief Statistician of Canada, Ivan Fellegi, has argued that Canada is a net recruiter of talent when net migration is calculated internationally, not just in terms of the US; see 'Brain Drain or Brain Gain', presentation to the annual conference of the Association of Universities and Colleges of Canada (7 Oct. 1997).

14 *Globe and Mail* (10 July 1999): D2.

15 Based on calculations from Statistics Canada, *Labour Force Information* (8 Oct. 1998): Table 15.

16 Statistics Canada, *The Daily* (14 April 1998).

17 Statistics Canada, *The Daily* (14 Oct. 1998).

18 Patrice de Broucker, 'Job-related education and training—who has access?' *Education Quarterly Review* 4, 1 (1997): 10–31.

19 Gordon Betcherman, Kathryn McMullen, and Katie Davidman, *Training for the New Economy: A Synthesis Report* (Ottawa: Canadian Policy Research Networks Inc., 1998): 2.

20 National Research Network on New Approaches to Lifelong Learning, 'Lifelong learning profiles: findings from the first Canadian survey of informal learning', press release (11 Nov. 1998); based on a nationally representative sample of 1,500 adults, conducted in early fall 1998.

21 Graham S. Lowe and Harvey Krahn, 'Job-related education and training among younger workers', *Canadian Public Policy* 21, 3 (1995): 362–78.

22 Graham S. Lowe, Harvey Krahn, and Jeff Bowlby, *1996 Alberta High School Graduate Survey: Report of Research Findings*, School-Work Transitions Project, Report 97-1 (Edmonton: Alberta Education and Population Research Laboratory, University of Alberta, 1997).

23 D.W. Livingstone, 'The limits of human capital theory: expanding knowledge, informal learning and underemployment', *Policy Options* (July–August 1997): 9–13.

24 Conference Board of Canada, *Employability Skills Profile* (Ottawa: Conference Board of Canada, 1993).

25 Sid Gilbert and Michael R. Bloom, *Issues in Measuring and Assessing Employability Skills* (Ottawa: Conference Board of Canada. 1998).

26 John Myles and Gail Fawcett, *Job Skills and the Service Economy* (Ottawa: Economic Council of Canada, 1990).

27 Albert Tuijnman, 'The importance of literacy in OECD societies', in Organization for Economic Cooperation and Development/Statistics Canada, *Literacy, Economy and Society* (1995): 22.

28 Ibid.: 22, 23.

29 Organization for Economic Cooperation and Development, *Lifelong Learning for All* (Paris: OECD, 1996): 13.

30 Ibid.: 24

31 Harvey Krahn and Graham S. Lowe, *Literacy Utilization in Canadian Workplaces* (Ottawa: Statistics Canada and Human Resources Development Canada, 1998); a nationally representative sample survey of 5,660 individuals 16 years of age and older, with an employed subsample of 2,604.

32 Stan Jones, 'The practice(s) of literacy', in OECE / Statistics Canada, *Literacy, Economy and Society*: 139.

33 Ibid.:105.

34 Stan Jones, 'The distribution of literacy,' In OECE / Statistics Canada, *Literacy, Economy and Society*: 57, 60, 62.

35 Jones, 'The practice(s) of literacy': 90.

36 Organization for Economic Cooperation and Development, *Literacy Skills for the Knowledge Society* (Paris: OECD, and Ottawa: Human Resources Development Canada, 1997).

37 Ibid.: 3.

38 Ibid.: 46. This estimate is based on a country relying on a value-added tax on goods and services, like the GST.

39 Robert C. Allen, 'Employability for university graduates in the humanities, social sciences and education: Recent statistical evidence', Social Sciences and Humanities Research Council <www.sshrc.ca/english/resnews/researchresults/allen.pdf>, 1998.

40 Economic Council of Canada, *People and Jobs*: 185–6.

41 Gordon Betcherman, Kathryn McMullen, and Katie Davidman, *Training for the New Economy: A Synthesis Report* (Ottawa: Canadian Policy Research Networks Inc., 1998).

Chapter 6: Youth and Work

1 William Bridges, *JobShift: How to Prosper in a Workplace Without Jobs* (Don Mills: Addison-Wesley, 1994).

2 Jeremy Rifkin, *The End of Work: The Decline of the Global Labor Force and the Dawn of the Post-Market Era* (New York: Putnam, 1995): 209.

3 See, for example, Richard W. Judy and Carol D'Amico, *Workforce 2020: Work and Workers in the 21st Century* (Indianapolis: Hudson Institute, 1997); David B. Bills, ed., *The New Modern Times: Factors Reshaping the World of Work* (Albany: State University of New York Press, 1995).

4 Don Tapscott, *Growing Up Digital: The Rise of the Net Generation* (New York: McGraw-Hill, 1997).

5 Robert B. Reich, *The Work of Nations: Preparing Ourselves for 21st Century Capitalism* (New York: Alfred A. Knopf, 1991).

6 David K. Foot and Jeanne C. Li, 'Youth employment in Canada: a misplaced priority?' *Canadian Public Policy* 12, 3 (1986): 499–506.

7 Gordon Betcherman and René Morissette, *Recent Youth Labour Market Experiences in Canada* (Ottawa: Analytic Studies Branch, Statistics Canada, 1994): 9.

8 M. Burstein, N. Tienharra, P. Hewson, and B. Warrander, *Canadian Work Values: Findings of a Work Ethic Survey and a Job Satisfaction Survey* (Ottawa: Information Canada, 1975): 7.

9 Ivar Berg, '"They won't work": The end of the Protestant Ethic and all that', in James O'Toole, ed., *Work and the Quality of Life* (Cambridge: MIT Press, 1974): 30.

10 Harold L. Sheppard, and Neal Q. Herrick, *Where Have All the Robots Gone? Worker Dissatisfaction in the '70s* (New York: Free Press, 1972): 120.

11 OECD, *Employment Outlook* (Paris: OECD, July 1996): x, 148.

12 Even the right-wing Fraser Institute concludes that youth with the lowest levels of education face real problems and require assistance (although their proposals for market-based solutions would only make things worse, in my view); Fraser Institute,

'Youth Unemployment "Crisis" Overstated' (4 Feb. 1998) < http://www.fraserinsti-tute.ca/pps8.htm >.

13 OECD, *Youth Unemployment: Its Causes and Consequences* (Paris: OECD, 1980); OECD, *Employment Outlook* (Paris: OECD, July 1996).

14 Statistics Canada, *Labour Force Update. An Overview of the 1997 Labour Market* (Winter 1998): 29.

15 OECD, *Employment Outlook* (Paris: OECD, July 1996).

16 The employment–population ratio reports the proportion of a specific group in the total adult population that is employed. This is a more accurate measure of economic activity than the labour-force participation rate, which includes the unemployed as well.

17 Statistics Canada, 1981 and 1996 Censuses.

18 Gordon Betcherman and Norm Leckie, *Youth Employment and Education Trends in the 1980s and 1990s* (Ottawa: Canadian Policy Research Networks Inc., 1997): 8.

19 Ibid.: 16.

20 OECD, *Employment Outlook* (Paris: OECD, July 1996). .

21 Nonstandard work arrangements include part-time jobs, temporary work, own-account self-employment, and multiple job-holding. See Harvey Krahn, 'Nonstandard work on the rise', *Perspectives on Labour and Income* (Winter 1995): 35–42.

22 Statistics Canada, *Labour Force Update: An Overview of the 1997 Labour Market* (Winter 1998): 46.

23 Betcherman and Leckie, *Youth Employment*: 8; Harvey Krahn and Graham S. Lowe, *Work, Industry and Canadian Society*, 3rd edn (Scarborough: ITP Nelson, 1998): 84–6.

24 Richard Easterlin, *Birth and Fortune: The Impact of Numbers on Personal Welfare* (New York: Basic Books, 1980).

25 In a representative sample of Alberta grade 12 students in spring 1996, 65 per cent agreed or strongly agreed with the statement 'It will be harder for people in my generation to live as comfortably as previous generations'; Graham S. Lowe, Harvey Krahn, and Jeff Bowlby, *1996 Alberta High School Graduate Survey: Report of Research Findings* (Edmonton: Alberta Education and Population Research Laboratory, University of Alberta, 1997): 53.

26 Peter Shawn Taylor and Ian McGugan, 'Devoured by degrees', *Canadian Business* (September 1995): 34. Given their readership, it is perhaps not surprising that the authors advocate a market-based approach to skills that devalues the job-relevant knowledge provided in post-secondary programs.

27 Statistics Canada, *Historical Labour Force Statistics 1997* (1998). Note that workers aged 25–55 increased by 12.3 per cent, and those 55 and older by 4.9 per cent in the same period.

28 Data from the 1996 Census (Statistics Canada), based on tables prepared by my University of Alberta colleague Professor Wayne McVey.

29 This is the median age of retirement; David Gower, 'Measuring the age of retire-ment', *Perspectives on Labour and Income* (Spring 1997): 11–17.

30 For an overview of these theoretical positions see Andy Furlong and Fred Cartmel, *Young People and Social Change: Individualization and Risk in Late Modernity* (Buckingham, UK: Open University Press, 1997).

31 Statistics Canada, *The Daily* (14 Oct. 1997).

32 Data are for 1991; Monica Boyd and Doug Norris, 'Leaving the nest? The impact of family structure', *Canadian Social Trends* (Autumn 1995): 15.

33 Ekos Research Associates Inc., *Rethinking Government III*, Draft Report (8 Jan. 1997); Final Report (15 Aug. 1997).

34 Angus Reid Group, 'Younger Canadians' perspectives on work', *The Angus Reid Report* (July–Aug. 1997).

35 Graham S. Lowe and Harvey Krahn, 'Work aspirations and attitudes in an era of labour market restructuring: a comparison of two Canadian cohorts', *Work, Employment & Society* 14, 1 (2000): 1–22.

36 Almost one thousand grade 12 students and close to six hundred University of Alberta fourth-year undergraduates were surveyed just prior to graduation in the spring of that year. Follow-up surveys were completed in 1986, 1987, 1989, and 1992. For details see Harvey Krahn and Graham S. Lowe, *The School–Work Transition in Edmonton, 1985–1992* (Edmonton: Population Research Laboratory, University of Alberta, 1993).

37 See James E. Cote and Anton L. Allahar, *Generation on Hold: Coming of Age in the Late Twentieth Century* (Toronto: Stoddart, 1994).

38 Jeffrey Frank, *After High School: The First Years*, First Report of the School Leavers Follow-up Survey (Ottawa: Statistics Canada and Human Resources Development Canada, 1996).

39 Harvey Krahn and Graham S. Lowe, *1997 Alberta Graduate Survey: Labour Market and Educational Experiences of 1994 University Graduates* (Edmonton: Population Research Laboratory, University of Alberta, and Alberta Advanced Education and Career Development, 1998).

40 Karen Kelly, Linda Howatson-Leo, and Warren Clark, 'I feel overqualified for my job. . . .' *Canadian Social Trends* 47 (Winter 1997): 11–16.

41 Ruy A. Teixeira and Lawrence Mishel, 'Skills shortages or management shortage?' in David Bills, ed., *The New Modern Times: Factors Reshaping the World of Work* (Albany: State University of New York Press, 1995).

42 Government of Canada, *Take on the Future: Canadian Youth in the World of Work* (Report of the Ministerial Task Force on Youth, 1996).

43 Peter Calamai, *What Works: Corporate Success in Tackling the Youth Jobs Crisis* (Canadian Youth Foundation; commissioned by the Canadian Imperial Bank of Commerce, 1997).

44 This discussion has already begun. See, for example, Nadene Rehnby and Stephen McBride, *Help Wanted: Economic Security for Youth* (Ottawa: Canadian Centre for Policy Alternatives, 1997).

Chapter 7: 'Putting People First'

1 Catherine G. Johnson and Carolyn R. Farquhar, *Empowered People Satisfy Customers*, Report 92-92 (Ottawa: Conference Board of Canada, 1992): 1.

2 *Globe and Mail* (21 Oct. 1998): A1.

3 *Globe and Mail* (23 Oct. 1998): B1.

4 Tellier was the ninth recipient of the award, which is sponsored by The Caldwell Partners. Among the accomplishments cited were his negotiation of US-style collective agreements with CN unions and workforce reduction; see < www.ceoaward-canada.org >.

5   *Globe and Mail* (29 Oct. 1998): B1.

6   Johnson and Farquhar, *Empowered People Satisfy Customers.*

7   Business Council on National Issues, *Building a New Century Economy: The Canadian Challenge*, working paper (Ottawa: BCNI, 1993).

8   Canadian Auto Workers Union, *Statement on the Reorganization of Work* (1990).

9   For an overview of Taylorism see Daniel Nelson, *Frederick W. Taylor and the Rise of Scientific Management* (Madison: University of Wisconsin Press, 1980). On the efficiency craze in America, see Samuel Harber, *Efficiency and Uplift: Scientific Management in the Progressive Era, 1890–1920* (Chicago: University of Chicago Press, 1964).

10   Judith A. Merkle, *Management and Ideology: The Legacy of the International Scientific Management Movement* (Berkeley: University of California Press, 1980): 3.

11   I discuss the diffusion of scientific management into Canada in my book *Women in the Administrative Revolution: The Feminization of Clerical Work* (Toronto: University of Toronto Press, 1987): 34–41.

12   Gordon Betcherman, Kathryn McMullen, Norm Leckie, and Christina Caron, *The Canadian Workplace in Transition* (Kingston: IRC Press, 1994): 23.

13   Ibid.

14   A.T. Kearney Ltd. surveyed executives in 450 international businesses; *Globe and Mail* (28 Nov. 1997): B12.

15   Statistics Canada and Human Resources Development Canada, *The Evolving Workplace: Findings from the Pilot Workplace and Employee Survey* (Ottawa: Statistics Canada, 1998). The pilot was conducted in April 1996 and consisted of personal interviews with representatives in 748 establishments, and telephone interviews with 1,960 workers employed in these establishments. The results are not nationally representative, but do reflect particular industrial sectors and regions (e.g., finance and insurance in Quebec, education and health services in Atlantic Canada, communications and other utilities in Canada). For related research see Gordon Betcherman et al., *The Canadian Workplace in Transition*; Paul Osterman, 'Skill, training, and work organization in American establishments', *Industrial Relations* 34, 2 (1995): 125–46.

16   A point also emphasized in Gordon Betcherman, Kathryn McMullen, and Katie Davidman, *Training for the New Economy: A Synthesis Report* (Ottawa: Canadian Policy Research Networks Inc., 1998). Paul Osterman's US research also supports this view. See Osterman, 'How common is workplace transformation and who adopts it?' *Industrial and Labor Relations Review* 47, 2 (1994): 173–88; and 'Skill, training, and work organization'.

17   The list of organizational changes also included downsizing; re-engineering; integrating different functional areas; centralizing and closing decentralized suboffices; decreased centralization; greater use of part-time or temporary workers, increased overtime; adoption of flexible work hours; reducing management levels; more functional flexibility through job rotation; multi-skilling; Total Quality Management; increased use of external suppliers of goods and services; more interfirm collaboration in research, production, and marketing.

18   After extensively reviewing this research, sociologist Vicki Smith concluded that while some North American employers have transformed work structures, the diffusion of flexible and participative work designs is limited and the benefits for workers are inconsistent; Smith, 'New forms of work organization', *Annual Review of Sociology* 23 (1997): 320.

19   Murray Axmith & Associates Ltd., *1997 Canadian Hiring and Dismissal Practices Survey*. Manufacturing firms were overrepresented in the sample (22 per cent of respondents). Senior human resource managers provided the information.

20   Angus Reid Group and the Royal Bank, *Workplace 2000. Working Toward the Millennium: A Portrait of Working Canadians* (Fall 1997).

21   Ibid.: 2.

22   Ibid.: 4.

23   Towers Perrin, *Towers Perrin Workplace Index: How Canadian Employees Really Feel About their Work* (November 1995): 5. Based on a representative sample of 578 private sector employees (18 years and older) in large (300 +) firms, conducted in spring 1995.

24   Based on company documents provided by the human-resource departments at Telus (Edmonton) and Nova (Calgary).

25   *Globe and Mail* (23 May 1995): B1.

26   Adam Smith, *The Wealth of Nations* (Chicago: University of Chicago Press, 1976) [originally published in 1776].

27   *The Downsizing of America* (New York: Times Books, 1996): 294. This was a representative poll of American adults conducted in December 1995.

28   Jenny C. McCune, 'That elusive thing called trust', *Management Review* (July–August, 1998): 11–16.

29   Frederick F. Reichheld, *The Loyalty Effect: The Hidden Force Behind Growth, Profits, and Lasting Value* (Boston: Harvard Business School Press, 1996): 92.

30   Thomas J. Peters and Robert H. Waterman, Jr, *In Search of Excellence* (New York: Warner, 1982).

31   Joseph Peters, *An Era of Change: Government Employment Trends in the 1980s and 1990s* (Ottawa: Canadian Policy Research Networks Inc., 1999); Alberta data calculated from Statistics Canada's *The Labour Force*.

32   David Osborne and Ted Gaebler, *Reinventing Government: How the Entrepreneurial Spirit is Transforming the Public Sector* (New York: Plume, 1993): 38.

33   Ibid.: 254.

34   Christopher Clark, *Public Sector Downsizing: The Impact on Job Quality in Canada*. (Ottawa: Canadian Council on Social Development, 1997).

35   Human Resources Development Council, *Empowerment: A Hands-On Approach to Creating More Service-Oriented Relationships Between Clients, Employees, and Organizations in the Public Service of Canada* (Ottawa: Treasury Board Secretariat, Human Resources Development Branch, Government of Canada, 1992): 3.

36   Michael Hammer and James Champy, *Reengineering the Corporation: A Manifesto for Business Revolution* (New York: Harper Business, 1993).

37   For a critical appraisal of re-engineering, see John Micklethwait and Adrian Wooldridge, *The Witch Doctors. Making Sense of the Management Gurus* (New York: Times Books, 1996).

38   Thomas S. Kuhn, *The Structure of Scientific Revolution*, 2nd edn (Chicago: University of Chicago Press, 1970).

39   I have drawn on a prominent theory of organizational change, even though it has not been tested for work systems or organizational cultures; see Elaine Romanelli and Michael L. Tushman, 'Organizational transformation as punctuated equilibrium: an empirical test', *Academy of Management Journal* 37, 4 (1994): 1141–66.

40   Rosabeth Moss Kanter, Barry A. Stein, and Todd D. Jick, *The Challenge of Organizational Change: How Companies Experience It and Leaders Guide It* (New York: Free Press, 1992).

41   Statistics Canada, *Labour Force Update: The Self-Employed* 1, 3 (1997) Ottawa: Statistics Canada.

42   Jeffrey Pfeffer, *Competitive Advantage Through People: Unleashing the Power of the Workforce* (Boston: Harvard University Press, 1994).

43   Eileen Appelbaum and Rosemary Batt, *The New American Workplace: Transforming Work Systems in the United States* (Ithaca: ILR Press, 1994).

44   Osterman, 'Skill, training, and work organization': 144.

45   Gerald E. Ledford Jr. and Susan Albers Mohrman, 'Self-design for high involvement: a large scale organizational change', *Human Relations* 46, 1 (1993): 144.

46   Canada, *Collective Reflection on the Changing Workplace, Report of the Advisory Committee on the Changing Workplace* (Human Resources Development Canada, 1997).

47   Ibid.: 193.

48   Organization for Economic Cooperation and Development, *Lifelong Learning for All* (Paris: OECD, 1996).

49   MaryAnn McLaughlin, *Employability Skills Profile: What Are Employers Looking For?* Report 81-92E (Ottawa: Conference Board of Canada, 1992).

50   Arun Maira and Peter Scott-Morgan, *The Accelerating Organization: Embracing the Human Face of Change* (New York: McGraw-Hill, 1997): 217.

51   Peter M. Senge, Art Kleiner, and Charlotte Roberts, *The Fifth Discipline Fieldbook: Strategies and Tools for Building a Learning Organization* (New York: Currency Doubleday, 1994).

52   Ekos Research Associates Inc., *Tafelmusik Baroque Orchestra: Final Case Report*, Background Document for Lessons Learned on the Innovative Workplace (Ottawa: Evaluation and Data Development Branch, Strategic Policy, Human Resources Development Canada, 16 May 1997).

53   Peter M. Senge, *The Fifth Discipline: The Art and Practice of the Learning Organization* (New York: Doubleday, 1990).

54   Senge et al., *The Fifth Discipline Fieldbook*: 23.

55   Ibid.: 11.

56   Edgar H. Schein, *Organizational Culture and Leadership*, 2nd edn (San Francisco: Jossey-Bass, 1992): 364.

57   Chris Hendry, 'Understanding and creating whole organizational change through learning theory', *Human Relations* 28, 5 (1996): 621–41.

58   Maira and Scott-Morgan. *The Accelerating Organization*: 203.

59   Betcherman et al., *Training for the New Economy*: 59.

60   *Globe and Mail* (26 Dec. 1997): B7.

Chapter 8: Workplace Innovation

1   Quoted in Louis E. Davis and Charles S. Sullivan, 'A labour-management contract and quality of working life', in G. S. Lowe and H. J. Krahn, eds, *Work in Canada* (Scarborough: Nelson Canada, 1993): 245.

2   Donald Nightingale, *Workplace Democracy: An Enquiry into Employee Participation in Canadian Work Organizations* (Toronto: University of Toronto Press, 1982).

3   Ibid.: 194.

4   Ibid.: 188.

5   Auditor General of Canada, *Attributes of Well-Performing Organizations* (Ottawa: Minister of Supply and Services, 1989): 4.73.

6   Suzanne Payette, *Workplace Innovation: Overview 1996* (Ottawa: Workplace Information Directorate, Human Resources Development Canada, 1997).

7   Workplace Innovations Team, Industrial Relations, Human Resources Development Canada, 'Workplace innovation: dialogue on changes in the workplace', *Collective Bargaining Review* (November 1994): 89.

8   Payette, *Workplace Innovation: Overview 1996:* 24. This distinction is found in Thomas Kochan and Paul Osterman, *The Mutual Gains Enterprise: Forging a Winning Partnership Among Labor, Management and Government* (Boston: Harvard Business School Press, 1994), and Gordon Betcherman, Kathryn McMullen, Norm Leckie, and Christina Caron, *The Canadian Workplace in Transition* (Kingston: IRC Press, 1994).

9   Ekos Research Associates, *Lessons Learned from Workplace Innovation: Draft Progress Report* (Ottawa: Human Resources Development Canada, 1996).

10   Workplace Information Directorate, Human Resources Development Canada. 'Innovative workplace practices: case studies. Lessons from nine case studies', *Collective Bargaining Review* (October 1997): 81–8. This report also cites as supporting evidence a review of the recent Canadian research.

11   Edward T. Jackson and Gordon DiGiacomo, 'Innovative workplace practices: case studies', *Collective Bargaining Review* (January 1997): 85–9.

12   Cited in Canadian Labour Market and Productivity Centre, *Quebec Labour and Management Experiences with Workplace Innovation*, Background Document for Lessons Learned on the Innovative Workplace (Ottawa: Evaluation and Data Development Branch, Strategic Policy, Human Resources Development Canada, May 1997): 4.

13   Ibid.: 31–2; based on 19 case studies by the Quebec Department of Employment.

14   Kochan and Osterman, *The Mutual Gains Enterprise.*

15   This plant has been well documented; see Davis and Sullivan, 'A labour-management contract and quality of working life'; Tom Rankin, *New Forms of Work Organization: The Challenge for North American Unions* (Toronto: University of Toronto Press, 1990).

16   Gordon DiGiacomo, 'High involvement work reorganization at NB Tel', *Collective Bargaining Review* (January 1997): 91–9.

17   Summarized in Gordon Betcherman, *Lessons Learned from Innovative Workplaces: A Final Synthesis Report*, Background Document for Lessons Learned on the Innovative Workplace. (Ottawa: Evaluation and Data Development Branch, Strategic Policy, Human Resources Development Canada, July 1997): 19–23. Full details are presented in Betcherman et al., *The Canadian Workplace in Transition*, and Gordon Betcherman, Kathryn McMullen, and Norm Leckie, *Developing Skills in the Canadian Workplace: The Results of the EKOS Workplace Training Survey*, Study No. W 02 (Ottawa: Canadian Policy Research Networks Inc., 1997).

18   Betcherman et al., *The Canadian Workplace in Transition*: 58.

19 Ibid.: 69; also see Terry Wagar, *Human Resource Management Practices and Organizational Performance* (Kingston: IRC Press, 1995).

20 Betcherman, *Lessons Learned*: 3.

21 Ibid.: 8–9.

22 Based on Bryan D. Palmer, *Capitalism Comes to the Backcountry: The Goodyear Invasion of Napanee* (Toronto: Between the Lines, 1994).

23 Based on James Rinehart, David Robertson, Christopher Huxley, and the CAW Research Team on CAMI, 'CAW, worker commitment, and labor management relations under lean production at CAMI', in William C. Green and Ernest J. Yanarella, eds, *North American Auto Unions in Crisis: Lean Production as Contested Terrain* (Albany: SUNY Press, 1996).

24 Ibid.: 115.

25 Based on Valerie Preston, John Holmes, and Allison Williams, *Lean Production in a Greenfield Mill: A Case Study of 'Wild Rose 1'* (Kingston: IRC Press, 1996).

26 Ibid.: 10.

Chapter 9: Unions and the Quality Agenda

1 Nuala Beck, *Shifting Gears: Thriving in the New Economy* (Toronto: HarperCollins, 1992): 2.

2 Joseph H. Boyett with Jimmie T. Boyett, *Beyond Workplace 2000: Essential Strategies for the New American Corporation* (New York: Dutton, 1995): xiv.

3 Richard J. Barnet, 'The end of jobs', *Harper's* (September 1993): 49.

4 David F. Noble, *Progress Without People: New Technology, Unemployment, and the Message of Resistance* (Toronto: Between the Lines, 1995): xi.

5 William Bridges, *JobShift: How to Prosper in a Workplace Without Jobs* (Reading: Addison-Wesley, 1994): 191.

6 Jeremy Rifkin, *The End of Work: The Decline of the Global Labor Force and the Dawn of the Post-Market Era* (New York: Putnam. 1995): 224.

7 International Labour Organization, *World Labour Report 1997–98: Industrial Relations, Democracy and Social Stability* (Geneva: ILO, 1997).

8 Ibid.

9 Ernest B. Akyeampong, 'The rise of unionization among women', *Perspectives on Labour and Income* 10, 4 (1999): 36.

10 See, for example, Jerry Zeidenberg, 'The just-in-time workforce', in G.S. Lowe and H.J. Krahn, eds, *Work in Canada: Readings in the Sociology of Work and Industry* (Scarborough: Nelson Canada, 1993).

11 Eileen Appelbaum and Rosemary Batt, *The New American Workplace: Transforming Work Systems in the Unites States* (Ithaca: ILR Press, 1994); Jeffrey Pfeffer, *Competitive Advantage Through People: Unleashing the Power of the Work Force* (Boston: Harvard Business School Press, 1994); Paul Osterman, 'How common is workplace transformation and who adopts it?', *Industrial and Labor Relations Review* 47, 2 (1994): 173–88; Gordon Betcherman, Kathryn McMullen, Norm Leckie, and Christina Caron, *The Canadian Workplace in Transition* (Kingston: IRC Press, Queen's University, 1994).

12 John O'Grady, *Direct and Indirect Evidence on the Extent of Changes in Work Organization in Canada* (Toronto: Secretariat, Ontario Premier's Council on

Economic Renewal, 1993); Gordon Betcherman, 'Workplace transformation in Canada: policies and practices', in Bryan Downie and Mary Lou Coates, eds, *Managing Human Resource in the 1990s and Beyond* (Kingston: IRC Press, Queen's University, 1995).

13   Betcherman et al., *The Canadian Workplace in Transition*: 58.

14   Don Wells, 'Are strong unions compatible with the new model of human resource management?' *Relations industrielles/Industrial Relations* 48, 1 (1993): 56–85; James Rinehart, Christopher Huxley, and David Robertson, 'Worker commitment and labour management relations under lean production at CAMI', *Relations industrielles/Industrial Relations* 49, 4 (1994): 750–75.

15   William C. Green and Ernest J. Yanarella, eds, *North American Auto Unions in Crisis: Lean Production as Contested Terrain* (Albany: State University of New York Press, 1996).

16   CAW/TCA Canada, *CAW Statement on the Reorganization of Work* (North York: Canadian Auto Workers Research Department, 1990); Christopher Shenck and John Anderson, eds, *Re-Shaping Work: Union Responses to Technological Change* (Don Mills: Ontario Federation of Labour, Technological Adjustment Research Programme, 1995); Nancy Jackson, ed., *Training for What? Labour Perspectives on Job Training* (Toronto: Our Schools/Our Selves Education Foundation, 1992).

17   Harvey Krahn, 'Non-standard work on the rise', *Perspectives on Labour and Income* 7 (Winter 1995): 35–42; these data are for the labour force aged 15 to 64.

18   Statistics Canada, *Monthly Labour Force Survey* (December 1995): section C, Table 1.

19   Colin Lindsay, Mary Sue Devereaux , and Michael Bergob, *Youth in Canada*, 2nd edn (Ottawa: Statistics Canada, 1994): 27.

20   Krahn, 'Non-standard work on the rise': 36.

21   Rachel Bernier, 'The Labour Force Survey: 50 years old!' in Statistics Canada, *The Labour Force* (November 1995): C-5; Nathalie Noreau, 'Involuntary part-timers', *Perspectives on Labour and Income* 6 (Autumn 1994): 26.

22   Statistics Canada, *Labour Force Update: Canada–US Labour Market Comparisons* 2, 4 (1998).

23   R. Morissette, J. Myles and G. Picot, *What Is Happening to Earnings Inequality in Canada?* No. 60, Business and Labour Market Analysis Group, Analytic Studies Branch (Ottawa: Statistics Canada, 1993).

24   Harvey Krahn, *Quality of Work in the Service Sector*, General Social Survey Series Analysis Series No. 6 (Ottawa: Statistics Canada, 1992).

25   This and subsequent references to the 1994 General Social Survey report my analysis of the micro-data file.

26   Grant Schellenberg and Christopher Clark, *Temporary Employment in Canada: Profiles, Patterns and Policy Considerations* (Ottawa: Canadian Council on Social Development, 1996): 19.

27   Statistics Canada, *Labour Force Update: An Overview of the 1997 Labour Market* 2, 1 (1998): 18.

28   Bernier, 'The Labour Force Survey: 50 years old!': C-8

29   Statistics Canada, *Historical Labour Force Statistics 1997*.

30   Harvey Krahn and Graham S. Lowe, *Work, Industry and Canadian Society*, 3rd edn (Scarborough: ITP Nelson, 1998): 57.

31   Ibid.: 62.

32 These projections are based on data provided by the COPS group at Human Resources Development Canada, National Headquarters. They reflect the demand for labour only and do not take into account attrition.

33 Brad Edmonson, 'Work slowdown', *American Demographics* (March 1996): 7.

34 National Centre on Education and the Economy, *America's Choice: High Skills or Low Wages! Report of the Commission on the Skills of the American Workforce* (Rochester: NCEE, 1990): 3.

35 Mary Lou Coates, *Is There a Future for the Canadian Labour Movement?* Current Issues Series (Kingston: Industrial Relations Centre, Queen's University, 1992); Pradeep Kumar, *Unions and Workplace Change in Canada* (Kingston: IRC Press, Queen's University, 1995).

36 Richard B. Freeman, 'What does the future hold for US unionism?' *Relations industrielles/Industrial Relations* 44 (1989): 25–46.

37 Diane Galarneau, 'Unionized workers', *Perspectives on Labour and Income* 8 (Spring 1996): 43–52.

38 Statistics Canada, *1994 General Social Survey*, microdata file. Union membership is calculated as a percentage of all wage and salary earners, excluding the self-employed. When I wrote this section, this was the only reliable source of national data available on the characteristics of union membership. However, beginning in 1997, Statistics Canada's monthly Labour Force Survey has asked questions about union membership and collective bargaining coverage, although a detailed microdata file is not available. According to the Labour Force Survey, 30.5 per cent of paid employees were union members in 1998 and collective bargaining coverage was 33 per cent (a measure of union members plus a small number of others covered by collective agreements but who are not union members, often for religious reasons). See Ernest B. Akyeampong, 'The rise of unionization among women', *Perspectives on Labour and Income* 10 (Winter 1998): 30–43.

39 This includes durable and non-durable manufacturing between 1990 and 1997; Statistics Canada, *Historical Labour Force Statistics, 1997*: 24–34.

40 John Myles, 'Post-industrialism and the service economy', in Lowe and Krahn, eds, *Work in Canada*: 126–7.

41 G. Picot, J. Baldwin and R. Dupuy, *Have Small Firms Created a Disproportionate Share of New Jobs in Canada? A Reassessment of the Facts*, No. 71, Business and Labour Market Analysis Group, Analytic Studies Branch (Ottawa: Statistics Canada, 1994).

42 Statistics Canada, 1994 General Social Survey, microdata file. See also Akyeampong, 'The rise of unionization among women': 41.

43 For details of the trends discussed here see Krahn and Lowe, *Work, Industry, and Canadian Society*, especially Chapter 4.

44 Leroy O. Stone, ed., *Dimensions of Job–Family Tension* (Ottawa: Statistics Canada, Family and Community Support Systems Division, 1994): 11.

45 Judith Frederick, 'Are you time crunched?' *Canadian Social Trends* 31 (Winter 1993): 7–8.

46 Alberta Government, Personnel Administration Office, *Balancing Work and Family: Survey Results* (Edmonton: July 1991).

47 The Work and Eldercare Research Group, *Work & Family: The Survey* (Guelph: CARNET: The Canadian Aging Research Network, Gerontology Research Centre, University of Guelph, 1993).

48 Leroy Stone and Donna Lero, 'Factors in job-family tension: a perspective from the National Child Care Survey and the Total Work Accounts System', in Stone, ed., *Dimensions of Job-Family Tension:* 23–4.

49 Ernest B. Akyeampong, 'Absences from work revisited', *Perspectives on Labour and Income* 4 (Spring 1992): 44–53.

50 Stone, *Dimensions of Job-Family Tension:* 12.

51 Brenda Lipsett and Mark Reesor, 'Flexible work arrangements', in Paul-André Lapoint, Anthony E. Smith, and Diane Veilleux, eds, *The Changing Nature of Work, Employment and Workplace Relations: Selected Papers from the xxxivth annual CIRA conference* (Quebec: Canadian Industrial Relations Association 1998): 34–5.

52 Noah Meltz and Anil Verma, *Developments in Industrial Relations and Human Resource Practices in Canada: An Update from the 1980s,* Queen's Paper in Industrial Relations, 1993–8 (Kingston: Industrial Relations Centre, Queen's University, 1993).

53 Deborah H. Hurst, 'Work and Family Organizational Change: A Case Study of Barriers and Resistance', doctoral dissertation, Department of Sociology, University of Alberta, 1996.

54 Gordon Betcherman and René Morissette, *Recent Youth Labour Market Experiences in Canada*, Analytic Studies Branch, Research Paper Series No. 63 (Ottawa: Statistics Canada, 1994): 1.

55 Statistics Canada, 1989 and 1994 General Social Survey (GSS), microdata files.

56 Statistics Canada, 1994 GSS, microdata file.

57 For details see Harvey Krahn and Graham S. Lowe, 'Transitions to work: results of a longitudinal study of high school and university graduates in three Canadian cities', in D. Ashton and G.S. Lowe, eds, *Making Their Way: Education, Training and the Labour Market in Canada and Britain* (Toronto: University of Toronto Press, 1991): 130–70.

58 Canadian Labour Market and Productivity Centre, *Canada: Meeting the Challenge of Change—A Statement by the Economic Restructuring Committee* (Ottawa: CLMPC, 1993).

59 David Ross and Richard Shillington, *Flux: Two Years in the Life of the Canadian Labour Market* (Ottawa: Statistics Canada, 1991): 5.

60 Andrew Heisz, 'Changes in job tenure in Canada', *Canadian Economic Observer* (January 1996): 3.1–3.9 (Statistics Canada).

61 Statistics Canada, 1994 GSS, microdata file.

62 Richard B. Freeman, 'The future for unions in decentralized collective bargaining systems: US and UK unionism in an era of crisis', *British Journal of Industrial Relations* 33, 4 (1995): 533–4; Dorothy Sue Cobble, 'Organizing the postindustrial work force: lessons from the history of waitress unionism', *Industrial and Labor Relations Review* 44, 3 (1991): 419–36; AFL-CIO, *The Changing Situation of Workers and Their Unions*; A Report by the AFL-CIO Committee on the Evolution of Work, Publication No. 165 (Washington, DC: AFL-CIO, 1985); John Chowcat, 'Flexible unionism', *New Statesman & Society* (27 Oct. 1995): 31–2.

63 Graham S. Lowe, *The Human Resource Challenges of Education, Computers and Retirement*, General Social Survey Analysis Series No. 7 (Ottawa: Statistics Canada, 1992): 51–4.

64 Graham S. Lowe and Harvey Krahn, 'Job-related education and training among younger workers', *Canadian Public Policy* 21, 3 (1995): 362–78.

65   Statistics Canada, 1994 GSS, microdata file. The extent of overqualification in respondent's current job is 19.2 per cent versus 25.1 per cent, members and non-members respectively.

66   See, for example, MaryAnn McLaughlin, *Employability Skills Profile: What are Employers Looking For?* (Ottawa: Conference Board of Canada, 1992); Michael Bloom, *Profiles of Partnerships: Business—Education Partnerships that Enhance Student Retention* (Ottawa: Conference Board of Canada, 1991).

67   Graham S. Lowe, 'Computers in the Workplace', *Perspectives on Labour and Income* 9 (Summer 1997): 29–36.

68   See especially Shoshana Zuboff, *In the Age of the Smart Machine: The Future of Work and Power* (New York: Basic Books, 1988); Robert Karasek and Töres Theorell, *Healthy Work: Stress, Productivity, and the Reconstruction of Working Life* (New York: Basic Books, 1990); Melvin Kohn and Carmi Schooler, *Work and Personality: An Inquiry into the Impact of Social Stratification* (Norwood: Ablex, 1983).

69   Richard Locke, Thomas Kochan, and Michael Piore, 'Reconceptualizing comparative industrial relations: lessons from international research', *International Labour Review* 134 (1995): 150.

70   D'Arcy Martin, *Thinking Union: Activism and Education in Canada's Labour Movement* (Toronto: Between The Lines, 1995): 120.

71   Graham S. Lowe, *CUPE Staff Workload Study*, Report submitted to the Joint Project Management Committee (Ottawa: CUPE, November 1990).

72   AFL-CIO, *The Changing Situation of Workers and Their Unions*.

73   Peter F. Drucker, *Post-Capitalist Society* (New York: HarperBusiness, 1993): 16.

Chapter 10: Creating a Higher Quality of Work

1   Marshall McLuhan, 'Learning a living', in Fred Best, ed., *The Future of Work* (Englewood Cliffs: Prentice-Hall, 1973): 103.

2   Peter F. Drucker, *Post-Capitalist Society* (New York: HarperBusiness, 1993): 16

3   Government of Canada, *Speech from the Throne*, October 1999.

4   Angus Reid Group, *The Angus Reid Report*, 11, 6 (November–December 1996): 26–7.

5   See CPRN's web site: < www.cprn.org >.

6   *Globe and Mail* (23 Jan. 1997): A3.

7   *Globe and Mail* (2 Feb. 1999): B4.

8   Human Resources Development Canada, 'Emerging employment patterns and their implications for labour policy', presentation to the Canadian Association of Labour Law Administrators, 23 Sept. 1998, Summerside, PEI.

9   For a good overview from a Canadian perspective, see Canadian Labour Market and Productivity Centre, *Workplace Innovation in Europe: A Review of the Literature and Findings of Case Studies*, Background Document for Lessons Learned on the Innovative Workplace (Ottawa: Evaluation and Data Development Branch, Strategic Policy, Human Resources Development Canada, May 1997).

10   Ibid.: 12.

11   Commission of the European Communities, *Green Paper: Partnership for a New Organisation of Work*. COM (97) 128 final. Brussels (16 April 1997): ii.

12   This report is available on the Internet at < www.house.gov/eeo/oversight/awp/awp.htm >.

13 Wellford W. Wilms, *Restoring Prosperity: How Workers and Mangers Are Forging a New Culture of Cooperation* (New York: Times Business, 1996).

14 *Report on Business Magazine* (July 1999): 129.

15 Catherine G. Johnson and Carolyn R. Farquhar, *Empowered People Satisfy Customers,* Report 92-92 (Ottawa: Conference Board of Canada, 1992): 1.

Index